KANT'S *CRITIQUE OF PURE REASON*

THIS WAY UP

A fresh series of guides to the central works of the philosophical canon suitable for student readers. The books provide clear and authoritative exposition of each text's central ideas and their importance in the history of philosophy. The series aims to make the texts less forbidding for the beginning reader and provide a reliable source of guidance to which way is up.

KANT'S *CRITIQUE OF PURE REASON*
AN INTRODUCTION AND INTERPRETATION

JAMES R. O'SHEA

ACUMEN

© James R. O'Shea 2012

Excerpts from Immanuel Kant, *Critique of Pure Reason*, translated and edited by Paul Guyer and Allen W. Wood (Cambridge: Cambridge University Press, 1998), © Cambridge University Press, reprinted with permission of the publisher and editors.

This book is copyright under the Berne Convention.
No reproduction without permission.
All rights reserved.

First published in 2012 by Acumen

Acumen Publishing Limited

4 Saddler Street
Durham
DH1 3NP

ISD, 70 Enterprise Drive
Bristol, CT 06010

www.acumenpublishing.com

ISBN: 978-1-84465-278-5 (hardcover)
ISBN: 978-1-84465-279-2 (paperback)

British Library Cataloguing-in-Publication Data
A catalogue record for this book is available from the British Library.

Printed and bound in the UK by MPG Books Group.

For Karina, Betty and James

CONTENTS

Preface		ix
	INTRODUCTION	1
	A brief sketch of Kant's life and the historical context	1
	Approaching the text of Kant's *Critique of Pure Reason*	11
1	**METAPHYSICS AND THE "FIERY TEST OF CRITIQUE"**	**13**
	1.1 Rational metaphysics: the highest aims of speculative reason	13
	1.2 'Appearances' versus 'things in themselves': Kant's transcendental idealism	26
2	**WAKING FROM DOGMATIC SLUMBERS: HUME AND THE ANTINOMIES**	**40**
	2.1 Hume's scepticism and the problem of synthetic *a priori* judgments	40
	2.2 The Antinomies of Pure Reason	50
	2.3 Elusive totalities and the interests of reason: Kant's critical solution	62
3	**SPACE AND TIME AS FORMS OF HUMAN SENSIBILITY**	**78**
	3.1 Space and time as pure forms of sensory intuition	82
	3.2 Assessing Kant's transcendental idealism concerning space and time	97
	3.3 The problem of affection and 'things in themselves'	106

4	THE CATEGORIES OF UNDERSTANDING AND THE THINKING SELF	116
	4.1 Conceptual thinking: the categories as *a priori* forms of understanding	116
	4.2 The Transcendental Deduction of the Categories	132

5	ONE LAWFUL NATURE	158
	5.1 Applying categories to the world in the Principles of Pure Understanding	158
	5.2 Substance and causality, self and nature: a metaphysics of experience	173

6	CONCLUSION: PURE REASON'S ROLE IN KANT'S METAPHYSICS OF NATURE	205
	6.1 Clipping the wings of pure speculative reason	205
	6.2 Kant's critique of speculative theology in "The Ideal of Pure Reason"	207
	6.3 The validity of pure reason's immanent regulative principles	214

	Bibliography	225
	Index	231

PREFACE

The aim of this book is to provide a clear introduction to the central arguments of the *Critique of Pure Reason* at a level designed for both undergraduate and graduate students as well as any other readers interested in the main contentions and arguments of Kant's revolutionary book. In order to achieve a relatively fluid and readable introduction to such a notoriously difficult text, it was agreed to limit the scholarly engagement with other commentaries and with disputes in the secondary literature to just the occasional in-text reference to particularly influential recent contributions by (primarily English-language) commentators on Kant, without any apparatus of notes. I have also had to make decisions about which sections of the book to treat in depth and which to treat more briefly, and the index is the way to locate the latter discussions. Within the restricted scope of this book, however, what follows is not a superficial introduction to Kant's thought but rather an attempt to analyse, explain and assess the main lines of argument that occur in most of the more famous sections of the *Critique*. In places in each chapter I have also taken matters more deeply and have not held back from offering my own reconstructive interpretations of Kant's views, some of which may be of interest to more experienced readers of Kant.

There are many high-quality commentaries on Kant's *Critique of Pure Reason* currently available in English, some of which are listed in the Bibliography, so that one has to feel some trepidation in offering a new one. In my experience of teaching and writing on the *Critique* over the past twenty-five years, however, it is remarkable how many students, lecturers and professors continue to express the desire for a comparatively short and introductory but non-superficial explanation of Kant's fundamental conceptions and interconnected strategies of argumentation in the *Critique*. I have also been encouraged in this work by many students, colleagues and fellow Kant scholars, and for their encouragement I am especially grateful. I hope this book will be of some small help in guiding at least some readers to a better grasp of one of the most exciting and influential books in the history of philosophy.

I do fancy that the present introduction has some features that distinguish it from other books with a similar purpose, as those who are already familiar with Kant's work will recognize in what follows. In particular I have departed from tradition and included a substantial discussion of the Antinomies in Chapter 2, before engaging with Kant's positive arguments in the Transcendental Aesthetic and Transcendental Analytic. In a letter to Herz written in 1781, the year in which the *Critique* was published, Kant indicated that if he were himself to attempt to write a more popular introduction to its central themes, he would begin with the "Antinomy of Pure Reason", since a colourful presentation of the arguments on both sides of those irresolvable metaphysical disputes would give "the reader a desire to get at the sources of this controversy": the controversy concerning the reach of pure reason and the possibility of metaphysics. In addition, in a letter much later in life to Garve in 1798, Kant stated that it was the Antinomies "that first aroused me from my dogmatic slumber and drove me to the critique of reason itself, in order to resolve the scandal of ostensible contradiction of reason with itself". One cannot really understand what Kant is saying from the very start, in the Prefaces and in the Introduction to the *Critique*, unless one has a good idea of what he really means by 'pure reason' in the first place, and this is what it is hoped the relatively early detailed discussion of the Antinomies will supply. However, the discussion of Hume's scepticism in the first section of Chapter 2 would be sufficient if one wants to skip the Antinomies and move straight to the Aesthetic and Analytic.

For reasons of economy I include only a brief discussion of Kant's "Ideal of Pure Reason" and his criticism of the traditional proofs of God's existence. This occurs at the start of the concluding chapter in relation to the overall role of the *idea* of God in Kant's Critical Philosophy. However, Chapter 2 on the Antinomies will have given a detailed introduction to reason's problematic idea of the experience-transcending 'unconditioned' that is also at play in the negative arguments of the Ideal. The analysis of Kant's Transcendental Deduction and the unity of the apperceptive self in Chapter 4 appropriately ends with a discussion of Kant's critique of the traditional doctrine of the soul in the "Paralogisms of Pure Reason". In this way, all the main themes of Kant's lengthy Transcendental Dialectic are introduced along the way of gradually developing the themes of Kant's own positive account of human knowledge and his immanent metaphysics. The hope is that this will give the reader a more substantive sense of the important role of the Dialectic in motivating the overall argument of the *Critique* throughout its internal development.

I also attempt to give a sense of the main lines of dispute concerning the nature of Kant's *transcendental idealism* right away in the first chapter, and then again in Chapter 2 in relation to the Antinomies and in Chapter 3 on space and time in the Aesthetic. I do not heavy-handedly push any particular approach to that vexed interpretive issue, although Kant's transcendental idealism becomes more plausible in those places where I present something like the non-traditional 'double aspect' interpretation of that doctrine.

The reader may wish to know the background of my own views on Kant. These become more visible in the later chapters of the book, perhaps most overtly in my analyses in Chapter 5 of Kant's First and Second Analogies on substance and causality (I have for the most part omitted discussion of the very interesting Third Analogy for reasons of space), and in the Conclusion on the role of regulative maxims in Kant's system. In my 1992 doctoral dissertation at the University of North Carolina at Chapel Hill ("Problems of Substance: Perception and Object in Hume and Kant") I had focused on issues concerning substance and identity over time in Hume and Kant, and in subsequent articles I offered more detailed interpretations of Kant on substance, causality and the regulative maxims of reason (O'Shea 1996b; 1997). I have referred to my own articles at several points in what follows merely because they might help to fill out my particular way of putting things in this book, not because those articles are superior to the thousands of other helpful articles on these topics to be found in the secondary literature on Kant. Although the general purpose of this book has limited my discussions of these topics on this occasion, I hope that some of what I am able to say here might be of interest as interpretations of Kant's views.

I owe the original development of my interest in and understanding of Kant to the late Jay F. Rosenberg of Chapel Hill and Bielefeld, Germany, who, among other things, encouraged me to spend what turned out to be a fruitful research year at the Georg-August Universität in Göttingen during 1996–97. In recent years my understanding of Kant has benefited from my own work on the philosophy of Wilfrid Sellars. I emphasize the Kantian aspects of Sellars's views in *Wilfrid Sellars: Naturalism with a Normative Turn* (2007), and more recently in "How to be a Kantian *and* a Naturalist about Human Knowledge: Sellars's Middle Way" (2011). I do not, however, offer an overtly Sellarsian reading of Kant in this book. Finally, I have discussed the influence of Kant's views on Hilary Putnam, Sellars, P. F. Strawson and other recent thinkers in "Conceptual Connections: Kant and the Twentieth-Century Analytic Tradition" (2006), which is contained in the highly recommended *A Companion to Kant*, edited by the outstanding Kant scholar Graham Bird (2006b).

On the primary text, I have used the now standard 1998 Cambridge University Press translation of the *Critique of Pure Reason* by Paul Guyer and Allen Wood. This is the translation that can best be relied on to stay very close to Kant's original German. Where these are available I have also used all the other Cambridge translations of the *Works of Immanuel Kant*, with page references to the marginal page numbers of the Akademie-Ausgabe (Ak.) edition of Kant's works. All bold text in Kant's texts is as those editions have reproduced them from the originals. Finally, I follow a practice common among philosophers of using 'single' quotation marks for mentioning items and for 'scare quotes', while reserving "double" quotation marks for actual quotations from authors and titles and I am grateful to Steven Gerrard and Acumen for allowing this convention to be used here.

    I would like to thank the following people for giving me feedback or for otherwise supporting or encouraging my work on this book: Lilian Alweiss, Graham Bird, John Callanan, Bill deVries, Steven Gerrard, Ciaran McGlynn, Fintan Neylan, John Pauley, Vasilis Politis, Jay Rosenberg, Jens Timmermann and Kate Williams. I am grateful to my colleagues in the School of Philosophy for their support, and to University College Dublin for a generous President's Research Fellowship award during the tenure of which this book was written. I am especially grateful to my family for the true joys that keep all the rest in perspective.

INTRODUCTION

Immanuel Kant (1724–1804) was perhaps the most profound thinker of that period of modern history known as the Enlightenment, or the Age of Reason. Kant has also arguably been the philosophical figure who has had the greatest overall influence on the subsequent development of Western philosophy from the late eighteenth century to the present day. This introduction will provide just a few details of Kant's biography and discuss some of the more important intellectual influences on his philosophical development, followed by a few remarks on the text of the *Critique of Pure Reason*. The proper explanation of Kant's philosophical views and of such terms used below as 'metaphysics', '*a priori* knowledge', 'rationalism' and 'empiricism' will begin in Chapters 1 and 2. For an in-depth and up-to-date biography of Kant, one that simultaneously makes for good reading and explains Kant's personal and philosophical development, I particularly recommend Manfred Kuehn's *Kant: A Biography* (2001), to which I am indebted here; and see also Ernst Cassirer's earlier *Kant's Life and Thought* ([1918] 1981).

A BRIEF SKETCH OF KANT'S LIFE AND THE HISTORICAL CONTEXT

'Emanuel' (later changed by Kant to 'Immanuel') Kant was born on 22 April 1724, in the city of Königsberg, which today is Kaliningrad, Russia, located on the Baltic Sea between Poland and Lithuania. During Kant's life, Königsberg was the capital of East Prussia under the rule of Frederick William I, King of Prussia until 1740, whose reign was followed by Frederick II ('Frederick the Great') until 1786, Frederick William II until 1797, and Frederick William III until 1840. Kant was the fourth of nine children, only four of whom survived early childhood. Throughout his life, Kant was grateful for the exemplary virtue and industry he saw in his parents. His father was a harness-maker and his mother was the daughter of a harness-maker in Königsberg, where

Kant was subsequently to live and work his entire life. In fact, Kant is reputed never to have ventured far beyond the borders of Königsberg except, so to speak, in his extraordinarily capacious grasp of what was then the known geography of the planet. Physical geography was a subject of study that Kant would later introduce to his own University of Königsberg. Kant was a student at this university from 1740 to 1746, and then later on a lecturer from 1755, after serving in the intervening years as a private tutor. He eventually became professor of logic and metaphysics from 1770 until his retirement from teaching in 1796.

Kant's earlier childhood education from the age of eight to sixteen had been at the *Collegium Fridericianum*, with its overbearing Pietist religious instruction that Kant later described as intellectually stifling. The principal of the school was Albert Schultz (1692–1763), a professor of theology who had been a student of one of the most important so-called 'rationalist' philosophers of the German Enlightenment, Christian Wolff (1679–1754), and who some say recognized Kant's talent. Kant's parents were deeply religious followers of Pietism, a protestant evangelical movement that emphasized inner repentance and rebirth along with personal devotion to God and practical acts of charity, as opposed to the theological intellectualism and the orthodox emphasis on outer ritual that the Pietists regarded as perversions of true Christianity.

Throughout his life Kant retained a respect for the purely moral aspects of religion and for the calm dignity of his parents' faith. On Kant's own way of thinking, however, these admirable qualities of character ought always to be based, ultimately, on universal motives of moral duty and on a conception of the intrinsic dignity of persons, motives that he argues are grounded on impartial principles of human reason rather than on religious faith or doctrines. Kant held in disdain all the ubiquitous aspects of conventional religious practice that require belief in matters that go beyond what can be shown to be grounded in universal morality and to be supportable by human reason alone. Consequently, like so many other intellectuals of the Enlightenment period, he was not a churchgoer. In the chapters to follow, however, we shall see that pure reason's *idea* of God nonetheless plays an important role throughout Kant's philosophy, including an argument to the effect that we must 'postulate' (although we cannot prove) God's existence, from a 'purely practical' or moral perspective, in order to further the ideal rational ends or 'highest good' of human morality.

Interestingly, and no doubt controversially, in his recent book *Kant: A Biography*, Kuehn contends that Kant himself actually "had no faith in a personal God. Having postulated God and immortality" in his philosophy, Kuehn suggests, Kant "himself did not believe in either. His considered opinion was that such beliefs were just a matter of 'individual needs'. Kant himself felt no such need" (2001: 2–3). This biographical claim is disputed by those interpreters who hold that Kant did maintain a purely reason-based religious faith. Whatever the truth may or may not have been about Kant's personal views on religion, however, his philosophical views on the nature of morality and on the limits of human knowledge represented a sharp turn away from traditionally theocentric foundations and towards a grounding in the nature of human reason alone, while also arguing in favour of the intellectual respectability of and rational warrant for religious faith.

As to his personal characteristics, Kant would later gain the reputation of having been absurdly mechanical in his daily habits and routines, his neighbours reputedly setting their clocks by the times of departure of his daily walks. Before roughly the age of forty, however, Kant apparently cut an elegant figure – including a youthful period scraping together money for university fees by playing billiards – and throughout his life he was a socially entertaining and vivacious host of intellectual dinner parties. From age forty or so onwards, however, Kant's character and demeanour did take on something of the rigid professorial routine for which he is famous. At any rate, one of Kant's students, the Romantic poet and philosopher Johann Gottfried Herder (1744–1803), offered a glowing reminiscence of Kant's thought and character in the following famous passage:

> I have enjoyed the good fortune to know a philosopher, who was my teacher. In the prime of life he had the happy cheerfulness of a youth, which, so I believe, accompanied him even in grey old age. His forehead, formed for thinking, was the seat of indestructible serenity and peace, the most thought-filled speech flowed from his lips, merriment and wit and humor were at his command, and his lecturing was discourse at its most entertaining. In precisely the spirit with which he examined [the philosophers] Leibniz, Wolff, Baumgarten, and Hume and pursued the natural laws of the physicists Kepler and Newton, he took up those works of Rousseau which were then appearing, *Émile* and *Héloïse*, just as he did every natural discovery known to him, evaluated them and always came back to unprejudiced knowledge of Nature and the moral worth of mankind. The history of nations and peoples, natural science, mathematics, and experience were the sources from which he enlivened his lecture and conversation; nothing worth knowing was indifferent to him; no cabal, no sect, no prejudice, no ambition for fame had the least seductiveness for him in comparison with furthering and elucidating truth. He encouraged and engagingly fostered thinking for oneself; despotism was foreign to his mind. This man, whom I name

with the utmost thankfulness and respect, was Immanuel Kant; his image stands before me to my delight.
(Herder, *Letters on the Advancement of Humanity*, letter 79, in Cassirer [1918] 1981: 84)

To whatever degree Kant's actual character lived up to this fine portrait, Kant's extraordinary *intellectual* career certainly confirms the astounding range of interests and accomplishments recorded in this passage. It is to a brief synopsis of some of the historical and intellectual influences on that career that I now turn. There are many dimensions of Kant's intellectual career and of the Enlightenment period in general that one might choose to highlight in the space of a few short remarks, but it is perhaps most fruitful to focus on Kant's search, throughout his career, for the proper method for developing what he called a *metaphysics of nature* on the one hand, and a *metaphysics of morals* on the other.

With regard to the study of nature in general, the astounding success of the modern scientific revolution was most strikingly represented in the new sun-centred and mathematically law-governed universes of Nicolaus Copernicus (1473–1543), Galileo Galilei (1564–1642), Johannes Kepler (1571–1630), René Descartes (1596–1650) and Isaac Newton (1642–1727). This fundamental reconception of the 'nature of nature', as it were, demanded a fundamental rethinking not only of the nature of the physical universe but also of the nature of knowledge and of the human being. As we shall see in Chapters 1 and 2, it is helpful (if often misleading when one really gets down to the details) to make use of the traditional distinction between *rationalist* and *empiricist* philosophical responses to such deep-seated intellectual challenges.

Rationalist philosophers such as Descartes contended that what was most powerful and revealing about the new science was, as Galileo had insisted, that the book of nature is written in the language of pure mathematics. ('Cartesian coordinates' are named after Descartes, the discoverer of analytic geometry.) On Descartes' view, our knowledge of reality should thus be seen to be primarily an achievement of pure intellect or '*a priori*' reasoning; that is, reasoning or cognition that is essentially independent of, although it may be confirmed by, our partial and often misleading sensory experiences of the world. Crucially, Descartes further argued that our rational scientific knowledge of nature is itself based at the most fundamental level on a direct, inner and equally *a priori* cognition of the nature of our own rational souls. According to Descartes (at any rate, on standard readings of his view), we have knowledge of our own souls as perfectly 'simple' (i.e. non-compound, non-spatial) and hence immortal metaphysical substances. Furthermore, Descartes argued, this *a priori* knowledge is also the basis for a purely rational demonstration of the existence of God as the 'infinite substance' that sustains all of creation. So the wonderful, mathematically demonstrable mechanistic machinery of physical nature, for Descartes, is thus supported by a foundation of even more certain rational demonstrations of the existence of God and of our own immortal souls. Benedict de Spinoza (1632–77) in Holland and Gottfried Wilhelm Leibniz (1646–1716) in Germany would subsequently build on and critically transform central aspects of this general Cartesian rationalist outlook. The views of Leibniz in particular remained enormously influential in the philosophical climate in which Kant's own views were nurtured in eighteenth-century Germany and Prussia.

Like Descartes, Leibniz was a mathematical genius and a polymath as well as a philosopher who was deeply knowledgeable of, and impressed by, the new mathematical physics. Leibniz and Newton independently discovered the mathematical calculus at roughly the same time, leading to a famous dispute at the time as to which of the two – the German or the Englishman – should be recognized as its true discoverer. In his metaphysics Leibniz sought to harmonize two broad themes. The first concerns what, for Leibniz, is our *a priori* theoretical knowledge of God's omniscient rational governance of all the metaphysically fundamental immaterial souls or substances that (according to Leibniz's famous doctrine of '*monads*') make up all of reality at its deepest level. And the second is the picture of nature's mathematically lawful physical phenomena in space and time, phenomena that, according to Leibniz's rationalism, only confusingly reveal themselves to us in our sense experiences and are only rationally clarified and apprehended in logic, mathematics, physics and metaphysics. For Leibniz, the non-substantial 'relational' physical phenomena in space and time that are revealed merely '*a posteriori*' to our senses turn out, when more adequately grasped by pure *a priori* intellect, to be in a divinely ordained *pre-established harmony* with the logically necessary unfolding of the essential natures of the underlying immaterial substances or monads. This harmonious rationalist outlook is reflected in the title of one of Leibniz's important later essays: "The Principles of Nature and Grace, Based on Reason" (1714). It notoriously is supposed to follow on purely rational grounds, according to Leibniz, that our divinely governed world must be *the best of all possible worlds*, a view that, after the horrifying and seemingly senseless destruction of humanity that was wrought by the Lisbon earthquake of 1755, was later lampooned by the French Enlightenment thinker Voltaire (1694–1778) in his short novel *Candide* (1759).

Leibniz's rationalist metaphysics was a deep influence not only directly on Kant, but also on many of those who had a direct impact on Kant's own early philosophical development. Such thinkers include Christian Wolff, Martin Knutzen (1713–51; Kant's most prominent teacher in Königsberg) and Alexander Baumgarten (1714–62; a Wolffian philosopher whose philosophical texts were used by Kant for many of his lectures over the years). Kant's own metaphysical views were in many respects – but certainly not in all respects, as we shall see in a moment – fundamentally Leibnizian throughout at least the first half of what is called his 'pre-Critical' period. The pre-Critical period covers the years from Kant's first publication in 1747 up until roughly 1770 and the publication of his crucial and transitional 'Inaugural Dissertation': *On the Form and Principles of the Sensible and Intelligible World*. This pre-Critical period was followed by a so-called 'silent decade' of intense thinking, writing and rewriting that eventually culminated in the publication of his *Critique of Pure Reason* in 1781. This initiated a decade and a half of astounding productivity in which all the major works of Kant's Critical Philosophy were published. Here is a selection of some of Kant's major works throughout his career, leaving out many important shorter essays (many of Kant's important pre-Critical works have been conveniently collected and translated in *Kant: Theoretical Philosophy, 1755–1770*).

Pre-Critical period
Thoughts on the True Estimation of Living Forces (1947)
Universal Natural History and Theory of the Heavens (1755)
New Elucidation of the First Principles of Metaphysical Cognition (1755)
Physical Monadology (1756)
The Only Possible Argument in Support of a Demonstration of the Existence of God (1763)
Attempt to Introduce the Concept of Negative Magnitudes in Philosophy (1763)
Observations on the Feeling of the Beautiful and the Sublime (1764)
Inquiry Concerning the Distinctness of the Principles of Natural Theology and Morality (1764)
Dreams of a Spirit-Seer Elucidated by Dreams of Metaphysics (1766)
Concerning the Ultimate Ground of the Differentiation of Directions in Space (1768)
On the Form and Principles of the Sensible and Intelligible World (Inaugural Dissertation) (1770)

Critical period
Critique of Pure Reason (1781/1787; the 'First *Critique*')
Prolegomena to Any Future Metaphysics (1783)
Groundwork of the Metaphysics of Morals (1785)
Metaphysical Foundations of Natural Science (1786)
Critique of Practical Reason (1788; the 'Second *Critique*')
Critique of the Power of Judgment (1790; the 'Third *Critique*')
Religion within the Boundaries of Mere Reason (1793)
Toward Perpetual Peace (1795)
The Metaphysics of Morals (1797)

The Conflict of the Faculties (1798)
Anthropology from a Pragmatic Point of View (1798)
Logic (Jäsche) (1804)
Opus Postumum (Kant's final incomplete project, published posthumously)

(Note that some interpreters take Kant's views to have changed to a 'post-Critical' outlook after 1790, although I am not inclined to think so myself. Note also that the Second and Third *Critiques* were seen to be necessary by Kant only after he had written the First *Critique*.) After a few remarks on the Critical period, I shall focus the remainder of this brief Introduction on some of the most important pre-Critical influences on Kant's philosophical development.

Particularly important for Kant's Critical Philosophy are, of course, the three main '*Critiques*' listed above. In the *Critique of Pure Reason*, sometimes called the 'First *Critique*', Kant on the one hand launched sharp and systematic criticisms of traditional rational metaphysics, but on the other hand he also argued, against sceptical empiricism, in favour of the necessity of an *a priori* rational metaphysics that is restricted to the bounds of the world of sense experience in space and time. As will be noted briefly in Chapter 1, Kant then argued in the *Critique of Practical Reason* or Second *Critique* (together with the rightfully highly regarded and relatively brief *Groundwork* of 1785) for a pure *a priori* basis in human reason alone for the universal obligations or duties of *morality*. Finally, the *Critique of the Power of Judgment* examined our 'reflective judgments' of taste in aesthetics and of organic 'purposiveness' in teleology. In this Third *Critique* Kant attempted to display the overall purposive unity in nature that overcomes the seeming 'gulf' that had separated the two metaphysical domains grounded by his First and Second *Critiques*: the lawfully determined physical world on the one hand, and our irreducible (non-deterministic) moral freedom on the other. The other works of Kant's Critical period were then built on the foundations that had been laid by those three *Critiques*.

Turning to the pre-Critical period, the developing character of Kant's thinking during these decades was influenced not only by the broadly rationalist, Leibnizian metaphysical background discussed above, but also by many other crucial intellectual developments of the time. In Britain, the resounding achievements of Newton's new physics rightly seemed to Kant, as to so many of his intellectual contemporaries, to have uncovered the true mechanics and the dynamical gravitational forces sufficient to mathematically predict and explain the movements of every material substance throughout the entire physical universe. This caused an intense rethinking by the pre-Critical Kant and by many of his philosophical and scientific colleagues of Leibniz's fundamental metaphysics of entirely self-sufficient and – in that sense – causally 'windowless' monads. How could the 'pre-established harmony' among Leibniz's metaphysical monads, a harmony that was supposed to be sustained by God without requiring any *causal interactions* between the monads, plausibly account for the sorts of lawful and universal causal interactions in nature that were entailed by Newton's view? Did God perhaps after all establish lawful causal interactions and influences among the immaterial monads in such a way as to reflect the truth of Newton's physics? Kant wrestled directly with such issues during various stages of his pre-Critical period.

Newton had characterized his revolutionary physics as based most fundamentally on the *experimental* scientific method. This helped to inspire the systematic development of enormously influential *empiricist* accounts of the nature and limits of human knowledge, for example by such thinkers as John Locke (1632–1704) in England and David Hume (1711–76) in Scotland. Impressive weight and impetus were thus added to the general empiricist contention that our knowledge of reality is fundamentally based not on allegedly purely intellectual *a priori* proofs of God's best possible universe of immaterial souls or monads (although the role of God was certainly important for Newton's own overall views), but rather on the methodical and patient 'historical' and empirical observation of both the inner psychological and outer physical worlds that are revealed in *human sense experience.* These broadly empiricist outlooks, just as much as Leibnizian rationalism, had a powerful impact not only on Kant but on many of the distinguished thinkers who, at one stage or another, were working in Germany and who directly influenced Kant. Such thinkers included the genius Swiss-born mathematician and pro-Newtonian critic of Leibniz's metaphysics Leonhard Euler (1707–83); the important scientist and Kant correspondent Johann Heinrich Lambert (1728–77), whose philosophical thinking uniquely combined elements of both rationalism and Lockean empiricism; the Jewish physician and philosopher Marcus Herz of Berlin (1747–1803), who had provided the official defence of Kant's Inaugural Dissertation while a medical student in Königsberg, and whose sound knowledge of, and critical perspective on, Kant's thought is reflected in their important correspondence over many years; and finally the German and Danish polymath Johann Nicolaus Tetens (1738–1807), whose two-volume work of 1777, *Philosophische Versuche über die menschliche Natur und ihre Entwicklung* (Philosophical essays on human nature and its development), represented a substantial German development of many of the psychological and empiricist philosophical themes characteristic of Locke and Hume in Britain, and which made a strong impact on Kant in the years just prior to the *Critique of Pure Reason*. (Eric Watkins has recently produced an excellent, affordable volume of short translated selections from the works of many of the less-well-known empiricist and rationalist thinkers mentioned above [see Watkins 2009].)

So the scientific revolution, along with the resulting critical quest for a reformed *metaphysics of nature*, was one central Enlightenment theme that weighed heavily in the development of Kant's thought, and which involved both broadly rationalist and empiricist lines of thinking as sketched above. An equally important theme, however, was the similarly critical examination that took place throughout the Enlightenment period of the *foundations of morality* and of the fundamental nature of moral–political 'right' or justice, culminating in the declarations of the 'universal rights of man' that were embodied in the American Revolution of 1776 and the French Revolution of 1789. Two particularly important thinkers in this regard for Kant were the German philosopher and theologian Christian August Crusius (1715–95), and the brilliant but enigmatic philosopher and adopted hero of the French Revolution Jean-Jacques Rousseau of Geneva (1712–78). Crusius was a systematic Pietist thinker who sharply criticized the all-comprehensive determinism that was inherent in the 'principle of sufficient reason' of the rationalist philosophers Leibniz and Wolff, defending instead a 'voluntaristic' conception of both God's freedom and human freedom. The idea of freedom also figured centrally in Rousseau's idealized conception of a democratic republic in *The Social Contract* (1762), particularly in his conception of the legislative 'General Will' of free citizens, whom Rousseau conceives as *autonomously binding themselves to self-created laws* in service of the common good.

These emphases on moral and political freedom were also supported, although in characteristically more empiricist or naturalist ways, by the 'natural' moral philosophers of the Scottish Enlightenment. In particular, Francis Hutcheson of Ireland and Scotland (1694–1746) and, once again, Hume were thinkers who made a particularly powerful impression on Kant during much of his pre-Critical period. These philosophers argued that the fundamental sources of our moral distinctions lie in *human nature and experience* rather than in pure *a priori* reasoning. On their view the source of the binding authority of moral principles rests, for instance, in an instinctive 'moral sense', or in our natural moral sentiment of approval of whatever is experienced to be useful or agreeable whether to ourselves or to other people.

Kant's developing thoughts about the nature of morality involved grappling along all of those intellectual dimensions. To what extent were our judgments of moral and political right based on pure *a priori* rational conceptions of the perfectibility of our nature under God's divine ordinance, as the Leibnizian and Wolffian metaphysicians held? Or was God's moral law established as the law of nature in the very different way that Pietist thinkers such as Crusius argued? Or yet again, was the alternative perspective of the Scottish moral philosophers the truly enlightened view, and our moral distinctions in fact derive from our own natural and instinctive moral sense as cultivated by experience? And finally, as his thinking progressed, a perhaps even more striking impression was made on Kant that there might be key insights to be mined and refined in Rousseau's passionate defence of the intrinsic moral goodness of the human being as naturally possessed of a *self-legislating free will*.

The heterogeneous rationalist and empiricist lines of thinking crudely sketched above had profound effects on Kant's continuously evolving search, throughout both his pre-Critical and Critical periods, for a systematic philosophy that would encompass in one reasoned view both a *metaphysics of nature* and a *metaphysics of morals*. That is, what Kant sought was the right method for an overall philosophical account that would systematically explain and ultimately unite two very different domains of rational inquiry. On the one hand was the search for the fundamental principles of an *a priori* rational science or 'metaphysics' of the nature of all existing things, encompassing both a general 'ontology' (from the Greek *to on* for 'being') as well as the three fundamental subject matters of 'special metaphysics': the nature of the human being ('rational psychology', on the *soul*), of the entire physical *cosmos* in space and time ('rational cosmology') and of *God* ('rational theology'). On the other hand, Kant simultaneously sought the fundamental grounds and principles of morality and justice as concerned not so much with the *nature* of existing things, but rather with the sources and validity of all our beliefs concerning what *ought* and *ought not* to be or be done. The somewhat eclectic works of Kant's pre-Critical period in particular show him struggling brilliantly to systematically develop, at times with a healthy measure of scepticism, the often conflicting philosophical insights and claims discussed above: concerning the essential nature of the cosmos, concerning the sources and limits of human knowledge, and concerning the true foundations of morality.

But it was the publication of Kant's *Critique of Pure Reason* in 1781 that would dramatically change the intellectual world in ways that are still being vigorously debated today. The *Critique* was the culmination of over a decade of Kant's ever more radical rethinking of the very nature and possibility of a rational metaphysics of any kind whatsoever. *A priori* metaphysics both of nature and of morals were indeed achievable, Kant would argue over the next two decades in developing his systematic 'Critical' or 'Transcendental Philosophy'. But they would be possible, he argued, only in the light of a devastating *critique* of all extant rationalist and empiricist conceptions of the founding principles of metaphysics and of morality that had been developed throughout the Western philosophical tradition from Plato and Aristotle to Leibniz and Locke, and including the abandonment of much of Kant's own pre-Critical outlook, too. In the place of all previous accounts of the nature of both theoretical metaphysics and practical morality, in Kant's new 'critical' view, would be a radically new *transcendental* conception of both our *a priori* rational cognition of nature and the universal rational grounds of our moral freedom and moral obligations. Our investigation of these exciting developments, however, begins in Chapter 1.

APPROACHING THE TEXT OF KANT'S *CRITIQUE OF PURE REASON*

The first edition of Kant's *Critique of Pure Reason* or First *Critique* appeared in 1781, but in a second edition in 1787 Kant rewrote and replaced significant portions of the text. These two editions are known as the A and B editions, respectively. Since much of the A-edition material that Kant deleted remains valuable for understanding his thought, all good editions and translations of Kant's First *Critique* include in the margins the paginations from both the A and B editions as these appeared in the standard German edition of Kant's work, and today everyone refers to passages of the First *Critique* using these page numbers. For example, Kant's preface in the first edition, often referred to as the 'A-Preface', is retained in all standard editions of the First *Critique*, followed by the 'B-Preface'. It is standard practice when referring to or quoting passages from the First *Critique* to use only the appropriate A and B marginal page numbers. When a passage is common to both editions, authors cite both marginal numbers, for example 'A41/B58' (or 'A41=B58'). In addition to the two prefaces, separate references are also made to the 'A-Deduction' and the 'B-Deduction', the 'A-Paralogisms' and the 'B-Paralogisms' and so on, in those cases where Kant replaced large portions of the relevant sections of the text for the second edition. One quickly gets used to all these standard conventions. The following is a list of the main contents and divisions of Kant's *Critique of Pure Reason*:

The A-Preface
The B-Preface
The Introduction
I. Transcendental Doctrine of Elements
(A) Transcendental Aesthetic (on Space and Time)
(B) Transcendental Logic
(1) Transcendental Analytic
    (a) Analytic of Concepts
        (i) Metaphysical Deduction (of the Pure Categories)
        (ii) Transcendental Deduction (in both A and B editions)
    (b) Analytic of Principles
        (i) On the Schematism
        (ii) Principles of Pure Understanding
            a. Axioms of Intuition
            b. Anticipations of Perception
            c. Analogies of Experience (Substance, Causality, Reciprocity)
            d. Postulates of Empirical Thought (and "Refutation of Idealism")
        (iii) Phenomena and Noumena (in both A and B editions)

   (iv) Appendix: the Amphiboly of Concepts of Reflection
(2) Transcendental Dialectic (the Logic of Illusion)
  (a) Paralogisms of Pure Reason (in both A and B editions)
  (b) Antinomy of Pure Reason
  (c) Ideal of Pure Reason
  (d) Appendix to the Transcendental Dialectic
II. Transcendental Doctrine of Method
(A) The Discipline of Pure Reason
(B) The Canon of Pure Reason
(C) The Architectonic of Pure Reason
(D) The History of Pure Reason

During the course of Chapter 1 it will become clear that to some of the main headings above correspond important distinctions made by Kant between different fundamental cognitive faculties (and correspondingly different kinds of mental representations), which we can sum up by anticipation as follows (reading down each column):

	Transcendental **Logic**	
Transcendental **Aesthetic**	Transcendental **Analytic**	Transcendental **Dialectic**
faculty of sensibility	faculty of understanding	faculty of reason
intuitions	concepts	ideas

One important terminological point to note right away is that what the term 'idea' means for many (particularly empiricist) philosophers will be very different from what Kant means by an idea (*Idee*) of reason. The latter is more like a purely abstract thought or concept or principle, whereas when Locke or Hume writes about 'ideas in the mind' they typically have in mind something much more like a perception or a mental image. Kant's own term for a mental *representation* (or 'presentation') in general is *Vorstellung*. See A319–20/B376–7 in the *Critique of Pure Reason* for Kant's own terminological distinctions.

Rather than attempting to explain these distinctions here, however, it will be best if we start on the task of coming to grips with Kant's fundamental concerns in the *Critique of Pure Reason*.

CHAPTER 1

METAPHYSICS AND THE "FIERY TEST OF CRITIQUE"

> The advantage is entirely on the side of pneumatism [the metaphysics of the soul], even though pneumatism cannot deny that radical defect through which its entire plausibility dissolves into mere haze when put to the fiery test of critique.
> (Kant, *Critique of Pure Reason*, A406/B433)

1.1 RATIONAL METAPHYSICS: THE HIGHEST AIMS OF SPECULATIVE REASON

When the *Critique of Pure Reason* appeared in 1781, it was clear that Kant intended both to tear down and to rebuild, on entirely new ground, one of philosophy's most prized and ancient disciplines: *rational metaphysics*. But what is rational metaphysics? And why did Kant believe that 'pure reason' stands in need of criticism? In this chapter and the next we shall be focusing primarily on Kant's criticisms of traditional metaphysics, with brief glimpses ahead to Kant's own revolutionary 'transcendental' or 'critical' solution to the problems of metaphysics, to be examined more thoroughly in subsequent chapters.

What is metaphysics?

In his *Lectures on Metaphysics*, Kant certainly makes clear to his students the high esteem in which he holds metaphysics. (These lectures were delivered over several decades at the University of Königsberg and were transcribed by capable students.) Here is one sample:

> Metaphysics is the spirit of philosophy. It is related to philosophy as the spirit of wine is to wine. It purifies our elementary concepts and thereby makes us capable of comprehending all sciences. In

> short, it is the greatest culture of the human understanding.
> (Kant, *Lectures on Metaphysics* [Mrongovius, 1782–3], 286=29:940)

The term 'metaphysics' derives from the ancient Greek term *meta*, meaning 'after' or 'beyond', and *ta phusika*, which refers to Aristotle's (384–322 BCE) works on nature or natural philosophy, including his *Physics*. Aristotle's natural philosophy investigated the principles of change or movement of all kinds of natural bodies in the cosmos, both living and non-living, and including the eternal motions of the celestial bodies and heavenly spheres. *Metaphysics*, by contrast, was the traditional title given to Aristotle's famous work on 'First Philosophy' concerning the nature of 'being *qua* being', in which he investigated certain fundamental philosophical matters beyond those treated in his *Physics*.

Metaphysics for Aristotle, and for much of the subsequent tradition of Western philosophy, was basically the reasoned search for the first principles and *causes* of all existing things. Aristotle's *Metaphysics* inquired into the '*substance*' (*ousia*) or primary being of all natural things, and it culminated in arguments for the existence of a highest 'divine' principle as the 'unmoved mover' or final unchanging cause of all changing things. Principles pertaining to *substance* and *causality*, as allegedly necessary principles discovered by pure reason, will be seen throughout this book to be central not only to the traditional metaphysics that Kant wants to destroy, but also, on different grounds (as we shall see in Chapters 3–5), to the radically different 'critical' metaphysics of sense experience that Kant wants to defend. Such principles of substance and causality in 'general metaphysics' were traditionally applied in 'special metaphysics' in alleged proofs or rational demonstrations of the existence of such final causes and ultimate substances as God, the soul and free will.

In his *Lectures on Metaphysics*, Kant recognizes Aristotle as "the founder of metaphysics" and offers the following helpful clarification of his own understanding of the meaning of the term 'metaphysics'. The passage is worth quoting in full since it sketches the big picture that we shall be exploring throughout our first two chapters in particular:

> According to the sense of the word, metaphysics is a science of nature which is limited to the rational part, and to that insofar as it can be cognized without experience [i.e. *a priori*]. Metaphysics is physics beyond the empirical cognition of nature: here one expected a great field, without determining it or being able to determine it according to its boundaries. One came upon three objects here which lay beyond the boundaries of the cognition of nature, and were discovered and cognized merely *a priori* or

through human understanding alone. These are:
1. God, i.e., the first beginning of all things.
2. Freedom, i.e., a faculty of human beings for acting in accordance with reason, independent of all natural influence, with resistance against all sensory impulses and powers of nature.
3. Immortality, i.e., the object of investigation of the understanding, to what extent the soul, as a being on its own, will survive the physical human being.

All three are pure concepts of reason that simply cannot be exhibited in appearance, which therefore can merely be thought. One can therefore call them supersensible objects, noumena, i.e., objects of the understanding, and oppose them to the phenomena <phaenomenis>. (Kant, *Lectures on Metaphysics* [Vigilantius (K_3), 1794–95], 419=29:947)

So metaphysics for Kant is a science of pure reason as opposed to an empirical or experimental science such as physics. As such, metaphysics investigates nature *a priori*, that is, without dependence on any particular sense experiences (more on '*a priori*' below). This rational science has as its highest aim the *a priori* cognition of three non-sensory objects of pure thought in particular: the 'supersensible' (i.e. non-sensory, purely thinkable) *noumenal* objects, God, freedom and immortality. 'Noumena' are purely intelligible objects, from the Greek term '*nous*' for intellect. (By 'pure', Kant basically means 'no sensation' [A20/B34].) So whereas sensible 'phenomena' are objects that appear to our senses – we can see or touch or hear them, for instance – the three intelligible noumena are, as Plato had put it by analogy with sight, 'invisible' objects of pure thought. They are conceived as lying 'beyond' the boundary of the phenomena of sensible (i.e. sense-perceivable) nature in space and time in general.

Kant uses the technical terms *sensory intuition* and *sensibility* to refer to our receptive capacity to sensorily represent or be aware of particular sensible objects in general (where 'sensible' here means 'capable-of-being-sensed' rather than 'reasonable', etc.). 'Intuition' (*Anschauung* in German) is a technical term in Kant that refers to any kind of *direct or 'immediate' cognition of particular objects*, for example, of *this* object *here-now* before me. As Kant uses the term 'intuition', while a Divine Being might, for all we know, have a purely '*intellectual* intuition' that simultaneously *creates* the particular world or particular objects that it knows, our human form of intuition is a merely *receptive* or sensory intuition. Real objects must be *given* to our senses, directly or indirectly, if we are to have any knowledge of them.

Metaphysics, then, certainly has far-reaching and noble aspirations, according to Kant. In his groundbreaking *Critique of Pure Reason*, however,

Kant makes it clear that in his view metaphysics as practised throughout the entire history of philosophy has utterly failed to achieve its worthy aims. In particular, Kant will argue in detail that metaphysics, despite its lofty pretensions, has failed to rationally justify our belief in the existence of the three "noumena" or intelligible objects of pure thought: God, free will and our immortal souls. More basically, Kant will argue that such foundational principles in 'general metaphysics' as those of substance and causality themselves cannot be proved either by pure reason or by means of sense experience. Rather, as we shall see him argue in later chapters, such *a priori* metaphysical principles are in fact provable or warrantable, but only in so far as they can be shown to be principles that are *necessary for the possibility of any experience at all*. What the latter really means will not become clear, of course, until we present Kant's own positive views in later chapters. The upshot, however, will be that on Kant's view there *are* demonstrably valid *a priori* metaphysical principles of substance and causality, but they can be shown to be valid only in so far as they demonstrably make possible, and are restricted to, the world of possible sense experience in space and time. Such principles are demonstrably *invalid*, he will attempt to show, in their inevitable attempted application to such allegedly purely intelligible objects or noumena as God, immortal souls, free will or the 'cosmos as an unconditioned whole' (cf. Chapter 2 on the Antinomies of Pure Reason).

As we shall see, Kant argues that this failure of purely speculative reasoning is not merely accidental or temporary but is rather a permanent incapacity due to certain systematic limitations that are inherent in the nature of human reason itself. This crucial point is put succinctly in the opening sentence of Kant's Preface to the *Critique* in its first (A) edition:

> Human reason has the peculiar fate in one species of its cognitions that it is burdened with questions which it cannot dismiss, since they are given to it as tasks by the nature of reason itself, but which it also cannot answer, since they transcend every capacity of human reason. (Avii)

Exploring the meaning and implications of the overall view of human reason and metaphysics expressed in the two passages quoted above will form the central business of this chapter and the next. To start with, however, we need to bring to the surface several important distinctions that are presupposed by Kant both in the passages quoted above and throughout the two Prefaces and the Introduction to the *Critique of Pure Reason*. Let us begin with one idea that is clearly implicit in the passage from Kant just quoted, namely, that human reason is characterized by more than one fundamental kind or "species" of cognition.

Theoretical reason versus practical reason

Kant's entire Critical Philosophy is based on a fundamental distinction between *speculative* or *theoretical* reason on the one hand, and *practical* reason on the other. Roughly put, theoretical reason has as its *ideal* goal the complete, logically systematized cognition of the nature and origin of all existing things (more on this in Chapter 2). Theoretical reason thus investigates how things *are*, indeed *must* be. Practical reason, by contrast, is primarily concerned with what *ought* to exist as a result of our own freedom of will and action.

The term 'practical' in Kant is thus typically used in a quite general way to refer to the realm of free human action and choice. Practical philosophy treats of the necessary principles that govern, or more importantly ought to govern, free human action in general. Practical reason thus aims at right reasons and motives concerning what can and ought to be the case across the various domains of human action, whether in morality or religion, history or politics. Speculative or theoretical reason, by contrast, aims at sound intellectual reasoning in the quest for ultimate conclusions concerning the necessary principles that are true of all existing things. (Kant sometimes uses the terms 'theoretical reason' and 'speculative reason' interchangeably, but at other times he reserves the term 'speculative' for the traditional attempts to prove matters that lie beyond the bounds of sense experience.)

So in relation to the shorter passage quoted above (i.e. Avii), Kant's *Critique of Pure Reason* will demonstrate that theoretical or speculative reason (not practical reason or morality) is somehow by its nature tasked with answering certain ultimate metaphysical questions concerning God, freedom and immortality – the ultimate causes and substance of all things – that it nonetheless, by its very nature, *lacks the capacity to answer*. To take one of the most important topics in Kant's philosophy, mentioned several times already: does there really exist such a thing as *free will* at all, given that (as Kant also holds) every particular event in nature is determined in accordance with the universal principle of causality, as instantiated, for example, in the laws of Newtonian physics? Kant will seek to demonstrate that it is *impossible either to prove or to disprove*, by theoretical reasoning, that there exists such a thing as genuine free will. And the same is true of the propositions that God exists and that we each possess an 'immaterial' spiritual soul that will enable us to survive the perishing of our material bodies. What pure reason *can* demonstrate, Kant will argue, is that reason, in principle, *cannot* resolve such traditional metaphysical questions from the traditional speculative theoretical perspective. More generally, as we shall see beginning in Chapter 2, Kant argues that the most fundamental 'first principles' that are appealed to not only in general metaphysics but in science and by common sense, too – for example, that 'Every event must have some cause', or that 'Throughout every change, substance (or matter) persists' – themselves cannot be proved on any of the traditional grounds, whether of reason or of sense experience, whether by rationalists or empiricists.

But pure *practical* reason is another matter. In the end Kant will argue that it is the undeniable reality of our *internally recognized, rationally self-imposed moral obligations* that ultimately serves to establish – from a practical (rather than theoretical) point of view – the objective reality of free will. To take just one relevant consideration, how could we rightfully be *blamed* – or perhaps more centrally, blame ourselves – for actions that we recognize we ought not to have performed, if in fact it were the case that all our actions and volitions are *causally determined* by physical and psychological laws of nature that ultimately stretch back in time before we were born? For in that case, it seems, whatever we in fact do is causally necessitated to occur by events that are ultimately outside our control. But moral reality would make no sense, Kant argues, if we could not *really*, at that very same time, have acted otherwise than we in fact did.

This joint or co-implicative reality of freedom and morality, however, is known solely from the perspective of what Kant calls the *practical standpoint* of inner moral deliberation itself. From the *theoretical standpoint* by which we have knowledge of all objects in general, Kant argues that we can neither prove nor disprove that we have genuine free will in light of the equally compelling but contradictorily opposed claim of natural causal determinism (see Chapter 2 below on Kant's Antinomies). But as just indicated, the recognized reality of morality implies that we must have genuine free will. So in the end Kant argues that it is solely from the practical perspective of action and will, that is, solely from within the standpoint of practical reason's own *necessarily binding idea of the moral ought* (as Kant also argues), that the existence of God and our souls can ultimately be indirectly supported on moral grounds rather than by means of speculative theoretical arguments or proofs. For Kant contends that the overall rational requirements of morality alone support a form of rational faith (*Glaube*) in the existence of God and immortality.

Denying speculative knowledge, making room for rational faith

The above *practical* upshot of the *Critique of Pure Reason* – namely, to secure for pure reason a rationally justifiable faith in the reality of God, free will and the soul – is what Kant means to refer to when he famously remarks in the second (B) edition Preface that he has found it necessary "to deny [or set aside] **knowledge** [*das Wissen aufheben*] in order to make room for **faith** [*Glaube*]" (Bxxx). Kant does not mean that he has found it necessary to deny any kind of knowledge of objects within the entire universe in space and time, that is, within the phenomenal realm of perceivable objects. The "deny knowledge" aspect refers to his attempt to demonstrate in the *Critique* the utter fallaciousness of *theoretical* reason's cherished arguments intended to prove the existence of God, freedom and immortality. The futility of these arguments is what Kant attempts to demonstrate in roughly the entire second half of the *Critique*, namely the Transcendental Dialectic, as we shall see beginning in Chapter 2 on the Antinomies of Pure Reason. Furthermore, traditional speculative metaphysics not only fails to support religious belief but inadvertently continually threatens to undermine the intellectual foundations of religious belief. This effect had become increasingly evident not only to Kant but to many other thinkers of the eighteenth century and wider Enlightenment period. Traditional metaphysics has this self-destructive effect, Kant will argue, by unintentionally making it no more reasonable to conclude that God exists, for example, than to conclude with the materialist that God does not exist.

As briefly mentioned above, however, Kant in the end contends that purely 'practical' considerations pertaining to the ultimate ends of our moral freedom successfully support a rational *moral proof* of the existence of the two noumenal objects additional to freedom, that is, God and immortality. Kant's argument here is based on the idea that it is an objective moral requirement, independent of any assumptions about God, to seek to promote and to strive for a *highest good* in which, contrary to what we currently find, human happiness would be found in proportion to one's moral goodness or virtue. Hence it is 'practically rational' (i.e. rational from the practical perspective of morality) to 'postulate' the real possibility of such a highest good as the object of our moral endeavours. But, as Kant argues in a late section of the First *Critique* entitled "The Canon of Pure Reason" (A795–831/B823–59), only practical reason's *a priori* postulation of the existence of God and immortality can make sense, for us, of that objectively rational requirement of human morality. This is roughly because there is no prospect of our moral endeavours in nature alone, without the support of God and human immortality, being able to achieve such a highest (i.e. all-inclusive, most complete) good.

In a subsequent 'Second *Critique*', the *Critique of Practical Reason* (1788), Kant sums up his argument as follows (note that 'duty', in Kant's account of morality, refers to internally and autonomously self-imposed universal moral obligations, not to duties that are 'heteronomously' imposed by any external authority, whether it be God or the State):

> Now, it was a [moral] duty for us to promote the highest good; hence there is in us not merely the warrant but also the necessity, as a need connected with duty, to presuppose the possibility of this

> highest good, which, since it is possible only under the condition of the existence of God, connects the presupposition of the existence of God inseparably with duty; that is, it is morally necessary to assume the existence of God. (*Practical Reason*, 5:125)

However, Kant continues by immediately seeking to clarify the complex epistemic status of his argument's conclusion:

> It is well to note here that this moral necessity *is subjective*, that is, a need, and not *objective*, that is, itself a duty; for, there can be no duty to assume the existence of anything (since this concerns only the theoretical use of reason). ... What belongs to duty here is only the striving to produce and promote the highest good in the world, the possibility of which can therefore be postulated, while our reason finds this thinkable only on the presupposition of a supreme intelligence [i.e. God]. (*Practical Reason*, 5:125–6)

The grounds for our objective moral obligations lie in pure practical reason and are independent of any belief in God, for Kant. But morality requires us to pursue the highest good and Kant argues on both theoretical and practical grounds that the existence of God and human immortality are required to make sense of the possible achievability of the highest good. Hence Kant concludes that reason *overall* demands the postulation and firm belief in the existence of God and our immortal souls.

A full examination and evaluation of Kant's argument here, as in every case we shall encounter, would raise many questions to reflect on and debate. For example, is Kant right that there are universal moral obligations grounded in pure practical reason in the first place? And if he is, is he also right that one of those purely rational obligations is to promote the highest good in his sense? And if moral duty does require us to promote the highest good as far as we able to do so, why does the latter also require us to assume that such a state of perfection is really achievable? And if Kant is right about the latter, is he also successful in arguing that God and immortality are required in order to conceive the possible achievability of such a condition?

Kant takes on the task of arguing for each of his claims, and it is up to the reader to reflect on both Kant's texts and those of his commentators in the attempt to interpret and ultimately evaluate the success of his arguments. In this short book we shall have to pick and choose which arguments to pursue in further detail. While I shall not pursue the important details of Kant's attempted 'moral proof' for God's existence on this occasion, we should at least keep in view the following intended conclusion: namely, it is the practical standpoint of morality, rather than the theoretical standpoint

METAPHYSICS AND THE "FIERY TEST OF CRITIQUE"

of traditional metaphysics, that is supposed to rescue us from the fallacious abyss that Kant argues continually confronts theoretical reason in these speculative, experience-transcendent domains. In the end, then, Kant denies pure reason's speculative metaphysical knowledge of God, freedom and immortality. Precisely by doing so, however, he seeks to secure the rational respectability and objectivity of practical reason's undeniable founding presupposition (in the case of human freedom) and derivative need-based 'postulations' (in the case of God and our immortal souls) of those same three 'noumenal objects'. This is arguably the most important overall result in Kant's own eyes of his *Critique of Pure Reason*, however different the ultimate significance of his work might be for most philosophers of the twentieth and twenty-first centuries (as we shall see primarily by implication in later chapters).

The First *Critique* is thus a critique of pure reason in its speculative or theoretical rather than practical uses. So how exactly is it that in the First *Critique* pure speculative reason finds itself subjected to a "fiery test of critique" at the hands of Kant? In this chapter let us continue to tease out more of the basic scaffolding of Kant's critical framework, leading up to a more detailed sketch of his account of the problems of pure reason in relation to the traditional aims of metaphysics.

A priori *versus* a posteriori, *pure versus empirical*

In order to understand the problematic yet unavoidable tasks that are set by pure theoretical reason, and hence the question of the very possibility of metaphysics, we need a basic grip on Kant's general notion of '*a priori*' knowledge or cognition. The following distinctions can be a bit tedious, but they are just as important in philosophy today as they were in Kant's own time.

Kant tells us that "**cognitions *a priori***" (i) are characterized by strict *universality* and *necessity* (for example, in 'every ... must ...' judgments such as '*every* event *must* have a cause'); and (ii) are in some sense *knowable independently of all sense experience* (B2–3; cf. A1–2). Mathematical knowledge, for example, as embodied in judgments or propositions such as '2 + 2 = 4', is thought by Kant and by many other philosophers to provide a clear example of *a priori* knowledge. For such judgments, when true, are generally thought to be universally and necessarily true, and to be knowable independently of whatever the particular course of my or your or anyone else's sense experiences happens to have been. This last point requires further clarification, however.

What does 'independent of all experience' mean? Of course, a person has to be born, has to grow up, has to learn a language, has to acquire the relevant concepts and so on in order to be able to grasp any mathematical

21

propositions at all. And this will be accomplished in the course of experience in very different ways depending on each person's experiential history. But the idea of *a priori* knowledge is that once one has come to acquire the relevant concepts by whatever means, it can be shown that the ground of truth and evidence for such demonstrable truths as '2 + 2 = 4' holds independently and irrespective of the particularities of *any* such experiential history. That is roughly the sense in which *a priori* knowledge holds independently of all sense experience (cf. Kitcher 2006).

Does '*a priori*' mean 'innate', then: in some sense, inborn knowledge? Does it refer to what is 'prior *in time*'? Kant in fact rejected the idea, often attributed to him but more commonly to his so-called *rationalist* predecessors Descartes, Spinoza and Leibniz, that *a priori* knowledge consists in the possession of *innate ideas* in the mind or soul from the start: specific ideas that lie ready to be awakened by the stimulus of sense experiences (compare Plato's dialogue the *Meno*). For Kant it is not the ideas or representations themselves that are innate but rather the *faculties* or powers of the mind (of sensibility and understanding) themselves that by their very nature enable us to have what he calls an 'original acquisition' of the relevant *a priori* representations in response to experience over time (cf. Kant's *On a Discovery*: "The *Critique* admits absolutely no divinely implanted [*anerschaffene*] or innate [*angeborne*] representations" [Kant–Eberhard Controversy, 312–13=8:221–3]). It is certainly true for Kant that we do not acquire *a priori* knowledge from the senses. But we do *acquire* our *a priori* knowledge over time, according to Kant: namely, through reflection on the activities and products of our cognitive faculties as they operate both in response to sense experience and in our actions. It is especially important in most cases to take Kant's '*a priori*' to mean *not* '*prior to* sense experience *in time*', but rather something like '*independent of* sense experience as to its source and justification'. In the order of time, sensory stimulation can come first.

The possibility of *a priori* knowledge – in particular, 'synthetic' *a priori* knowledge, as we shall see at the outset of Chapter 2 – is one of the most central concerns in the First *Critique*. In fact, the term *transcendental*, which occurs so frequently throughout Kant's Critical or Transcendental Philosophy, is defined by Kant in terms of the possibility of *a priori* cognition: "I call all cognition transcendental that is occupied not so much with objects but rather with our mode of cognition of objects insofar as this is to be possible *a priori*" (A11–12/B25). (For an important contrast between 'transcendental' in this sense and the term 'transcendent', see A296/B352.)

A posteriori cognitions, by contrast to *a priori* cognitions, are *empirical* in the sense that their source and ultimate justification lie in our experiences of objects that are *given* to our senses, either directly or indirectly. Empirical judgments or propositions that are cognizable only *a posteriori*, such as that '*the Eiffel Tower is in Paris*', or that '*force equals the product of mass and acceleration*' ('$F = ma$'), ultimately have some sensory experiences or other as their source and primary justification.

Note that this is so even if (as in the '$F = ma$' example) such empirical knowledge involves the construction of highly abstract scientific theories and is precisely expressed by means of mathematical laws, as in mathematical physics. For if the motions of bodies in the universe had been very *different* from what we have experienced them to be, then the resulting laws in mathematical physics would have been quite different, too. In this sense it is *contingent* that our universe contains the laws of physics that it does: that is, the universe could have been governed by other physical laws determining the sequence of events in nature. So even such general *a posteriori* knowledge as that '$F = ma$' contrasts in this respect with such *a priori* knowledge as '2 + 2 = 4'.

To elaborate on this last point just a bit (the next five paragraphs take several matters a little more deeply and can be skipped if need be), the case of the status of the laws of physics is actually quite complex on Kant's view. In his book *Metaphysical Foundations of Natural Science* (1786; *MFNS*), Kant argues that while the precise quantitative laws of Newtonian physics are not instances of *a priori* knowledge, but are rather *a posteriori* discoveries, Newton's physics does have a very close relationship to certain more general *a priori* metaphysical principles that are proved in the Critical Philosophy. For example, while the philosopher cannot prove purely *a priori* that matter is governed by the particular quantitative laws of gravitational attraction that were discovered by Newton, Kant does attempt to prove on ('impure') *a priori* grounds that *every* possible movable body in any humanly knowable world *must be* subject to physical forces of attraction and repulsion in general, as part of the very concept of a movable material body occupying space. (For more on these sorts of issues, see Chapter 5.)

The mention here of 'impure' *a priori* knowledge appeals to Kant's distinction between 'pure' and 'mixed' or impure *a priori* knowledge. Among "*a priori* cognitions", Kant tells us, "those are called **pure** with which *nothing empirical* is intermixed" (B3, second italics added). For example, '2 + 2 = 4' is a *pure a priori* proposition, since a mathematician could construct the relevant proof in what Kant calls 'pure imagination' or 'pure intuition' alone, whatever her particular *a posteriori* experiences might have been (in the sense discussed earlier). An *impure a priori* proposition, by contrast, is one that includes some empirical concept that ultimately derives from sense experience as an essential part of its content, but nonetheless the proposition as a whole is still knowable *a priori*, independently of the experience of any particular empirical objects at all.

For instance, as we shall see later on, the 'category' of *causality* for Kant is a *pure a priori* concept that derives from certain purely formal aspects of our understanding of *any possible sense experience* of objects in general. So the *a priori* principle of causality, roughly that 'every experienceable event must have some determining cause', does not have as its source or derive its justification from the experience, *a posteriori*, of any particular given object or other (although, as Kant will crucially argue, the causal principle necessarily *applies to* all such objects of possible experience). By contrast, the more particular proposition that 'every *motion in space* has a cause' is an *impure a priori* truth, because the concept of *motion*, according to Kant, is a very general empirical concept that is ultimately derived from sense experiences. So it works out roughly this way: (i) the *pure a priori* causal principle is proved in the *Critique of Pure Reason*; (ii) the *impure a priori* causal principle as applied to moving bodies in general is proved in the *Metaphysical Foundations of Natural Science*; and (iii) the particular *a posteriori* mathematical–physical laws of motion and gravity that fall under those *a priori* principles are discovered by Newton and other scientific inquirers (and perhaps in some respects, like (ii), such laws might be deducible *a priori* given various further *a posteriori* assumptions, as Michael Friedman [1992] has argued).

Strictly speaking, although I shall not always make this explicit in stating Kant's principles, there are really two different kinds or levels of necessity involved in Kant's causal principle and in fact (on my reading) in all his other synthetic *a priori* principles, too. First, the content of each such principle represents that a particular kind of first-order objective necessity obtains among the empirical objects of our experience themselves. For example, an event of empirical kind *A* (releasing an object) causally necessitates the occurrence of an event of kind *B* (the object falling); or, for a different example, physical objects and events in space and time are subject to laws or principles of arithmetic and geometry (e.g. '2 + 2 = 4'). But second, what Kant will argue in the *Critique* is that principles that represent objects as themselves obeying necessary laws in this way can themselves be proved, at the 'transcendental' or philosophical level of analysis, to be *necessarily applicable* to, or *objectively valid* in relation to, all our possible experience of the world. That is, Kant will argue that such principles or laws, which say the world *must always* be such-and-such a way, *must* themselves have objectively valid application to experience, if any experience of objects whatsoever is to be possible for us.

So, for example, the *a priori* principle of causality for Kant, in the end, will really technically be something like this: 'Necessarily (= a transcendental necessity, i.e. if experience is to be possible): for any given event, call it *B* (for example, a loud noise), there existed *some* preceding kind of event or other, call it *A* (perhaps a detonated bomb), such that events of *A*'s type (bomb-detonations) are *universally and necessarily* followed by (i.e. they causally necessitate or produce) events of *B*'s type (loud noises).' As shorthand, however, I shall usually simply state the principle as 'every event must have a cause', or 'necessarily, every event has a cause', and we shall not worry about this technical point. But in the long run I think it is essential to a correct understanding of Kant's overall philosophy to distinguish the necessity that forms part of the *content* of such principles or laws (e.g. 'A causally necessitates B') from the transcendental or philosophical question of whether such laws in general are themselves objectively valid in the sense of being, for example, *necessary for the possibility of our having any experience* or cognition of the world at all. Explaining what the latter means is one of the central tasks of the *Critique of Pure Reason* and it will be one of the central tasks of this book, too.

Returning to the main point, then, whereas *a priori* knowledge tells us what is necessarily and universally the case, and does so independently of any particular history of experience, *a posteriori* knowledge "tells us, to be sure, what is, but never that it must necessarily be thus and not otherwise" (A1). This is the crucial point: *a posteriori* experience tells us what is and what has been the case, but cannot tell us anything about what *must always* be the case; whereas *a priori* knowledge consists in precisely such universal and necessary truths. (Kant's famous distinction between *analytic* and *synthetic* judgments, and the pivotal question, "How are synthetic judgments *a priori* possible?" (B19), will be addressed at the start of the next chapter.)

Philosophy, and hence metaphysics, on Kant's view, has primarily to do with the nature and possibility of *a priori* knowledge rather than with *a posteriori* empirical knowledge *per se*. This is true in both theoretical and practical philosophy. In practical philosophy, for example, even if it were true that most, or even all, human beings happen to feel badly whenever they knowingly harm another innocent human being, that would be a merely *a posteriori* (although very welcome!) empirical truth about the psychological nature of all or most members of the human species. But on Kant's view the idea that is really central to morality – roughly, the idea that any free rational being whatsoever ought always to act in such a way as to respect the inviolable dignity of any other free rational being – is an objectively binding *a priori* principle or idea of pure reason. As we have seen, however, it is in the contrasting domain of pure *speculative* reasoning that Kant thinks human reason inevitably gets into trouble in its attempts to prove the existence of such 'pure intelligibles' or 'noumena' as God, free will and the soul. And we shall see in the next chapter that this led Kant to probe more deeply and to ask in a critical spirit whether, and if so how, even the most basic metaphysical principles of substance and causality can have any objective validity at all.

The general contrast between reason's pure *a priori* ideas of intelligible beings and our *a posteriori* sensory knowledge of empirical phenomena embodies another indispensable distinction that runs throughout Kant's Critical Philosophy. We had better introduce it here at the start.

1.2 'APPEARANCES' VERSUS 'THINGS IN THEMSELVES': KANT'S TRANSCENDENTAL IDEALISM

Sensible 'appearances' versus intelligible 'things in themselves'

In the long passage from the *Lectures on Metaphysics* quoted at the outset of the previous section, Kant indicates that the metaphysical ideas of God, freedom and immortality "are pure concepts of reason that simply cannot be exhibited in appearance, [and] which therefore can merely be thought. One can therefore call them supersensible objects, *noumena*, i.e., objects of the understanding, and oppose them to the *phenomena*" (italics added). (Note that Kant himself will argue, as we shall see in the next chapter, that noumena or things in themselves are *not* in fact 'intelligible' to us in the sense of being *understandable* by us. But they are putative objects of pure intellect (*nous*) or pure reason, and in this sense they are 'pure intelligibles' as opposed to 'sensible' objects or 'phenomena'. For Kant they will turn out to be intelligible only from the practical standpoint of morality.) Although both Kant and Kant scholars draw important distinctions between them in some contexts, initially we can assume that the followings terms are roughly equivalent: *appearances = phenomena* and *things in themselves = noumena*. Let us treat them as equivalent until some particular context requires us to distinguish them. (See for example Allison [2004: 57–60] for some of the relevant distinctions between them.)

The first point to be clear about in this connection is that by 'appearances' (or phenomena) Kant does *not* mean to be referring to anything that is in any sense *illusory* or not objectively real (see B69–70 on illusions). It is useful to think of Kant's use of the term 'phenomena' in the way that we use the phrase 'astronomical phenomena', for example, to refer to various objective, perceivable movements of physical bodies in space and time in general. Similarly, Kant's use of 'appearances' for the most part refers to objects in space and time that are capable of *making their appearance to our senses*, as I shall put it, in ordinary cases of objective perceptual cognition. The appearances, in this (objective) sense, are the ordinary empirical objects that appear on the spatiotemporal stage of common human experience and scientific inquiry.

In this primary sense you and I can both directly visually perceive the *same* particular 'appearance' or 'phenomenon' that is the physical Eiffel Tower in Paris: from different visual perspectives, of course. Other things being equal, the realm of appearances or phenomena for Kant should in this way be thought of as referring to all of the sorts of experienceable objects and processes that make up the ordinary spatiotemporal universe. This includes both the physical objects and events that are directly or indirectly accessible to our five 'outer' senses, as well as all those felt, remembered and introspected psychological states that Kant calls the objects of 'inner sense'.

Generally speaking, what Kant usually means to refer to by 'the appearances', then, are just the various sorts of objects and events that we eat for lunch, or theoretically postulate and confirm in physics, or introspectively encounter in our internal reflections. It can be a helpful corrective to remember, in particular, that Kant means to include among the empirical objects that 'appear to us' all the sorts of scientifically inferred but (as things stand) *not directly observable* entities in space and time that, for example, occur below the particular perceptual thresholds of our sense organs. As Kant puts the point in one place in the *Critique* (in relation to the *a priori* concept or 'category' of *actuality* or *existence*):

> Thus we cognize the existence of a magnetic matter penetrating all bodies from the perception of attracted iron filings, although an immediate perception of this matter is impossible for us given the constitution of our organs. For in accordance with the laws of sensibility and the context of our perceptions we could also happen upon the immediate empirical intuition of it in an experience if our senses, the crudeness of which does not affect the form of possible experience in general, were finer. Thus wherever perception and whatever is appended to it in accordance with empirical laws reaches, there too reaches our cognition of the existence of things. (B273–4)

"The laws of sensibility" (i.e. spatiotemporality) and "empirical laws" (such as physical laws of nature) appealed to in this passage are basically what I shall be drawing on whenever I refer to what is 'directly *or indirectly* intuitable' or perceivable by means of the senses.

Kant does not use the term 'appearances' to refer primarily to what some empiricist philosophers have called 'sense-data'. He is not primarily concerned with objects as they appear differently within the individual consciousnesses of different perceivers in particular conditions, although his analysis will highlight the essentially perspectival and situated nature of human experience in general. Nor is his focus on the 'presenting surfaces' of objects as opposed to their 'insides' and whatever scientifically postulated 'micro-processes' (as we would call them) are theorized to be going on in such objects (the latter micro-processes, on Kant's view, would *also* be lawful spatiotemporal appearances in his sense). When Kant's analysis of experience does require him to introduce more strict notions of 'appearance', he does so and we shall do so. In most contexts, then, it is safest to begin by thinking of Kant's 'realm of appearances' as roughly made up of all the *outer material bodies and inner psychological states* that science and common sense take our universe to contain.

Transcendental idealism

But if that is the case, why does Kant use the term 'appearance' and phrases such as "mere appearances to us" or "mere representations in us" at all, instead of simply referring to 'physical objects' and 'psychological states' or whatever the case may be? To answer this important question we can begin by appealing to the contrast we just saw Kant himself make, namely, between all the "phenomena" that can be "exhibited in appearance" to our senses in space and time on the one hand, in contrast to supersensible "noumena, i.e., objects of the understanding" such as God, free will and the soul on the other. Kant is making a general distinction between *two essentially different kinds of objects of thought*, about which we can then raise various questions. Such questions include whether, and in what sense, the objects to which such thoughts purport to refer really exist as we conceive them to be, or not. On the one hand we have concepts of the appearances or phenomena as the sorts of spatiotemporal objects that by their very nature are in principle perceivable by means of our senses, in the ways discussed above. On the other hand we have reason's ideas of purely intelligible, supersensible, noumenal objects such as God, free will and immaterial souls, thinkable objects that by their very nature are not spatiotemporal bodies and are thus not perceivable by means of our senses in Kant's wide sense.

Kant's much disputed doctrine of *transcendental idealism* is the general thesis that we have theoretical knowledge of things *only as appearances, not as they are in themselves*. This philosophical or 'transcendental' distinction between appearances to us and things in themselves arises "in regard to things when they are considered in themselves through reason, i.e., without taking account of the constitution of our sensibility" (A28/B44). Of course, as we have already seen, Kant argues that we do have a *pure practical cognition* of free will and objective morality, and thereby also of God and the soul, as 'noumena' or 'things in themselves' (understood with the important qualifications discussed above in §1.1). But unless such a 'practical' context of freedom and morality is explicitly indicated, let us follow Kant's predominant practice in the First *Critique* and use the term 'knowledge' or 'cognition' (*Erkenntnis*) primarily to refer to the *theoretical* cognition of objects. The present point, then, is that when encountering Kant's general distinctions between 'appearances versus things in themselves' or 'phenomena versus noumena', we not only have to grapple with issues pertaining to our alleged knowledge of such supersensible noumenal objects as God, free will and the soul, but also come to grips with Kant's general transcendental idealist thesis that our knowledge even of such ordinary spatiotemporal objects as trees, puppy-dog tails and "magnetic matter" is only a knowledge of such things 'as appearances' (or 'as they appear *to us*') and not of those things 'as things in themselves' (or 'as they are *in themselves*'). But what does *that* mean?

That is a good question and a fiercely disputed one among Kant's interpreters, both past and present. We have seen that the 'transcendental' in 'transcendental idealism' refers to inquiries into the possibility of *a priori* cognition. What about the 'idealism'? Philosophical idealism in general, in the relevant sense, always involves some kind of contrast with 'realism', both of which come in many different forms. Very roughly, idealists argue that certain fundamental aspects of reality, aspects that we might pre-philosophically have assumed to exist entirely independently of our minds, have in fact in some sense a '*mind-dependent*' existence. To begin with we can consider an example of an *empirically* mind-dependent entity or aspect, which we can then oppose to the more unusual, philosophical 'mind-dependence' involved in Kant's *transcendental* (as opposed to empirical) idealism.

Here is an example of a merely empirically ideal or empirically mind-dependent 'object' (which, again, must not be confused with Kant's *transcendentally* ideal 'phenomena'). If I see an after-image when I blink after a camera flash, I do not suppose that the green blob that appears intermittently to be on the white wall over there is an object that has any existence apart from, or independently of, my mind. The after-image is something – whatever it is – the existence of which depends on my visual apprehension of it. (Here, of course, we must distinguish the physical cause of my after-imaging – i.e. as involving various material processes in my retina, etc. – from the after-image as a green blob that appears in my visual field in roughly the same location as the white wall over there.) In short, the after-image, whatever it is – perhaps it is only a mentally represented item – exists when and only when *I sense it*. The after-image is thus a merely 'empirically ideal' object of or content in my own mental state.

But if after-images are perhaps empirically mind-dependent entities or 'represent*eds*' in this sense, one might reasonably expostulate that surely the wall and the camera that we all can see are entirely *mind-independent* entities. Why, then, does Kant describe such physical objects as the wall, too, as 'mere appearances to us'? In what sense are public material objects supposed to be 'transcendentally ideal'? Are rocks merely mind-dependent 'appearances', for instance, and not 'things in themselves'?

We can begin by noting that idealists come in different stripes about many different aspects of experience, but most idealists argue that certain important aspects (some argue that *all* aspects) of all ordinary physical objects, as such, are mind-dependent and hence depend for their very existence either on our minds or perhaps on God's mind, or both. *To be is to perceive or be perceived*, as the Irish philosopher Bishop George Berkeley (1685–1753) famously held in his defence of a particularly strong form of idealism.

We shall find that Kant's transcendental idealism is indeed *some* kind of idealism, but crucially different from Berkeley's or any other idealism prior to Kant's time. For it will involve the recognition, to put it crudely at first, that all empirical objects must be conceived, in ways to be explored throughout this book, with essential reference to *our* cognitive faculties: in particular, to our *a priori forms of sensibility* (see Chapter 3) and of *understanding* (Chapters 4 and 5). Empirical objects are 'appearances-to-us' in that sense, a sense that I have deliberately left entirely vague at this early stage. Kant's conception of objects as 'things in themselves', by contrast, concerns what must be true of objects as considered in some sense by 'pure reason' independently of those same *a priori* cognitive conditions of sensibility and understanding. To consider an object (of theoretical reason) 'as a thing in itself', Kant will argue, is to conceive it independently of those *a priori* conditions that enable human subjects to have any real knowledge of any object whatsoever. Hence it will turn out that we can have no (theoretical) knowledge of objects conceived as 'things in themselves'.

But all of those so-called 'transcendental *realists*' whom Kant takes himself to be opposing – and this will presumably include every philosopher who is not a transcendental *idealist* in Kant's sense – might reasonably ask: why should we think that the description of how objects *are* should require any *essential* reference to what it takes for human beings to have *knowledge* or cognition of them? Things are as they are; what it takes for human beings or any other being to have knowledge of them is quite another matter, says the transcendental realist. (In Chapter 2 we shall explore the opposed notion of 'transcendental realism' in detail, which Kant ultimately diagnoses as the mistake of taking the appearances to be things in themselves.) But Kant thinks that there is a crucial (in fact, 'transcendental') sense in which the legions of transcendental realists are mistaken in the ways that they handle this intuitive point.

Yes, there is a perfectly good sense in which empirical objects exist out there in space independently of my experiences of them and independently of your or anyone else's perceptions of them. This is what Kant calls his *empirical realism*, the essential flip-side of his transcendental idealism, and it constitutes his rejection of what he calls the *empirical idealism* of philosophers such as Berkeley (more on this below). But once we understand what it really takes for us to have knowledge of any objects whatsoever, Kant argues, we will discover that the transcendental realist's contrasting conception of objects 'as-things-in-themselves' is virtually empty.

That the notion of 'things in themselves' is *not entirely* empty will be due primarily to three factors: (i) the ideas of *practical reason* concerning freedom and morality, as discussed above; (ii) our essential *sensory passivity* with respect to knowledge of things in general, to be discussed briefly below and in Chapter 3; and (iii) the *regulative maxims* and ideals of reason, to be discussed briefly at the end of Chapters 2 and 5, and in the Conclusion. As far as our theoretical cognition of objects is concerned, however, the conception of 'things in themselves' or of the 'noumenal realm' primarily functions only as a *negative limiting condition* concerning the scope and limits of human knowledge. (See Kant's conception of "a noumenon in the **negative** sense", e.g. at B307–8.)

Although understanding these difficult matters will require the work of later chapters, it might be helpful by way of anticipation to lay out in Table 1.1 Kant's crucial and easily missed *twofold distinction* between 'appearances vs. things in themselves', that is, as understood in both an empirical sense and in a transcendental sense. Kant's own position is at one and the same time an *empirical realism* and a *transcendental idealism*. (For simplicity's sake, the following table focuses only on the case of 'outer sense' and our perception of material objects in space, setting aside the case of time and the objects of 'inner sense' as such.)

One can see from Table 1.1 that Kant regards such philosophical distinctions as between what is 'outside us vs. inside us', 'objective vs. subjective' and 'appearance vs. reality' to be systematically ambiguous between an empirical sense and a transcendental sense. For example, if someone asks, 'Do spatiotemporal objects such as tables exist merely "in our minds" according to Kant?', an answer should run along something like the following lines.

No, material objects such as tables do not exist in our minds; they exist outside our minds in space, objectively. That is Kant's empirical realism. In the transcendental sense, however, there is, as we might put it, both an aspect of general mind-dependence and of mind-independence. For Kant there is clearly a 'problematic' sense (to use Kant's own term) in which we can (in fact, we must) say that 'things in themselves' are *given* to us by affecting our sensibility, although the only cognition we have of things in general is as spatiotemporal objects, plus our own indispensable idea of free will. As Kant puts it in the B-Preface, "even if we cannot **cognize** these same objects as things in themselves, we at least must be able to **think** them as things in themselves. For otherwise there would follow the absurd proposition that there is an appearance without anything that appears" (Bxxvi). This problematic issue pertaining to the idea of unknowable 'things in themselves' as affecting our senses is often called the *problem of affection* in Kant, and we shall encounter it again at the end of Chapter 3. The present point is that in both this problematic 'transcendental' sense pertaining to 'things in themselves', and in the ordinary empirical sense pertaining to outer material objects in space, our minds do not 'create' the objects that we know; they do not exist merely 'in us'.

But our minds do contribute the all-comprehensive *a priori* forms of sensibility (space and time) and of understanding (the categories of causality,

Table 1.1 Kant's transcendental idealism and empirical realism.

	'Appearances' ('in us'; subjective; mind-dependent)	**'Things'** ('outside us'; objective; mind-independent)
Understood in the **empirical** sense	The sensations, perceptions, mental images, dreams, hallucinations, colour-blindness, etc., of particular people as such. Starting-point for **empirical idealism** (not for Kant). Empirically subjective.	Ordinary material objects and scientific processes outside us in space. **Kant's empirical realism.** Empirically objective.
In Kant's **transcendental** sense	**Kant's transcendental idealism:** material objects in so far as they conform to our *a priori* forms of sensibility (space and time) and understanding (the categories). Transcendental subjectivity.	**Noumenal 'things in themselves'** = things as thought by pure reason, not as conforming to our *a priori* forms of experience. Kant: *unknowable by us* (except *practically* re: 'idea of freedom'). **'Transcendental realists'** mistakenly treat appearances as things in themselves.

material substance, etc.) by means of which we do know things as objects of experience (phenomena). Kant's transcendental idealism is the thesis that we have knowledge of things *only as they appear* under those *a priori* forms of human cognition; we have no knowledge of them in so far as they are thought as 'things in themselves' or 'noumena'. (Again, here we set aside the key role of practical reason and freedom.) The knowledge we do have of things is captured in Kant's empirical realism: we have *a priori* knowledge of the necessary structure of the objectively real world of outer material and inner psychological 'phenomena'. The humanly knowable real world is an ever-expansive universe of experienceable objects that make their appearance to our senses in one vast three-dimensional space and one vast historical time-order.

Kant takes his position of transcendental idealism and empirical realism to represent a very sharp break from all of his philosophical predecessors, realist and idealist alike. Recognizing such a sharp break is not to deny that one cannot adequately understand Kant without understanding his predecessors and his historical context, which is also true. But one major task in attempting to evaluate Kant's unique view is to try to understand what he really means when he concludes that the entire realm of empirical objects in space and time has a certain status that consists in being knowable only as how such things are necessarily represented by us (the phenomenal realm) and not as how such things are or might be as things in themselves. Understanding what that 'transcendental ideality' really amounts to is one of the steepest challenges facing any reader of Kant's philosophy. For the moment we can perhaps tease out Kant's transcendental idealism just a bit further as follows.

Our senses are affected by a reality that is not of our own making. For example, there is a clear sense in which, when I open my eyes, just which layout of potential objects of knowledge will *appear to my senses* is not a matter of my free choice. I do not actively *choose* for there to appear to me to be a tree directly in front of me when I open my eyes. Rather, my senses are passively affected in a certain way, and as a result I immediately see or touch – that is, I sensorily *intuit*, to use Kant's technical term – a certain spatiotemporal scene directly present to me. Note that this important *sensory passivity thesis* is perfectly compatible with its also being true that our sense perception of objects, considered overall, is very much an active, exploratory and mutually conditioning engagement with our external environment, both biologically and conceptually.

In addition to the above aspects of sensory passivity in the experience, however, as a thinker who possesses the relevant concepts I shall also take the particular items that I perceptually encounter to be of various *kinds*: in this case, *to be a tree*. I see this object *as* a tree, as a living thing, as (at least implicitly, or so Kant will argue) a substantial material body that is causally affected in various ways and which will continue to exist when it is no longer perceived by me. In short, my perceptual experience of the scene before me is in this case structured by my *concept* of a tree. What I see is *this tree (here-now)*, which involves both the spatiotemporal presentation or *sensory intuition* of a particular object and a *general concept* under which that object falls. The particular empirical concept of a tree, as Kant will later explain, is an instance of the pure *a priori* conceptual category of a persisting material body or *substance* in space, subject to various *causal* influences.

The necessary combined role of sensory intuitions and concepts in human cognition – working together like the blades of a pair of scissors, to borrow a simile from William James – will be the basis for Kant's famous statement, later in the *Critique*, that "Thoughts without content are empty, intuitions without concepts are blind" (A51/B75). In the chapters to follow we shall see that Kant argues that all possible human experience of objects is necessarily structured by *space and time* as the pure *a priori* forms of our sensory intuition, and by twelve *categories* as the pure *a priori* forms of our conceptual understanding. For future reference (see Chapter 4), Kant's four groups of three pure *a priori* conceptual categories are as follows: (i) *Quantity*: unity, plurality, and totality; (ii) *Quality*: reality, negation, and limitation; (iii) *Relation*: substance, causality, and mutual interaction; and (iv) *Modality*: possibility, actuality, necessity.

So consider again my perceptual experience of the tree, first in relation to the role of space and time in my experience. I perceive the tree as existing *now*, and as *having existed* for some duration of time. I also perceive the tree as occupying a certain three-dimensional region of space in relation to the objects beside and beyond it. In fact, all of my 'outer' perceptual experiences whatsoever, whatever their particular sensory content or 'matter' might be, have this kind of spatiotemporal 'form' or structure in general (this is one of Kant's many 'matter–form' distinctions). Kant will argue that every object or occurrence in the world throughout the endless horizon of all possible human experience must be conceived as existing or as occurring at some point in time in some region of space, ultimately in some relation, however indirect, to the perspectival 'here and now' of perceptual experience (see Chapter 3).

Similarly, Kant's proposal is that all of my perceptual experiences are structured by one member of each of the four groups of *a priori* conceptual *categories*. In our simple example, perhaps I either implicitly or explicitly conceptualize the object as, for instance, *a large green tree*: more specifically, as an *actual* (Modality) *large* (Quantity) *green* (Quality) *tree* (Substance), 'intuited' here and now as situated in a certain region of space during a certain period of time. In roughly the first half of the *Critique of Pure Reason*, that is, in the Transcendental Aesthetic (discussed in Chapter 3) and in the Transcendental Analytic (Chapters 4 and 5), Kant famously attempts to prove that all possible human perceptual knowledge *must* be jointly structured in this way by space and time, the pure forms of human sensory intuition, and the categories, the pure forms of conceptual thinking. I mentioned earlier that the Transcendental Dialectic, which occupies roughly the second half of the *Critique*, investigates the 'logic of illusion' that leads speculative metaphysicians to the mistaken belief that pure reason can demonstrate ultimate truths concerning God, freedom and immortality (see Chapter 2). So apart from an important Transcendental Doctrine of Method that occurs at the end of the book, all of the basic 'transcendental elements' and cognitive faculties that form the main topics of Kant's First *Critique* have been introduced in this chapter, as was earlier anticipated in the Introduction in relation to Table 1.2 (note once again that 'idea' [*Idee*] in Kant refers to highly abstract concepts, principles or ideals of pure reason, not to perceptual image-like 'ideas' as used by Locke, Berkeley or Hume).

So as we have seen, Kant's transcendental idealism is the claim that we can know things only as they 'appear to us' *as represented* in conformity with our *a priori* forms of sensibility and understanding. In particular, Kant will argue

Table 1.2 Transcendental Doctrine of Elements.

	Transcendental **Logic**	
Transcendental **Aesthetic**	Transcendental **Analytic**	Transcendental **Dialectic**
faculty of sensibility	faculty of understanding	faculty of reason
intuitions	concepts	ideas

that we can know things only as *causally interacting material substances in one spatiotemporal universe of possible experience*. Ordinarily, of course, that might be taken to be knowing things as they are in themselves. So once again the perfectly reasonable question to ask at this point is why exactly does it follow from this, according to Kant, that we do not thereby represent and know such spatiotemporal material substances *as they are in themselves*? I have offered some suggestions above as to how Kant would begin to answer that question, and there will be further exploration of Kant's transcendental idealism. It might be helpful, however, to provide a brief statement of one of the main debates that has arisen in the secondary literature concerning both the nature and the validity of Kant's transcendental idealism. I shall adopt the terms that are most often used by Kant scholars in this connection. (For comprehensive overviews of the secondary literature on the topic of transcendental idealism, see Ameriks [2003: chs 2, 3].)

'Two aspects' or 'two worlds'?

Kant's transcendental idealism early on (Bxviii–xx) receives two formulations that may be taken to illustrate two widely contrasted and contested interpretations of what Kant's 'formal' or 'critical' idealism, as he also calls it (*Prolegomena*, 88=4:293, 163=4:375; cf. B518), amounts to: namely, the so-called 'two-aspect' (or 'double-aspect') as opposed to 'two-world' (or 'two-object') interpretations of what Kant intended by his transcendental idealism.

On the one hand, Kant states in the B-Preface that "our rational cognition *a priori* ... reaches appearances only, leaving the thing [*Sache*] in itself as something actual for itself but uncognized by us" (Bxx). This formulation might encourage the traditional *'two-world'* interpretation according to which the *ultimately real* things that are responsible for the appearances are what Kant calls the 'things in themselves', which we can in a sense think about and must postulate but which we cannot know or cognize as objects (i.e. of theoretical reason). On 'two-world' and similar interpretations, what we know are only the *appearances* of this unknown thing or things, whatever it or they may be, which affect us through sensation and to which we respond by 'constructing', as it were, a shared phenomenal world of appearances in space and time. Many well-known critics of Kant's transcendental idealism, such as G. W. F. Hegel (1770–1831) in the nineteenth century and the twentieth-century Oxford analytic philosopher P. F. Strawson in his book *The Bounds of Sense* (cf. 1966: pt IV), argue that Kant's two-world transcendental idealist metaphysics is plagued with multiple absurdities and internal inconsistencies. On these interpretations of Kant's view we can have no knowledge of the ultimately real, non-spatial, non-temporal 'thing or things in themselves' that timelessly 'produce' sensations in us (how? causally? yet unknowably?), and which we synthesize into a world of merely phenomenal sensory appearances in space and time. One's very self, for instance, is on this view supposed (incoherently) to be in reality a timelessly 'active' agent that exists 'outside' space and time, and yet at the same time to appear to one's own self, in the here and now, as a bodily being, a 'process' that involves a sensory 'self-affection' by those same, ultimately real and timeless noumenal activities on our merely phenomenally 'constructed' empirical selves. Many critical wedges have been driven into the cracks in this traditional picture of Kant's transcendental idealism.

On the other hand, just two pages earlier Kant had introduced the same contrast between appearances and things in themselves in these terms:

> … the same objects can be considered from two different sides, **on the one side** as objects of the senses and the understanding for experience, and **on the other side** as objects that are merely thought at most for isolated reason striving beyond the bounds of experience. (Bxviii–xix n.)

Highlighting the *two conceptual perspectives* that are taken on "the same objects" in the latter passage, many non-traditional '*two-aspect*' or 'two standpoints' interpretations (i.e. emphasizing two different *meta-philosophical points of view*) over the past half-century or so have contended that the heart of Kant's transcendental idealism is the idea that on his view "things are considered from this twofold standpoint" (Bxix, *fn.*). The rough idea behind two-aspect readings is as follows.

As we saw earlier, one of those standpoints or perspectives – the *human standpoint*, as it has been called, following Kant (e.g. Longuenesse 2005) – gives us genuine cognition of the objects as experienceable phenomena in objective empirical reality in space and time. The other standpoint, however, is the idealizing standpoint of pure theoretical reason or, as some have called it (for reasons that should become clear), the *theocentric standpoint*, or the

'God's-eye point of view' (cf. Allison 2004; Putnam 1981). (For an example of Kant's conception of our idea of 'things in themselves' as beginning with the idea of God and then working 'downwards', as it were, see "Some Remarks on Ludwig Heinrich Jakob's *Examination of Mendelssohn's Morning Hours*" [1786] in Kant's *Anthropology, History, and Education* [181=8:154].) This latter standpoint generates certain *ideas* or thoughts of pure reason that outstrip the bounds of possible experience, and thus fail to give us any theoretical cognition of any object whatsoever, thus leading to the inevitable errors and the 'transcendental illusions' of traditional speculative metaphysics (see Chapter 2). Our only valid cognitions of non-empirical 'objects' – or more properly of what Kant calls "an **object in the idea**" of reason, rather than a proper object of our understanding *per se* (A671/B699) – are based ultimately on purely *practical* or moral considerations as discussed earlier; that is, in relation to the practical reality of our free intentional actions and volitions as governed by the objective requirements, the highest ends and (in the case of justifying our ideas of God and immortality) the resulting derivative needs of human morality. We can have no cognition properly speaking of any such object that transcends the realm of possible experience, as all the 'ideas of reason' do. (Again, to be more precise we shall see towards the end of the next chapter and in the Conclusion that the ideas of theoretical reason also have a perfectly good *immanent* use within experience, rather than a use that is *transcendent* of experience, provided that such ideas of pure reason are treated merely as *regulative maxims* rather than as principles that are *constitutive* of possible experience.)

The double-aspect and related readings can then argue that when Kant characterizes 'things in themselves' (e.g. our own 'character' as free agents) as 'timeless' or 'non-spatial' when viewed from the practical perspective of our rational freedom, he need not and should not be read as asserting or postulating the existence of a special kind of deeply problematic *timeless entity* (although he does argue, in a different sense, that we are entitled to think of ourselves *as if* we were immaterial entities or souls, as a justifiable antimaterialist *regulative maxim* or 'idea' of reason). Rather, our free rational agency is positively conceived by Kant only within the practical standpoint that concerns our principled intentions, rational norms and objective duties. On Kant's view this practical standpoint is a rational conceptual framework of a radically different kind from, and conceptually *irreducible* to, the otherwise all-comprehensive theoretical-explanatory framework that is involved in our knowledge of the law-governed motions of all matter in space and across time. On this more congenial sort of interpretation of transcendental idealism, Kant's contention that our free rational agency is necessarily *not* conceived as a spatiotemporal causal process in the latter sense does not entail that our free agency *is* thereby being conceived positively as a special *non*-spatiotemporal process or activity taking place in a different realm of timeless and shapeless being. (We shall encounter a distinction similar to this last one during our examination of Kant's "Paralogisms of Pure Reason" at the end of Chapter 4.)

The general distinction between two-aspect and two-world interpretations of Kant's philosophy is itself not always clear or uncontroversial (to put it mildly), and it should certainly be taken with a grain of salt as one puts in the hard work of trying to figure out just what Kant's transcendental idealism might really amount to. (For recent discussions, see Bird [2006a: 41–4]; Van Cleve [1999: 143–50, "One World or Two?"]; and also Allais [2004].) Roughly speaking, however, 'two-world' and similar interpretations of Kant (such as Guyer [1987] and Strawson [1966] are often taken to be) have tended to argue that his transcendental idealism is the least plausible aspect of Kant's philosophy and should be *detached*, wherever possible, from Kant's more valuable and enduring insights concerning human knowledge and moral freedom. The less traditional 'two-aspect' and related interpretations, by contrast, have generally been articulated in *defence* of Kant's transcendental idealism as an essentially sound thesis that concerns the nature and proper limits of human cognition (see e.g. Allison 2004; Bird 1962, 2006a; Prauss 1974). On the two-aspect or 'two standpoints' interpretation, Kant's notion of 'things as they are in themselves' or 'noumena' is primarily a negative limiting concept, at least in the theoretical domain, as explained earlier. As such, however, the idea of things as they are in themselves, even on two-aspect views, remains a necessary correlate (in a sense that such interpretations attempt to clarify) of the true 'critical' perspective according to which genuine human knowledge of reality is restricted solely to objects that make their appearance to us *within* the vast and ever-expansive spatiotemporal world of possible experience.

Kant's 'Copernican' turn in metaphysics

We shall return to questions concerning the nature of Kant's transcendental idealism in the following chapters, in particular in Chapter 3 on space and time. There we shall put a bit more flesh on what has come to be known as Kant's *Copernican revolution* or Copernican turn in metaphysics, which is closely related to his transcendental idealism. This is based on the famous comparison Kant makes in the B-Preface between the heliocentric (i.e. sun-centred) scientific revolution in astronomy that had been initiated by the Polish astronomer, Nicolaus Copernicus (1473–1543), and the new conception of metaphysics and other *a priori* knowledge that Kant himself is proposing. The following is among the most famous passages in the *Critique of Pure Reason*:

> Up to now it has been assumed that all our cognition must conform to the objects; but all attempts to find out something about them *a priori* through concepts that would extend our cognition have, on this presupposition, come to nothing. Hence let us once try whether we do not get farther with the problems of metaphysics by assuming that the objects must conform to our cognition, which would agree better with the requested possibility of an *a priori* cognition of them, which is to establish something about objects before they are given to us. This would be just like the first thoughts of Copernicus, who ... tried to see if he might not have greater success if he made the observer revolve and left the stars at rest. (Bxvi)

According to the revolutionary view of metaphysics that Kant will defend, as briefly foreshadowed in this chapter, "the object (as an object of the senses) conforms to the constitution of our faculty of intuition" as well as to the constitution of our faculty of "understanding, whose rule I have to presuppose in myself before any object is given to me, hence *a priori*" (Bxvii). We shall need to explore Kant's substantive views in both the Transcendental Aesthetic and the Analytic in order to understand what it means – and what it does *not* mean – for *the objects to conform to our cognition* in this sense, for Kant. Certainly the more usual or 'common-sense' idea (which, however, on traditional 'non-critical' philosophical assumptions gives rise to what Kant regards as ultimately incoherent 'transcendental realist' outlooks) is that our cognition, in order to provide knowledge of objects in the world, must conform to those objects as they really are 'in themselves', rather than the reverse. But as I hope to show, there is much to be said in favour of Kant's so-called Copernican turn in philosophy, whether or not one ultimately concludes that central aspects of it ought to be accepted, or modified, or rejected. As indicated, Kant's own defence of an 'immanent' as opposed to 'transcendent' metaphysics will be based on his detailed arguments for the conclusion that within our sense experience itself there already lie certain *a priori* forms and principles of human sensibility (space and time) and understanding (the categories), and that these can be rationally justified in so far as they can be shown to be necessary for the very possibility of any experience or empirical knowledge whatsoever.

What needs to be further explored at the moment, however, is how it was that Kant was supposed to have been 'awakened' to see the need for such a radical critique of traditional rational metaphysics – a *Critique of Pure Reason* – in the first place, and thereby to see the need to distinguish between the knowable spatiotemporal universe of 'appearances' on the one hand, and the thought of unknowable 'things in themselves' on the other.

CHAPTER 2

WAKING FROM DOGMATIC SLUMBERS: HUME AND THE ANTINOMIES

> [B]y an unavoidable law of nature the question 'Why?' will pursue you, and require you to go beyond this point ... (A488/B516)

> This sort of investigation will always remain difficult, for it includes the *metaphysics of metaphysics*. (Letter to Herz, 1781)

2.1 HUME'S SCEPTICISM AND THE PROBLEM OF SYNTHETIC *A PRIORI* JUDGMENTS

In a famous passage from the *Prolegomena to any Future Metaphysics* (1783), a shorter (but no less difficult) book in which Kant attempted to restate the central themes of his *Critique of Pure Reason*, Kant writes that it was in fact his taking in points made by the Scottish philosopher and moderate sceptic David Hume that stimulated the 'critical' revolution in his own thinking (cf. A758–69/B786–97):

> I freely admit that it was the admonition by [or remembrance of: *Erinnerung*] *David Hume* that was the very thing that many years ago first interrupted my dogmatic slumber and gave a completely different direction to my researches in the field of speculative philosophy. (*Prolegomena*, 4:260)

(On the translation of '*Erinnerung*', see Beck [1969: 439]; Guyer [2008: 1].) One of the main aims of the *Critique of Pure Reason*, as we have seen, is to demonstrate that speculative metaphysics has never been based on a sufficiently self-critical prior scrutiny of the essential nature and limits of human reason itself. From this critical perspective Kant characterizes the philosophical doctrines of so-called pre-Critical rational metaphysicians as *dogmas* of pure reason, and he gives the otherwise estimable thinkers who defended such doctrines the unflattering title of *dogmatists* (Aix–x; cf. Bxxxv). Some of the philosophers Kant most admired, from Plato to Leibniz, turn out from this critical perspective to have been slumbering 'dogmatically' on the deceptively comfortable mattress of speculative metaphysics.

In the following chapters we shall explore in more detail how Hume's sceptical arguments relate to Kant's articulation of the "real problem of pure reason" as "falling under the formula of a single problem": namely, "**How are synthetic judgments *a priori* possible?**" (B19; cf. *Prolegomena*, §5). For the moment what we need is an initial grip on the relevant distinctions and an initial grasp of Hume's sceptical challenge in general.

Analytic versus synthetic judgments

In the section of the introduction to the *Critique* entitled "On the Difference Between Analytic and Synthetic Judgments", Kant writes:

> In all judgments in which the relation of a subject to the predicate is thought ... this relation is possible in two different ways. Either the predicate *B* belongs to the subject *A* as something that is (covertly) contained in this concept *A*; or *B* lies entirely outside the concept *A*, though to be sure it stands in connection with it. In the first case I call the judgment **analytic,** in the second **synthetic.** ... One could also call the former **judgments of clarification,** and the latter **judgments of amplification** [or 'ampliative' judgments]. (A7/B11)

Consider the hackneyed example of an *analytic* judgment (it is not Kant's example): 'All bachelors are unmarried'. The subject-term concept of a *bachelor* includes by definition the constituent concepts *unmarried* and *male* (among other concepts pertaining to eligibility, appropriate age, etc.). The predicate-term concept, *being unmarried*, is thus in some sense already "(covertly) contained" within the subject-concept *bachelor*. For this reason analytic judgments are sometimes said to be merely 'true by definition' or 'true in virtue of the very meanings of the terms'. Note also that on this account the assertion 'this bachelor is married', that is, the denial of an analytic truth, implicitly contains a *conceptual contradiction*: 'this unmarried male is married'. This is why Kant says that the "supreme principle of all analytic judgments" is the merely formal-logical "principle of contradiction" (roughly, it cannot be the case that *both A and not-A* are true of the same subject in the same respect). This is "a general though merely negative criterion of all truth" (A150–51/B189–90).

Analytic truths merely 'tease out' and clarify the containments and entailments that hold among mere concepts in virtue of their conceptual content, and they do so independently of any questions concerning whether or not anything actually *exists* in reality corresponding to those concepts. It follows that merely analytic judgments are in principle *knowable a priori*, that is, independently of the contingencies of sense experience (provided, that is, that one possesses the relevant concepts at all, as was explained in §1.1 in relation to the term '*a priori*'). No one is likely to receive a research grant to carry out empirical research on the question 'Are bachelors unmarried?'

Kant's own example of an analytic judgment is the proposition 'All bodies are extended' (A7/B11), the truth of which requires some thinking through. *Being extended* just means 'extended *in space*', that is, occupying a space; and the very concept of a *body*, as opposed, for example, to the concept of a 'spirit', is of something that has spatial attributes. If one conceives of something that does *not* take up any space whatsoever, however small, then whatever it is that one might be conceiving, it is not a body.

By contrast with analytic judgments, an example of a *synthetic* judgment would be 'Most bachelors wear deodorant' or, to take Kant's own more interesting example, 'All bodies have weight' (cf. A7–8/B11–12). The concept of a *body*, as the concept of a *space-occupier*, does not by its mere definition rule out the logically consistent conceivability of *weightless* space-occupants or bodies. Hence, even if it happens or happened to be true in our universe that all bodies do have some weight or other (perhaps owing to a universal law of gravity), this would be a synthetic rather than an analytic truth about bodies *per se*.

Since synthetic truths are not merely definitional truths, the knowledge of such truths requires some way of establishing that the two distinct concepts that are asserted together in the judgment are in fact correctly predicated one of the other. So how do we gain knowledge of true judgments that are not merely analytically true in virtue of conceptual containments alone? The answer, of course, is that we typically find out 'what's true of what' by learning such facts, directly or indirectly, from our *experience* of the ways of the world. Hence the vast majority of (a strict empiricist would argue, *all*) synthetic judgments are established *a posteriori* by means of sense experience.

Before proceeding to Hume's sceptical argument, I should alert the reader to the fact that both the analytic–synthetic distinction and the *a priori–a posteriori* distinction have come under attack since the middle of the twentieth century, and disputes concerning the nature and validity of these distinctions are still very much alive today (see e.g. Boghossian & Peacocke [2001] regarding the *a priori*, and Juhl & Loomis [2009] on analyticity). A classic work in this regard was W. V. Quine's "Two Dogmas of Empiricism" ([1951] 1963), which basically argued that there is no rigorous way of distinguishing 'truths of meaning' or 'conceptual truths' (i.e. analytic *a priori*) from 'truths of empirical fact' (synthetic *a posteriori*). The meaning and empirical content of all truths, Quine argued, can be assessed only holistically in relation to the pragmatic virtues of whole theories and in relation to the tasks of translation and the interpretation of languages. From a different direction, Saul Kripke's *Naming and Necessity* ([1972] 1980) argued that there are necessary truths about the world that are discoverable *a posteriori*, hence challenging Kant's tight link between necessity and the *a priori*. (For defences of Kant's views in relation to these recent disputes, see e.g. Bird [2006a: chs 3–5]; Hanna [2001]. For a brief overview of twentieth-century views in relation to Kant's general distinctions in this regard, see O'Shea [2006]; or for more depth on the history of these issues since Kant, see Coffa [1991].)

Hume's most important sceptical arguments, when translated into Kant's terminology, essentially press the question of whether there can be any knowledge that is not of the two familiar kinds just mentioned. That is, do we possess any knowledge that is not based ultimately either on experience (i.e. Kant's synthetic *a posteriori* judgments, which Hume had called 'matters of fact') or on the merely abstract, formal-logical clarification of how our concepts are internally related to or 'contained in' one another (i.e. Kant's analytic *a priori* judgments, which Hume had called 'relations of ideas')? Or in Kant's formulation: *are there any objectively valid synthetic a priori judgments?* And if there are, what is the source of our knowledge of them?

Hume's sceptical challenge and the principle of causality

Hume's overall philosophy is far more subtle and complex than the following brief and partial characterization will suggest, but certainly the sceptical and empiricist sides of Hume's arguments sought to demonstrate that *all* our knowledge concerning the existence of things is ultimately derived from sense experience, *a posteriori* (where the latter includes the empirically discoverable aspects of our own instinctive human nature, too). But if Hume is right and there are no necessary truths concerning the nature and existence of things, then rational metaphysics, whether as traditionally conceived or as eventually reconceived by Kant himself, would be dead in the water.

For consider again one of the most important *a priori* principles in rational metaphysics, a principle that Hume rightly put at the centre of his investigations: the general *causal principle* that *every event has a cause*. (For the moment we shall not worry about how best to formulate or interpret this principle.) Not only in rational metaphysics but in ordinary experience and in Newton's physics, too, for example, it is assumed that any given happening or event *must* have been produced or caused by some preceding event or other (whatever the exact cause may turn out to be, and whether it is ever in fact discovered or remains undiscovered). In accordance with the principle of causality, then, *whenever* the preceding type of event occurs (i.e. the cause), the subsequent type of event (i.e. the effect) follows *necessarily*.

Those awaiting the guillotine, for example, no doubt trembled at the prospect. For they knew – not to put too fine an edge on it – that head removals cause death (and that the blade of the guillotine will do such and such when it is released, and so on). Discovering the causes of most kinds of event is of course not always as straightforward as this example suggests. For example, I may never be able to find out just what complex set of events caused my car engine to break down yesterday. But *some* complicated conjunction of events did cause that result, we assume, and hence would do so again if the circumstances were either exactly the same or the same in relevant respects. This is the *deterministic* aspect of natural causal laws that generates the ostensible conflict between free will and causality in nature mentioned in Chapter 1. Both Hume and Kant agree that the assumption of causal necessity is central to all of our beliefs about how the world works, and the rational metaphysicians have also tended to agree with this as well. (There are of course many important philosophical questions one could raise about indeterminacy in physics and about causal lawfulness in general, but we shall need to keep our focus here within manageable limits.)

What Hume's sceptical arguments claim to demonstrate, however, is that the general principle of causality, and all of our common-sense beliefs that particular kinds of event causally necessitate other particular kinds of event (and hence would do so again, etc.), *cannot be rationally supported* on the basis of the only two kinds of knowledge that are available to us: namely, analytic *a priori* 'relations of ideas' and synthetic *a posteriori* 'matters of fact'. For all that we can show by any factual or logical *reasoning*, Hume argues, it is no less likely that the *next* head removal will be followed, not by death, but by anything you care to imagine! Hume concludes that it is not reason but only our habitual expectations or habits of inference, as generated *a posteriori* by the contingent uniformities of our past experiences, that compel us to believe that head removals causally necessitate death and hence are best avoided if possible.

It might seem that the obviously correct response to Hume is that the sciences of biology and physics explain why head removals necessitate death, and that this is why we can justifiably make that simple causal inference. But to that response Hume has a convincing reply along the same lines as above. For by what reasoning and based on which facts do you have any evidence at all to support your belief that the laws of nature, as captured in our best current scientific theories, will continue to be the same *outside* the totality of past experience? For example, on what *a posteriori* factual or *a priori* logical bases do you know, or do you judge with any rational warrant at all, that *the laws of nature themselves* will not change tomorrow?

Hume's answer: not by any reasoning at all, but only as a result of the deep habits of expectation and belief that are produced in us by the constant uniformities of past experience. Hume argues that reason is powerless to justify our most basic beliefs in the causal coherence or even the very 'mind-independence' of the external material world. "CUSTOM or HABIT", concludes Hume's affable scepticism, "is the great guide of human life" (Hume [1748] 2000: §5, paras 5 and 6). Hume in the end has various *a posteriori* pragmatic recommendations to make as to why we should regulate our beliefs in certain ways and not others, and anyway, as he emphasizes, in daily life we literally *cannot*, by our very nature, suspend our instinctive habit of belief in causal necessity and in the persistence and independence of external material bodies. But rational justification? Not for those most basic beliefs, Hume argues, despite what all the philosophers have been telling you.

Let us sum up Hume's sceptical argument – which is sometimes called 'Hume's fork' because of the two-pronged nature of its attack (i.e. justified by experience? justified by reason?) – and translate it into Kant's terminology, as applied to the case of causality, as follows.

On the one hand, the principle that 'every event must have some cause' is not merely analytically true, *a priori*. The mere definition or analysis of the concept of *a happening* or event does not include or 'covertly contain' such a causal principle. Or, to put it another way, one does not logically *contradict* oneself (asserting '*A* and *not-A*') with the mere thought that some event occurs without any necessitating cause.

On the other hand, neither can the *'every … must …'* principle that every event must have a cause be rationally justified on the basis of the facts of sense experience, *a posteriori*, no matter how uniform and comprehensive such patterns of past experience have been. For no particular hypothesis offered as an answer to the question 'Do the events that we have *not yet* experienced follow the same general patterns as the events we *have* experienced?' can be supported on rational grounds more than any other hypothesis, however outlandish (as long as it fits the data of *past* experience), based solely on the experienced patterns themselves. (Note that the concept of *probability* will not help here either, unless we make certain assumptions that Hume would challenge in the same way. On Hume's own resulting view, by the way, probability consists in the relative strengths of our habits and vivacity of belief, which will be proportional to the relative frequencies of past experience.)

Kant believes that Hume's sceptical argument is a profound wake-up call to reason (and so also, as we shall see later in this chapter, are Kant's own Antinomies of Pure Reason). Our unavoidable and instinctive beliefs in the causal principle and in necessary causal connections are rationally supportable neither by the evidence of 'matters of fact' and experience (synthetic *a posteriori*) nor by logical or mathematical 'relations of ideas' (analytic *a priori*), nor by both combined. Furthermore, the same sort of sceptical challenge confronts our instinctive belief that there exists an external world of material bodies 'out there' at all. According to Hume, such basic beliefs ultimately have their source, not in reason, but in the contingent regularities of past experience and the habits of belief that such regularities produce. A handy and familiar way of capturing Hume's sceptical challenge in terms of Kant's question, 'How are synthetic *a priori* judgments possible?' is by means of Table 2.1.

As traditionally understood, *empiricists* such as Locke and Hume hold that all knowledge belongs to the top-left and bottom-right boxes only, because for empiricists all knowledge is either derived from sense experience or concerns merely analytic conceptual truths or formal-logical relations. By contrast, the *rationalists* (or 'intellectualists', as Kant calls them) from Plato to Descartes and Leibniz hold that the truths of rational metaphysics are *a priori* necessary truths about the existence of things. Such rationalist 'first principles' might amount to synthetic *a priori* truths (i.e. in the top-right box) that are allegedly *self-evident* or grasped by the 'natural light of reason' alone. (Kant will reject such claims to self-evidence.) Or the rationalist might claim that the top-left 'analytic' box is more robust than one might have thought and includes such substantive metaphysical principles as the principles of causality and substance. Such a rationalist might argue, for example, that real existential or matter-of-factual conclusions about the world *would* follow if only we had a *fully adequate* grasp of all of the *a priori* logical consequences that really flow from a perfectly complete concept or

Table 2.1 Kant's box: analytic/synthetic, *a priori*/*a posteriori*.

	Analytic	Synthetic
A priori	**Hume's 'relations of ideas'** Necessarily true, but merely in virtue of internal relations among meanings of concepts. Proves nothing about existence.	Are there any necessary truths about matters of fact and existence, i.e. synthetic a priori truths? Hume: No. Kant: Yes.
A posteriori	(None.) (Once one has acquired the relevant concepts, mere analytic truths can be known without appeal to experience.)	**Hume's 'matters of fact'** Contingent truths of experience. Provides facts about existing things, but no necessity. The opposite is thinkable without logical contradiction.

Idea of something: for example, if we could only grasp that Idea as conceived in God's creative intellect.

As noted in the Introduction, the 'empiricism–rationalism' distinction is of course only a tidy philosophical idealization, and it is a distinction that is only problematically applied to the complex views of actual historical and living philosophers. But it is a useful idealization, nonetheless, and one that is in no small part due, historically, to Kant himself (see the final section of the *Critique of Pure Reason*, 'The history of pure reason', A852–5/B880–83). Kant will argue against all of the above forms of traditional empiricism and traditional rationalism. Like the rationalists, Kant will argue that there are indeed substantive *a priori* necessary truths about reality and existence, but unlike the rationalists Kant will systematically reject all of the ways of attempting to justify such claims that have been proposed prior to his own *Critique of Pure Reason*. Like the empiricists, Kant is very much concerned that his own justification of synthetic *a priori* knowledge (i.e. the top-right box) does not involve any cognitively unusual or mystical or otherwise dubious sources of justification or knowledge. On some interpretations of Kant's view, in fact, his own defence of synthetic *a priori* truths (top-right box) can ultimately, when his full story is in, be *explicated* in terms of analytic conceptual truths (top-left box) and factual truths (bottom-right box) concerning the nature of human conceptualized experience. Such a view would see in the *Critique of Pure Reason* a kind of non-traditional and distinctively Kantian 'rational empiricism'. We shall be exploring what to make of Kant's own account of knowledge in subsequent chapters.

Once one gets the hang of 'Hume's fork', and if one is also open to another strong dose of useful philosophical idealization, then one can see the rationale behind most of the other famous *sceptical challenges* that have arisen in the history of philosophy and which continue to arise in philosophy today. In relation to any philosophically problematic concept 'X' (see Table 2.2 for some examples), the Humean sceptic will ask, to put it in simplified terms: do we strictly speaking observe X by means of the senses? If the answer is no, then we have no *a posteriori* knowledge of X. Perhaps, then, we have *a priori* knowledge of the *necessity* of X? But then the sceptic asks: is it at least logically conceivable, that is, coherently thinkable in some possible scenario without any internal logical contradiction, that all the facts of experience might be, or could have been, just as they are but *without* the existence of X? If the answer is yes, the sceptic argues, then neither can we have any *a priori* 'demonstrative' knowledge of X. Table 2.2 shows some classic sceptical problems, listed in the first column, followed by the sceptic's answers to those two questions in the next two columns.

Hume himself thought that the soundness of such sceptical arguments does *not* entail that we should stop believing in the existence of other minds,

Table 2.2 Classical sceptical challenges.

Sceptical problems	Observed via the senses (*a posteriori*)?	Is the opposite *thinkable a priori*, that is, without internal logical contradiction?
Problem of the 'External World' (Descartes, Hume):	No Sense experiences *alone* do not answer Descartes' challenge: 'Is it possible that I am dreaming right now?'	Yes It is at least merely *logically possible* that I am dreaming, or that I am a 'brain in a vat' and so on, right now.
Problem of 'Induction' (or 'Hume's Problem'):	No The evidence of all *past* observation and experience warrants no claim about what *will* happen in the future.	Yes There is no logical self-contradiction in the bare idea that all the laws of nature change tomorrow.
Problem of 'Causal Necessity' (Hume):	No Example: when one billiard ball causes another ball to move, we do not *see* any 'necessitation' (Hume).	Yes There is no logical contradiction involved in imagining *anything* to follow upon some event.
Problem of 'the Self' (Hume's 'bundle theory' of the self):	No We are not aware of 'the self' in our inner or outer experiences, but only of the changing 'bundle' of mental and material states themselves.	Yes It is quite conceivable that only those changing experiences might exist, without what philosophers call the identical 'self' or 'soul'.
Problem of 'Other Minds' (e.g., how do I know that you have a mind?):	No We can perceive other people's behaviour and their brain-states, but not their states of consciousness themselves.	Yes It is at least coherently thinkable or imaginable that others could be mere '*automata*' without any inner consciousness.

in an external world of material bodies, in natural causal laws and inductive probabilities, and in the identity of the self through the changing flux of experience. We *cannot* suspend such beliefs in real life anyway, Hume emphasized, once we leave 'the closet' of philosophical reflection; and I would argue that Hume has significant points to make about the overall 'reasonableness', in a wider sense, of such common-sense beliefs (cf. O'Shea 1996a). But what those arguments do demonstrate, for Hume, is that our *most basic* and unavoidable beliefs about reality are not given *any* direct support by any reasoning whatsoever, whether factual or logical, contrary to what the philosophers, empiricist and intellectualist alike, have insisted. As Hume notoriously expressed his general conclusion (metaphorically and ironically, of course, since Hume was one of the great Enlightenment defenders of a free press rather than one of the all-too-real book burners of past and present):

> When we run over libraries, persuaded of these principles, what havoc must we make? If we take in our hand any volume; of divinity or school metaphysics, for instance; let us ask, *Does it contain any abstract reasoning concerning quantity or number* [i.e. mere 'relations of ideas']*?* No. *Does it contain any experimental reasoning concerning matter of fact and existence?* No. Commit it then to the flames: For it can contain nothing but sophistry and illusion.
> (Hume [1748] 2000: §12)

Kant in an important sense agreed with the negative force of Hume's scepticism in relation to its target, and in particular in relation to all attempts by previous philosophers to exhibit the rational justification for any of our beliefs about reality that are not strictly derivable from sense experiences. (Consequently, Kant was known to some of his contemporaries such as Mendelssohn – with only partial justification – as the 'German Hume'; cf. Kuehn [2001: 256, 351].) Neither *a posteriori* sense experience nor the analytic *a priori* clarification of concepts can validate synthetic *a priori* truths about the necessary structure of reality. Analytic truths are conceptually necessary, but they entail nothing about the existence or non-existence of things. *A posteriori* truths report the contingencies and particularities of past and present existence as experienced, but can tell us nothing about how things *must* be, universally and necessarily, or even about how things can reasonably be expected to be if we propose to step off of the roof of a skyscraper.

The force of this general sceptical argument is an important part of what helped to wake Kant from his dogmatic slumber, and forced him to pursue the question: *how are synthetic judgments a priori possible?* The possibility not only of rational metaphysics but of reason as the source of any knowledge at all, however commonsensical, hangs in the balance. In the following chapters we shall see how Kant attempted to reply, in an indirect but powerful way, to Hume's sceptical challenge. In the next section, however, we shall explore another way in which sceptical challenges to reason developed within Kant's own emerging conception of the limits of pure theoretical reason.

2.2 THE ANTINOMIES OF PURE REASON

We have seen that Kant attributed his awakening from his dogmatic slumber to his remembrance of Hume. Later in life, in 1798, at the age of seventy-five, Kant wrote the following in a letter to Christian Garve concerning what it was that woke him from his dogmatic slumber:

> It was not the investigation of the existence of God, immortality, and so on, but rather the antinomy of pure reason – "The world has a beginning; it has no beginning [...]: There is freedom in man, vs. there is no freedom, only the necessity of nature" – that is what first aroused me from my dogmatic slumber and drove me to the critique of reason itself, in order to resolve the scandal of ostensible contradiction of reason with itself.
> (Kant, Letter to Garve, 21 September 1708, *Correspondence*; 552=12:257–8)

Here Kant suggests that he was roused from his dogmatic slumber by the *antinomy of pure reason*, a topic that eventually formed the title of the long second chapter (A405–567/B432–595) of the First *Critique*'s Transcendental Dialectic or *'logic of illusion'* (cf. A60/B85, A131/B170, A293/B349ff.).

An 'antinomy' in general, for Kant, is "a contradiction in the laws ... of pure reason" (A407/B434, from the Greek '*anti-*', against, plus '*nomos*', law – in this case, incompatible laws of reason). Each of the four antinomies, as we shall see further below, takes the form of a conflict between two apparently contradictory propositions, a '*Thesis*' and an '*Antithesis*' (e.g., as above, "There is freedom in man, vs. there is no freedom", from the Third Antinomy). Each opposed proposition is presented as the conclusion of a formally valid and seemingly sound chain of reasoning. The result is that each opposed conclusion (seemingly) *must* be true and yet *both* of them (apparently) *cannot* be true together. That is why the Antinomy of Pure Reason is a wake-up call to pure reason, demanding an explanation of the apparent internal contradictions in reason's own house. This is one important way in which Kant conceives his *Critique* to be an exercise in true self-knowledge centred on a reflective search for internal rational coherence. The *Critique of Pure Reason* is a *trial* in which reason must give an account of itself in light of its own demonstrable and inherent tendency to self-destruct (see the A-Preface, Axi–xiii).

In an earlier letter to Herz in 1781, the same year in which Kant's long anticipated book finally appeared in print (after a so-called 'silent decade'), Kant commented on how the problems that arise in the antinomies would be a good way to present the difficult reasonings of his *Critique* to a wider audience:

> This sort of investigation will always remain difficult, for it includes the *metaphysics of metaphysics*. Yet I have a plan in mind according to which even *popularity* might be gained for this study, a plan that could not be carried out initially ... Otherwise I would have started with what I have entitled the 'Antinomy of Pure Reason', which could have been done in colorful essays and would have given the reader a desire to get at the sources of this controversy [concerning metaphysics].
> (Kant, Letter to Marcus Herz, after 11 May 1781, *Correspondence*; 181=10:269–70)

Both Hume's sceptical arguments and Kant's antinomy of pure reason have in common, as we shall see, the attempt to demonstrate the impossibility of achieving any sound rational arguments, independently of experience, for any synthetic *a priori* conclusions about reality. Hume's general contention – in this respect, too, similar to Kant's own antinomies – was that sceptical dilemmas inevitably result from the systematically contrary tendencies of reasonings on the one hand and our natural beliefs on the other, both equally *unavoidable principles of human nature*. So it is understandable why Kant referred at different times to both Hume and to the antinomies as the source of his awakening from dogmatism (cf. Hume [1739] 2000: bk I, pt iv, §7, hereafter *Treatise*, 1.4.7; Kuehn 1983, 2001: 472 n.42). Both of them certainly represent direct challenges to the very possibility of rational metaphysics. For as we have seen, metaphysics, "the **queen** of all the sciences" (Axiii), was traditionally supposed to consist in a set of *a priori* proofs or rational demonstrations concerning the ultimate nature and existence of things in general. But both Hume's scepticism and Kant's antinomies are supposed to show that metaphysics, as traditionally understood, must continually fail in its aims.

What is 'reason'?

In order to understand what Kant really means by an 'antinomy' we first need to explore in more detail what exactly he means by 'reason' itself. The relevant sections here occur at the start of both the Transcendental Dialectic (A293–338/B349–96) and the Antinomy of Pure Reason (A405/B432ff.). "Reason", Kant tells us, "considered as the faculty of a certain logical form of cognition, is the faculty of inferring, i.e., of judging mediately (through the subsumption of a condition of a possible judgment under the condition of something given)" (A330/B386). Kant's terminology is off-putting, but what he is referring to here is basically deductively valid inference as formalized in the traditional logic of syllogisms. ('Syllogism' in German is *Vernunftschluß*, an 'inference of reason'.) As Kant further explains:

> In every syllogism I think first a rule (the *major* [premise]) through the understanding. Second, I subsume a cognition under the condition of the rule (the *minor* [premise]). Finally, I determine my cognition through the predicate of the rule (the *conclusion*), hence *a priori* through reason. (A304/B360–61)

To clarify what Kant means by all of this let us spell out an example that Kant himself briefly uses at one point. Consider the formally valid 'categorical' syllogism below, that is, a syllogism of the valid form: 'All *A* are *B*; All *B* are *C*; therefore, All *A* are *C*.' I will add Kant's technical terminology to the right:

1. All humans are mortal.   (= the given universal 'rule' or *major* premise; human is its 'condition', and *mortal* is its 'predicate')
2. All scholars are human. (= the *minor* premise; the cognition, '*x* is a scholar', is subsumed under the condition, '*x* is human')
3. So, all scholars are mortal. (= the *conclusion*; i.e., logical reasoning has thus *a priori* 'determined' the cognition, 'scholars are mortal', "through the predicate of a rule," i.e. '*x* is mortal', by means of the mediating *middle term*, '*x* is human')

Our logical faculty of pure reasoning in this way seeks to discover *logical entailments* among judgments with the aim of *systematically unifying* our cognition in relation to the diverse or 'manifold' cognitions of objects that are continually provided to our reason by our understanding in its particular judgments in response to ongoing experience.

The faculty of understanding, as briefly mentioned in Chapter 1, subsumes given sensory intuitions under the categories in various judgments about appearances (i.e. about objects in space and time). The second-order or higher-level 'materials' with which reason occupies itself are not sensory intuitions but rather the resulting judgments and rules of understanding themselves. For as indicated in the example above, reason seeks to inferentially relate such judgments as premises that logically necessitate given conclusions, thus 'unifying' cognition through mediating concepts or 'middle terms'.

This way of showing how a cognitive judgment is necessitated by other cognitions through *logical* relations among universal concepts is what, following Kant, I shall call the *logical postulate (or logical maxim) of pure reason* (see A307–8/B364, A498/B526). I shall refer to the *principles of understanding in experience* as a kind of summary of Kant's views on how judgments subsume sensory cognitions or intuitions of objects under general conceptual rules (e.g. in such judgments as '*x* is a scholar' or 'if *x* is a scholar, then *x* is mortal'). As we briefly saw in Chapter 1 and shall see in more detail in upcoming chapters, Kant holds that the possibility of experiencing any sensible objects at all requires certain *a priori* forms of sensibility (space and time) and understanding (the categories). By the 'experiential principles of understanding', then, I mean to refer to the resulting *a priori* principles of possible experience taken together. Such principles will include, for instance, Kant's own defence of the principle that every experienceable event necessarily has some determining cause (to be examined in Chapter 5).

Kant sums up his overall account of the cognitive role of theoretical reason in terms of what he calls *the unity of reason* (cf. Neiman 1994):

> If the understanding may be a faculty of unity of appearances by means of rules, then reason is the faculty of the unity of the rules of understanding under principles. Thus it [i.e. reason] never applies directly to experience or to any object, but instead applies to the understanding, in order to give unity *a priori* through concepts to the understanding's manifold cognitions, which may be called 'the unity of reason', and is of an altogether different kind than any unity that can be achieved by the understanding.
> This is the universal concept of the faculty of reason.
> (A302/B359)

Kant explains that usually the judgment that one seeks to rationalize as a logical conclusion initially confronts reason as *a task* to be accomplished or a problem for reason to solve by *finding* an appropriate middle term under which the relevant cognition can be subsumed (cf. A304–5/B361). An *explanatory* question arises, in other words, and sets a task for reason to search among the ongoing products of the understanding with the aim of discovering whether a given cognition can be successfully deduced *a priori* through logical reasoning from other such cognitions. For example, to continue with our rather artificial case, reason might ask the question in relation to the isolated judgment 3: '*Why* are scholars mortal?' This sets reason the task of finding a condition (perhaps, *being human*) that belongs to a given major premise or rule (1. 'All humans are mortal') and under which this cognition can also be subsumed in a given minor premise (2. 'All scholars are human').

Through purely logical reasoning the conclusion ('All scholars are mortal') is in this way 'mediately inferred' from the major premise, and thus from a "rule that **is also valid for other objects of cognition**" (A305/B361). Reasoning in this way thus *unifies* 'many-under-one', so to speak, and thereby *systematizes* our knowledge by showing how a particular judgment is logically entailed by premises that also logically relate to a wider range of kinds of cognition (e.g. in relation to all the non-scholarly humans who are also mortal, and so on). The 'logical postulate of reason' in this way demands that we seek to achieve an ever more embracing *systematic unity of reason* in relation to the given diverse cognitions of our understanding.

In this reasonable ongoing search to explain 'Why', as completely as possible, the logical postulate of reason demands that we now repeat the process in relation to our newly found explanatory premises in turn. That is, we search for 'pro-syllogisms' further back that will provide still more comprehensive logical conditions from which we could deduce our new major premise in its turn, and so on, potentially *ad infinitum*. Reason thus seeks further logically adequate conditions that will enable us to subsume each explanatory premise in its turn, until (the goal of reason is) some adequate reason can be found to *cease* pursuing the 'Why?' questions in relation to the given 'conclusion' from which we started.

What theoretical reasoning thus ultimately aims for in this process of achieving logically sufficient explanations is some premise that is such that, while much knowledge (and in the ideally comprehensive case, *all* knowledge) follows *from* it, it does not itself depend on any further premises as its logical 'conditions'. For if reason cannot eventually rest in what Kant calls an *'unconditioned'* condition – in effect, an ultimate premise with no further 'if's to be raised about it, or as Kant puts it: "a completeness in the series of premises that together presuppose no further premise" A416/B444) – then in that case the logical subsumption of each premise would depend on subsumption by further conditioning premises *ad infinitum*. As Kant puts this point in relation to the given major premise or universal rule discussed above (i.e. 'All humans are mortal'):

> Now since this rule is once again exposed to this same attempt of reason, and the condition of its condition thereby has to be sought (by means of a prosyllogism) as far as we may, we see very well that the proper principle of reason in general (in its logical use) is to find the **unconditioned** for conditioned cognitions of the understanding, with which its unity will be **completed**. (A307/B365)

Let us hazard a (no doubt misleading) 'practical' analogy. Suppose that Mary will receive a much needed loan from John, but *only if* John has received a loan from Sally, who was depending on Bill's receiving a loan from Amy who had been relying on a stressed bank that would issue loans *only if* the bondholders came through, which depended on ... and so on. No one ever sees actual cash unless this series of dependencies or conditions ultimately terminates in (what Kant calls) either an *unconditioned condition* or an *unconditioned totality*. That is, if in fact Mary does receive cash now (that is the 'conclusion' to be explained, so to speak), then either someone ultimately did provide cash *without* borrowing (an ultimately unconditioned 'Unmoved Mover' of finances, as it were); or alternatively, somehow the cash Mary sees today can be made sense of as resulting from an infinite succession of people each of whom depended on a loan from someone else, in an infinite past regarded as an actually completed totality. (The latter seems an apt description of the current state of our economy.)

Setting aside this dubious loan analogy, however, the real rationale behind the above *logical postulate of reason* is what Kant now proceeds to characterize as a genuinely *synthetic a priori* transcendental *principle of pure reason* (as I shall call it, again following Kant). The logical postulate, as we have seen, rationally enjoins us always to *seek* the completion of 'Why' conditions for given cognitions, with the ultimate aim of ultimately resting in some 'unconditioned' condition or totality of conditions. However, Kant now explains:

> But this logical maxim cannot become a principle of **pure reason** unless we assume that when the conditioned is given, then so is the whole series of conditions subordinated one to the other, which is itself unconditioned, also given (i.e., contained in the object and its connection).
>
> Such a principle of pure reason, however, is obviously **synthetic**; for the conditioned is analytically related to some condition, but not to the unconditioned.   (A307–8/B364; cf. A497–8/B525–6)

Or as Kant succinctly states this principle of pure reason at the outset of the Antinomies: "**If the conditioned is given, then the whole sum of conditions, and hence the absolutely unconditioned, is also given,** through which alone the conditioned was possible" (A410/B436).

The 'logical maxim of reason' justifies our continual search for logically sufficient conditions in the quest to find fully adequate 'unconditioned' explanations of given cognitions. The 'principle of pure reason', however, correspondingly demands that for any given 'conditioned' cognition in experience, there must also already be 'given', that is, *exist*, an *unconditioned* condition or totality, as the ultimately real explanation of the given cognition. Otherwise the 'loan' of logically sufficient explanations, as it were, would never actually be 'cashed', and the initial cognition would not find an adequate explanation.

The pure thought or concept of such an absolutely unconditioned condition or absolute totality is basically what Kant means by the *transcendental ideas* or *concepts of pure reason*, which are crucial idealizing representations or thoughts that play roles throughout Kant's entire philosophy (e.g. the idea of God). Kant compares his use of the term 'ideas' as pure concepts of the unconditioned to Plato's use of 'ideas' as eternal Forms or ideal archetypes (A313/B369; A326/B283). Both uses differ sharply, as we have noted several times, from the use of 'ideas' in Locke and other early modern philosophers in relation to broadly sense-perceptual or imagistic contents in the mind.

What we shall now watch unfold in Kant's Antinomy of Pure Reason, in brief capsule, is how the above *logical postulate of reason* and the existential *principle of pure reason* systematically conspire with the *experiential principles of understanding* mentioned earlier to generate the problematic highest aims of reason from which we started in Chapter 1 and from which, as we may recall, Kant's *Critique* began as well: "Human reason … is burdened with questions which it cannot dismiss, since they are given to it as tasks by the nature of reason itself, but which it also cannot answer, since they transcend every capacity of human reason" (Avii). In the end Kant will conclude that the Antinomies that he will examine involve the mistaken presupposition (by the 'transcendental *realist*') that the spatiotemporal cosmos exists as a 'thing in itself', and hence as an absolutely unconditioned totality. Kant will thus claim that the Antinomies serve as an indirect proof of his own transcendental idealism: we have knowledge only of an unending series of phenomena in space and time, not of the cosmos as an unconditioned totality. But let us continue to build up slowly to Kant's arguments for these conclusions. (The analysis of reason's explanatory principles given in this chapter is based partly on O'Shea [1997]; on transcendental illusion in general, see especially Grier [2001]; and for a succinct account of the logical structure and arguments of the antinomies, see Wood [2010].)

Reason's quest to explain the cosmos as a whole

Corresponding to three basic forms of logical syllogism – the categorical, hypothetical and disjunctive syllogisms – there turn out in Kant's 'architectonic' system to be three basic kinds of absolutely unconditioned unity about which reason forms its transcendental ideas. (I will not pause to explore this particular architectonic aspect of Kant's argument here; cf. A329–38/B386–96.) These three kinds of unconditioned unity traditionally corresponded to the three branches of '*special metaphysics*' in rational metaphysics I mentioned in the Introduction (whereas 'general metaphysics' treats of 'ontology', the science of being in general). So the three transcendental ideas and three corresponding subject matters of traditional metaphysics that are criticized in the three long chapters of Kant's Transcendental Dialectic turn out to treat of the following topics:

- the *soul* as the absolute unity of the subject as a thinking thing, the traditional subject of *rational psychology*, which will be subjected to "the fiery test of critique" in Kant's Paralogisms of Pure Reason (see the end of Chapter 4);
- the *cosmos* or World as an "absolute totality in the series of conditions for a given appearance" in space and time (A340/B398), the traditional subject of *rational cosmology*, which will be criticized here in Kant's Antinomies of Pure Reason; and
- **God** as the supreme being of all beings, the absolute totality in relation to the possibility of all things in general, the traditional subject matter of *rational theology*, which Kant subjects to criticism in the Ideal of Pure Reason (to be discussed at the start of our concluding chapter).

Since reason's idea of an unconditioned *free will* is a kind of 'uncaused causality', on Kant's view, it falls within his treatment of rational cosmology. So here once again we meet in these three branches of traditional special metaphysics the three highest aims of rational metaphysics discussed in Chapter 1: namely, our attempted cognition of the three supersensible noumenal objects: God, freedom and immortality (cf. B395 n.).

Let us turn without further ado to the arguments of the Antinomies themselves. As usual, Kant orders them 'architectonically' according to his four groups of *categories*: (i) Quantity, (ii) Quality, (iii) Relation and (iv) Modality (A415/B443). The theses and antitheses of the four antinomies are stated by Kant as shown in Table 2.3.

The Antinomies, unlike the Paralogisms (on the soul) and the Ideal (on God), are not concerned directly from the outset with any supersensible noumenal objects. Rather, the Antinomies are initially concerned only with explaining the various physical phenomena and events that make their appearance to our senses in one objective spatiotemporal universe or cosmos. Both sides of each antinomy thus start out from 'conditions' or 'dependencies' that are entailed by Kant's *a priori* principles of understanding in experience. For the latter require, as we shall see (especially in later chapters), that any spatiotemporal object that can make its appearance to us is necessarily *conditioned by*, or *dependent on*, certain prior experiential conditions of various kinds within the realm of possible experience.

What leads to difficulties concerning the 'unconditioned' in the Antinomies is that our reason and our understanding are, as it were, governed by two separate *a priori* laws or principles. According to Kant our reason by its very

Table 2.3 The four antinomes of pure reason.

	Thesis	Antithesis
First Antinomy (Quantity):	The world has a beginning in time, and in space it is also enclosed in boundaries.	The world has no beginning and no bounds in space, but is infinite with regard to both time and space.
Second Antinomy (Quality):	Every composite substance in the world consists of simple parts, and nothing exists anywhere except the simple or what is composed of simples.	No composite thing in the world consists of simple parts, and nowhere in it does there exist anything simple.
Third Antinomy (Relation):	Causality in accordance with laws of nature is not the only one from which all the appearances of the world can be derived. It is also necessary to assume another causality through freedom in order to explain them.	There is no freedom, but everything in the world happens solely in accordance with the laws of nature.
Fourth Antinomy (Modality):	To the world there belongs something that, either as a part of it or as its cause, is an absolutely necessary being.	There is no absolutely necessary being existing anywhere, either in the world or outside the world as its cause.

nature *legitimately* relies on both the 'principle of pure reason' and the 'principles of experiential understanding'. Rational metaphysicians, however, systematically misinterpret the proper use and significance of these principles in a way that naturally and inevitably generates the antinomial conflicts. For present purposes I shall not attempt to examine and assess the arguments of each Antinomy in full detail, but I will attempt to convey the structure of Kant's overall argumentative aims and conclusions in the Antinomies. (For further analyses see, among others, Al-Azm [1972]; Alexander [1956; i.e. the *Leibniz–Clarke Correspondence*]; Allison [2004]; Bennett [1974]; Grier [2006]; Rosenberg [2005]; Wood [2010].)

I. Consider, then, the "First Conflict of the Transcendental Ideas" (A427/B456ff.), that is, the First Antinomy, which begins by considering the magnitude of the sensible world in *time* (and then considers space). It is an objectively valid principle of understanding and possible experience that any event in nature that is 'given' to us (i.e. is experienceable as existing) *at* some point in time must be conceived *as having followed upon* some preceding moment in time. Since, of course, the same point applies to each previous moment in turn, the 'principle of pure reason' finally demands an answer to the question: how is this series of dependencies, on which the existence of the initial event itself depends, ultimately to be explained?

The proofs in the antinomies all work by *reductio ad absurdum*; that is, by showing that maintaining the opposite of what is to be proved would entail a logical contradiction or absurdity. So Kant puts the argument for the Thesis, that is, that "The world has a beginning in time", as follows:

> For if one assumes that the world has no beginning in time, then up to every given point in time an eternity has elapsed, and hence an infinite series of states of things in the world, each following another, has passed away. But now the infinity of a series consists precisely in the fact that it can never be completed through a successive synthesis. Therefore an infinitely elapsed world-series is impossible, so a beginning of the world is a necessary condition of its existence; which was the first point to be proved.
> (A427/B455)

Very roughly, the idea is that the past is what has already elapsed and hence has been completed. The principle of pure reason, as we have seen, requires some explanation for any such series of dependencies as the one generated here (i.e. 'this time *only if* a prior time, *only if* a still prior time ...' etc.). The conclusion in the Thesis is that "an eternity of actual states ... cannot have passed away, and so the world must have a beginning" (A431/B460).

Now consider Kant's argument on behalf of the Antithesis in this First Antinomy, that is, that the spatiotemporal "world has no beginning" in time:

> For suppose that it has a beginning. Since the beginning is an existence preceded by a time in which the thing is not, there must be a preceding time in which the world was not, i.e., an empty time. But now no arising of any sort of thing is possible in an empty time, because no part of such a time has, in itself, prior to another part, any distinguishing condition of its existence rather than its non-existence (whether one assumes that it comes to be of itself or through another cause). Thus many series of things may begin in the world, but the world itself cannot have any beginning, and so in past time it is infinite. (A428/B456)

The *a priori* principles of understanding in sensory experience entail that each state of such a world in time is conceived as conditioned by some such state in the preceding time. On the assumption that the material universe had an absolute beginning in time, however, the time prior to the alleged beginning of the material world would be entirely 'empty' of any existing matter. But as his "Remarks on the Antithesis" indicate (A431/B459ff.), Kant argues that the concept of such a sequence, that is, from an absolutely empty time to whatever the time is at which the entire matter of the world is supposed to have originated, is the thought of a sequence that would violate the *a priori* principles of experiential understanding. For there is "no distinguishing condition" in the thought of such an absolutely "empty time" to account for why the sensible world comes into existence at the time it does. Hence, the argument for the Antithesis concludes that the world had no beginning in time but is rather an *infinite totality* with respect to all past time. (Kant's remarks also seek to counter the riposte that *time itself* might have had a first beginning, hence without requiring any objectionable 'empty time': see A431/B459.)

Similar arguments are given in the First Antinomy in the case of the magnitude of the world in *space*. Basically, the principles of understanding in experience require that any given sensible space marks off a boundary that implies an enclosing space beyond its border, and so on for the thought of each more encompassing experienceable space. In the Thesis, the principle of reason is then taken to entail that the threatening infinite regress of enclosing spaces must terminate in an *unconditioned first member* of the series: a final outer spatial boundary enclosing all the matter-of-the-world. The Antithesis argues to the contrary that the concept of such an ultimate spatial boundary of the entire sensible world entails an *empty space* beyond that boundary, in violation of *a priori* principles of understanding and possible experience. Hence the sensible world must be infinite in spatial extent, and now the principle of pure reason demands that this infinite series of spaces is given (i.e. exists) as a whole, that is, as an *unconditioned totality*.

So now we are in a pickle. It cannot be true that the sensible world both *is* (Antithesis) and *is not* (Thesis) an infinite given magnitude in space and time. Something has to give. We cannot give up the *a priori* principles of understanding in experience, since these (as we shall see in later chapters) are necessarily true of any world that is experienceable by us. But neither can we give up the rational demand for fully adequate explanations, as embodied in the synthetic *a priori* principle of pure reason. Human reason's own cognitive principles are thus ostensibly at war with one another, although each of them is perfectly natural and unavoidable. It is this inevitable internal conflict or antinomy of pure reason – "a wholly natural antithetic" (A407/B433) – that Kant suggests woke him from his own 'dogmatic', pre-Critical slumber, rousing him from the unconditional but illusory comforts of traditional rational metaphysics.

II. Consider now the Second Antinomy, which concerns the *composition* or make-up of the spatiotemporal material bodies that appear to us in the sensible cosmos. In a nutshell, it is an *a priori* principle of experiential understanding that any spatially extended composite body fills a continuous space that is in principle further divisible into smaller spatial parts, and the same applies to *those* constituent parts in turn, and so on. Is every composite material body thus composed of smaller and smaller parts *ad infinitum*, 'downwards without end', so to speak? Or must the dependence of material wholes on material parts ultimately bottom out in perfectly 'simple' entities of some kind (i.e. entities that are not divisible into any real *parts*), absolute simples which compose all other things without themselves being composed of any 'deeper' constituent parts?

The argument for the Second Antinomy's Thesis follows the *a priori* principle of pure reason to argue, in effect, that the dependence of composites on the parts that compose them cannot be an infinite structure of dependencies in which composites are existentially dependent on ever smaller parts. Therefore, such composites and the cosmos as a whole must ultimately bottom out in unconditioned simple elements. The argument for the Antithesis, by contrast, is that this notion of perfectly simple entities composed of *no* space-filling material parts violates the principles of our understanding. For example, since the *a priori* principles of experiential understanding, according to Kant, entail that *space* has no smallest indivisible parts, neither can any sensible matter that *occupies* space have any such absolutely 'atomic' (i.e. strictly indivisible) parts.

The first two Antinomies thus concern the unconditioned unity of the cosmos with respect to its overall *magnitude*: "the age and size of the world," as Jonathan Bennett (1971) once aptly put it. The general form of Kant's *critical solution* to the first two antinomies will be different in kind from his critical solution to the third and fourth antinomies. Properly interpreted, both sides of the first two antinomies will turn out to be *false*, whereas both sides of the third and fourth antinomies will turn out to be interpretable as *true*. But let us first turn very briefly to the ideas behind the Third and Fourth Antinomies.

III. The Third Antinomy concerns *causality* in nature. As Kant puts it at the outset of the Thesis, "Causality in accordance with laws of nature" is an *a priori* principle of understanding in experience such that "everything **that happens** presupposes a previous state, upon which it follows without exception according to a rule" (A444/B472). The same principle of pure understanding requires that the cause, too, was itself a happening in nature that had *its* cause in turn. So again we have a series of dependent events, the sufficient explanation of which, according to the 'principle of pure reason', requires the existence of something unconditioned: in this case, a cause of happenings in nature that is *not itself naturally caused* or determined. The Thesis thus asserts the reality of what, as we saw in Chapter 1, is perhaps the most important concept of all in Kant's overall philosophy: the concept of *freedom*:

> Accordingly, a causality must be assumed through which something happens without its cause being further determined by another previous cause, i.e., an **absolute** causal **spontaneity** beginning **from itself** a series of appearances that runs according to natural laws, hence transcendental freedom, without which even in the course of nature the series of appearances is never complete on the side of the causes. (A446/B474)

Unfortunately, the Antithesis of the Third Antinomy begins from the same series of natural causes and argues, with what Kant intends to be equal soundness, that the concept of such an 'uncaused causality' is the (thoroughly problematic) concept of a production of events in nature 'out of nowhere', to put it crudely. But a production "such that nothing precedes it through which this occurring action is determined in accordance with constant laws" (A446/B474) violates the *a priori* principles of understanding and the possibility of experience. "Thus transcendental freedom is contrary to the causal law" and "hence is an empty thought-entity" (A447/B475).

IV. The Fourth Antinomy, finally, considers whether or not the series of dependent alterations in the world that is required by the principles of understanding, that is, with each alteration being contingent upon the existence of some prior one, must ultimately terminate (as demanded by the principle of pure reason) in the existence of an absolutely unconditioned *necessary being*, either in the world or outside it, as its ultimate cause. The Thesis argues yes, the Antithesis argues no. (We shall have occasion at the beginning of our concluding chapter to consider the role of reason's idea of *God* as the necessary 'being of all beings', to which this Fourth Antinomy provides a kind of transition: see A566/B594.)

2.3 ELUSIVE TOTALITIES AND THE INTERESTS OF REASON: KANT'S CRITICAL SOLUTION

Reason's interests and a sceptical representation of the Antinomies

Before turning to Kant's critical solution to the Antinomies, it will be helpful to explore some of Kant's remarks on both "the interest of reason in these conflicts" as well as a useful "sceptical representation" that he uses to illustrate all four of the conflicts.

In both the Thesis and Antithesis sides of the antinomial conflicts, Kant remarks, "philosophy exhibits such a dignity that, if it could only assert its pretensions, it would leave every other human science far behind in value" (A463/B491). Kant explains that the Thesis side of each antinomy, which he calls "the **dogmatism** of pure reason" (A466/B494), would satisfy the deepest interests not only of speculative rationalist metaphysics but also of practical reason and morality as well, since the Theses represent unconditioned conditions that are closely related to the ideas of God, freedom, and immortality:

> That the world has a beginning, that my thinking self is of a simple and therefore incorruptible nature [i.e. unlike composite bodies, 'simple' souls cannot perish by dissolution or 'corruption' into parts], that this self is likewise free and elevated above natural compulsion in its voluntary actions, and finally, that the whole order of things constituting the world descends from an original being, from which it borrows all its unity and purposive connectedness – these are so many cornerstones of morality and religion. The antithesis robs us of all these supports, or at least seems to rob us of them. (A466/B494)

On the other side, the assertions of the Antitheses defend "a principle of pure **empiricism**" according to which there is an actual infinite totality of empirical conditions in the objects or appearances that make up the boundless spatiotemporal material universe. The Antitheses portray (i) space and time as infinitely extensive, (ii) matter as infinitely divisible into ever smaller parts, (iii) every event as determined by an endless series of prior causes and (iv) all beings as contingent upon other finite beings for their existence. In short, the empiricist Antitheses conclude that nature provides an unending and infinitely rich domain of phenomena for our scientific and experiential understanding to explore. The empiricist or naturalist vision embodied in the Antitheses is clearly as attractive and compelling to Kant as the rationalist metaphysical vision embodied in the Theses (if only both of them were not ultimately illusory).

The boundless interest in discoveries about nature that would be encouraged by the infinite empirical totalities of the Antitheses, combined with the rejection of all epistemologically problematic supersensible conditions, Kant suggests, has strong appeal to philosophers and scientists in particular. Kant notes that in common life, however, most people prefer to believe in the epistemologically problematic but morally supportive 'supersensible conditions' of the Theses. Interestingly, Kant in fact suggests that part of the very appeal of such beliefs in the supersensible is precisely their apparent *insulation from intellectual criticism*, which is due to the fact that theoretical claims concerning such supersensible conditions can neither be intelligibly confirmed nor refuted by any possible experience (cf. A472–3/B500–501).

Such supersensible claims do, however, appear to directly contradict the natural scientific picture of the experienced world as the latter is 'totalized' in the Antitheses, hence the perennial conflict between the theses and the antitheses throughout intellectual history. For according to Kant, the 'principle of pure reason' leads the otherwise laudable defenders of pure empiricism, no less than the 'dogmatic' rationalist and traditional metaphysical defenders of the Theses, to draw 'unconditioned' conclusions that overreach what we can really understand. Such scientific naturalists do this, for instance, when they positively *deny* the existence of God, freedom, or immortality. That is,

> if empiricism itself becomes dogmatic in regard to the ideas [of pure reason] (as frequently happens), and boldly denies whatever lies beyond the sphere of its [sensory] intuitive cognitions, then it itself makes the same mistake of immodesty, which is all the more blameable here, because it causes an irreparable damage to the practical interests of reason. (A471/B499)

There are echoes of Kant's diagnosis of reason's clashing interests as expressed in the Antinomies in the American philosopher William James's well-known contrast, in his splendid book *Pragmatism* ([1907] 1978), between the two basic philosophical 'temperaments' that he suggests are exhibited in mixed degrees by all thinking people (Table 2.4; see James's opening lecture, "The Present Dilemma in Philosophy").

The similarities to Kant's diagnosis of the differing tendencies and interests embodied in the Theses and Antitheses of the Antinomies are clear. As we shall now see, Kant contends (as, by the way, James's pragmatist solution

Table 2.4 William James's *Pragmatism* on the two philosophical temperaments.

The 'tender-minded'	The 'tough-minded'
Rationalistic (going by 'principles')	Empiricist (going by 'facts')
Intellectualistic	Sensationalistic [i.e. sensation-based]
Idealistic	Materialistic
Optimistic	Pessimistic
Religious	Irreligious
Free-willist	Fatalistic
Monistic	Pluralistic
Dogmatical	Sceptical

would later suggest, too, in a different but related way) that the most fundamental source of these controversies is an underlying misconception on both sides about the reach of theoretical reason. And this 'transcendental illusion' also results in a parallel misconception about the real grounds for our practical interest in unconditioned freedom and universal morality. Kant's overall critical solution (again like James's) will attempt to satisfy the genuine interests of reason that are expressed on *both* sides of the Antinomies, but without their deceptive overreaches to the unconditioned.

Kant offers the following "sceptical representation" of all the conflicts in the Antinomies:

> if I could antecedently see about a cosmological idea [of reason] that whatever side of the unconditioned in the regressive synthesis of appearances it might come down on, it would **be** either **too big** or **too small** for every **concept of understanding**, then I would comprehend that since it has to do with an object of experience, which should conform to a possible concept of the understanding, this idea must be entirely empty and without significance because the object does not fit it no matter how I may accommodate the one to the other. And this is actually the case with all the world-concepts, which is why reason, as long as it holds to them, is involved in an unavoidable antinomy. (A486/B514)

The first three Theses as well as the fourth Antithesis, Kant goes on to explain, are in this way 'too small' for the *a priori* principles of our experiential understanding. For the latter principles entail – or so Kant argues against the three Theses and the fourth Antithesis – that we *cannot coherently stop* at the thought of such absolute borders on the ever expandable domain of possible experience. As Kant nicely puts it: "by an unavoidable law of nature the question 'Why?' will pursue you, and require you ... to go beyond this point" (A488/B516).

On the other hand, the first three Antitheses and the fourth Thesis are 'too big' for the understanding. The unconditionally complete yet infinite totalities of sensible reality that are asserted in the first three Antitheses, and the absolutely necessary being of the fourth Thesis, are 'too big' to be explained or justifiably asserted by our experiential understanding. Here I want to pause briefly to consider an important matter of philosophical dispute in relation to Kant's conception of infinity.

In relation to the various 'infinite totalities' considered above Kant is not claiming that there is anything wrong with our understanding of an infinite series *per se*. Nothing is unintelligible about what Kant calls the "true (transcendental) concept of infinity", despite the fact that this conception entails that "the successive synthesis of unity in the traversal of a quantum can never be completed" (A432/B460). This is what Kant calls "the mathematical concept of the infinite" as a quantum that "contains a multiplicity (of given units) that is greater than any number", that is, a notion of the infinite as what "would always remain the same" despite variation in units (A431–2/B459–60). In some ways the latter notion is perhaps even compatible with rudimentary aspects of Georg Cantor's later revolutionary conception of the mathematical infinite in the nineteenth century (cf. Rosenberg 2005: 178–9).

But as Bertrand Russell and others have pointed out in objection to Kant (cf. Russell [1914] 1956: 123), the Cantorian conception of infinity that would later be (and is now) widely accepted in mathematics does not build into the concept of infinity, as Kant's conception of infinity does, the idea of an infinitely "*successive synthesis*" of cognition that cannot be "traversed" within the limitations of an "empirical regress" of possible sense experience. It may well be true, such critics of Kant grant, that an infinite regress cannot be 'completed' if it is understood *in Kant's way*, as a task of human perceptual synthesis however indefinitely extended. But once the relevant mathematical notions are properly freed from the various experiential limitations that Kant mistakenly places upon them, these critics suggest, the cosmologist's application of them to physical reality need not generate any antinomies at all.

This is certainly an important matter of controversy, one that quickly runs beyond what we can properly explore here. But if the reader is interested in further researching this particular issue, one point to bear in mind is that Kant's concern here is not with the content of mathematical representations *per se*, nor even with the content of reason's totalizing ideas *per se*. His concern, rather, is with how far we can really intelligibly conceive *our ineliminably temporal and perspectival understanding of objects* to reach, when that understanding is thought of (as in the Antinomies) as being problematically extended to comprehend the spatiotemporal cosmos as a whole. Some commentators have defended Kant by arguing that in this epistemological context his arguments against the possibility of any coherent understanding of the sorts of 'infinite *given* magnitudes' required by the Antitheses do succeed in raising important issues (cf. e.g. Allison 2004; Buroker 2006; Posy 1983). Similar points of this kind might also be made in relation to other fascinating and worthwhile speculations as to how Kant's various views should be evaluated in light of subsequent developments in mathematics and natural science (e.g. in relation to the 'Big Bang' theory of the ultimate origin or 'beginning' of our entire spatiotemporal universe).

There are many other complex historical and conceptual issues to be raised both internal to Kant's Antinomies and in relation to subsequent developments in philosophy and science, but for our present purposes it is time to take a look at Kant's own "critical decision" or critical solution to the deep-seated Antinomy of Pure Reason.

Transcendental illusion and transcendental idealism

Kant indicates that the "entire antinomy of pure reason rests on this dialectical argument", which he partially states as follows: "If the conditioned is given, then the whole series of all conditions for it is also given; now objects of the senses are given as conditioned; consequently, etc." (A497/B525). Filling in the implicit conclusion here, and also filling in the roles of the relevant principles involved as explained above, we can now flesh out the 'dialectical' or fallaciously equivocating argument that Kant is suggesting lies behind the "entire antinomy of pure reason" as follows:

1. If the conditioned is given, then the whole series of all conditions for it, and hence the absolutely unconditioned, is also given, through which alone the conditioned was possible. (This is the *principle of pure reason*, e.g. A410/B436.)
2. Objects of the senses are given as conditioned. (This is in accordance with the *principles of understanding* and the possibility of experience.)
3. Consequently, *the whole series* of all conditions for given conditioned objects of the senses is also given.

Note that for something to be 'given' to our cognition, as Kant uses that term, is for that thing to have real existence. So the *conclusion* of this fallacious "dialectical argument", on which the Antinomies entirely rest, is therefore basically this: our conditioned experience of any real sensible object entails the real existence of the *whole series* of its conditions (and hence entails some absolutely *unconditioned* condition or totality of conditions).

Since that conclusion holds for each of the seemingly sound arguments for each of the seemingly contradictory conclusions in the Antinomies, what we need, and what Kant attempts to provide, is a diagnosis of the hidden error that is involved in the general dialectical argument form described above. Kant's diagnosis is this:

> [T]he major premise of the cosmological syllogism [i.e. (1) just above] takes the conditioned in the transcendental signification of a pure category, while the minor premise [i.e. (2)] takes it in the empirical signification of a concept of the understanding applied to mere appearances ... [i.e. this is a fallacy of equivocation that trades on two different meanings of 'conditioned']. This decep-

> tion is, however, not artificial, but an entirely natural mistake of common reason. For through common reason, when something is given as conditioned, we presuppose (in the major premise) the conditions and their series as it were **sight unseen**, because this is nothing but the logical requirement of assuming complete premises for a given conclusion, and no time-order is present ... Further, it is likewise natural (in the minor premise) to regard appearances as things in themselves and likewise as objects given to the mere understanding, as was the case in the major premise, where I abstracted from all conditions of intuition under which alone objects can be given. (A499–500/B528–9)

This diagnosis requires some explaining and some tying together of all the various threads discussed above.

We saw earlier that the *logical* postulate or maxim of pure reason demands that we try to find sufficient premises in order to explanatorily deduce given judgments as conclusions of arguments. A conclusion is in this sense *logically conditioned* by the full set of premises required by the best explanatory deduction that logically entails that conclusion. As a rational norm, then, what we are *seeking* to achieve or at least approximate in accordance with this 'logical postulate of pure reason' is an ideally complete and consistent *explanatory systematization* of all the empirical laws and factual judgments that are delivered by our understanding in its ongoing engagements with the objects of the senses. This logical postulate of reason, according to Kant, is in fact an *analytic a priori* truth:

> [T]he following proposition is clear and undoubtedly certain: If the conditioned is given, then through it a regress in the series of all conditions for it is **given** to us **as a task**; for the concept of the conditioned already entails that something is related to a condition, ... and so through all the members of the series. This proposition is therefore analytic and beyond any fear of a transcendental criticism. It is a logical postulate of pure reason to follow that connection of a concept with its conditions through the understanding, and to continue it as far as possible, which already attaches to the concept itself. (A498/B526)

Note, however, that the real explanatory goals that engage this logical postulate of pure reason require that we attempt to fully subsume under laws and logically systematize the empirical objects and events that appear to our senses and are judged by our experiential understanding. Hence, for Kant, the logical postulate of pure reason does *legitimately presuppose* the *real* or *transcendental* 'principle of pure reason' as a genuinely synthetic *a priori* principle: the principle, as we have seen, that if the sensible conditioned is given, then the absolutely unconditioned is also given (cf. A307–8/B364–5). Everything now hangs on how to correctly interpret this transcendental principle and hence the *real use* (i.e. in addition to the 'logical use') of pure reason in relation to the objects of cognition. (See Grier [2001], O'Shea [1997] and Kant's "Appendix to the Transcendental Dialectic" [A642–704/B670–732] for further important details on this complex issue.) Kant's diagnosis of pure reason's fallacious equivocation in the Antinomies can now be explained as follows.

First side of the equivocation: 'condition' taken to mean 'purely logical condition'. In relation to the real sensible objects that are given to us in the minor premise (2), Kant's diagnosis in the passage quoted above suggests that "common reason" unwittingly treats those sensible objects or "appearances as things in themselves and likewise as objects given to the mere understanding" (A499–500/B528–9). By "*mere* understanding" Kant here means the logical form of our thinking considered in abstraction from the principles of experiential understanding and possible experience. As we saw earlier, Kant defines '*transcendental realism*' in general, that is, all positions apart from his own transcendental idealism, as any position that *treats appearances as things in themselves* (e.g. A369). To think some object 'as a thing in itself', we may recall from Chapter 1, is to conceive it as a purely intelligible object or 'noumenon'. This is a conception of objects considered by pure reason alone, which, as the passage quoted above has it, results from our having "abstracted from all conditions of [sensory] intuition under which alone objects can be given" (A499–500/B528–9). If we thus treat the sensible objects that make their appearances to us in space and time as if they were 'things in themselves' or purely intelligible objects, then the merely analytically true 'logical postulate of reason' in the major premise (1) will have as its 'real' transcendental presupposition the claim that the absolutely unconditioned is thereby already constituted and exists as a completed totality in itself:

> If the conditioned as well as its condition are things in themselves, then when the first is given not only is the regress to the second **given as a task**, but the latter is thereby really already **given** along with it; [and so on for each condition], ... hence the unconditioned is thereby simultaneously given, or rather it is presupposed. ... Here the synthesis of the conditioned with its conditions is a synthesis of the mere understanding, which represents things **as they are** without paying attention to whether and how we might achieve acquaintance [*Kenntnis*] with them.   (A498/B526)

Kant's point here may be put this way. Suppose you merely sit back and *think* abstractly about what the thought of a 'conditioned object' in general might intelligibly be taken to require, that is, considered simply *as a thing in itself*, and employing just the general thought of a 'condition' (i.e. of an *if*, or an *only if*) in general. So regarded, what could then be more natural than to assume from the start the fulfilment of whatever *logical conditions* are entailed by the *thought* of any 'conditioned' or 'dependent' item whatsoever? From this purely logical but *'transcendental realist'* point of view, then, if a conditioned appearance is given; *and* if it is conceived in the minor premise (2) as a pure intelligible or 'thing in itself'; *then* it will indeed seem to follow *logically* that the absolutely unconditioned condition or totality of conditions must exist as well (A500/B528). For the unconditioned is thereby already logically presupposed or posited "**sight unseen**", as Kant put it colourfully above, as soon as the conditioned is given.

Second side of the equivocation: 'condition' taken to mean 'real empirical condition'. In order to actually arrive at the desired conclusion in (3), however, which concerns objects in so far as they make their appearance to our senses, a *real* and not merely *logical* meaning of 'being conditioned' must be presupposed in the minor premise (2). For in the conclusion the real existence of the unconditioned is supposed to follow from the conditioned givenness of objects *as sensible objects*. To get to this conclusion we must consider objects not merely as pure intelligibles but as objects that appear to us in space and time. Hence we must conceive them as subject to all of the various *spatiotemporal and causal conditions* (not merely logical conditions) that are involved in the possibility of experience in accordance with the *a priori* principles of pure understanding and sensibility.

Once the minor premise (2) is given this real interpretation in terms of sensible objects as such, however, a very different significance would consequently have to attach to the major premise (1) too. The 'logical postulate of reason' continues, as before, to presuppose some real, transcendental 'principle of pure reason'. But the latter is now conceived to entail the unconditioned, *not as a completed totality*, but in terms of the *necessarily unending task of uncovering the real explanatory conditions for any given conditioned*:

> in such a case one can very well say that a **regress** to the conditions, i.e., a continued empirical synthesis on this side [of the conditions] is demanded or **given as a task**, and that there could not fail to be conditions given through this regress.   (A499/B527)

This "rule of reason" is not what Kant calls "a **constitutive principle**" but rather a *regulative principle* of pure reason (A508–9/B536–7): "it cannot say

what the object is, but only **how the empirical regress is to be instituted** so as to attain to the complete concept of the object" (A510/B538).

With this general diagnosis now in place, consider once again the First Antinomy. Its Thesis asserts that the world as a whole is *finite* in time and space (i.e. had a beginning in time and has an outer spatial boundary), while the Antithesis asserts that the world as a whole is *infinite* in time and space. Surely the world as a whole must be either of finite or infinite magnitude in these respects! But Kant offers the following example: "If someone said that every body either smells good or smells not good, then there is a third possibility, namely that a body has no smell (aroma) at all, and thus both conflicting propositions can be false" (A503/B531). That is, 'x smells good' and 'x smells not good' are logical *contraries* rather than *contradictories*: both propositions can be false if the relevant presupposition is not fulfilled (in this case, the presupposition that x is among the bodies that have some smell or other).

Similarly, Kant concludes that all four Antinomies involve the mistaken presupposition that the spatiotemporal cosmos exists as a 'thing in itself', and hence as an absolutely unconditioned totality:

> If one regards the two propositions, 'The world is infinite in magnitude', 'The world is finite in magnitude', as contradictory opposites, then one assumes that the world (the whole series of appearances) is a thing in itself. For [so interpreted] the world remains, even though I may rule out the infinite or finite [empirical] regress in the series of its appearances. But if I take away this presupposition, or rather this transcendental illusion, and deny that it is a thing in itself, then the contradictory conflict of the two assertions is transformed into a merely dialectical conflict, and because the world does not exist at all (independently of the regressive series of my representations), it exists neither as **an in itself infinite** whole nor as **an in itself finite** whole. It is only in the empirical regress of the series of appearances, and by itself it is not to be met with at all. Hence if it is always conditioned, then it is never wholly given, and the world is thus not an unconditioned whole, and thus does not exist as such a whole, either with infinite or with finite magnitude. (A504–5/B532–3)

Similarly in relation to the Second Antinomy:

> I will have to say: the multiplicity of parts in a given appearance is in itself neither finite nor infinite, because appearance is nothing existing in itself, and the parts are given for the very first time through the regress of the decomposing synthesis, and in this

> regress, which is never given absolutely **wholly** either finite or infinite. (A505/B533)

Note that in stating above that the world and the empirical objects in it do not exist "independently of the regressive series of my representations", Kant is not saying that empirical objects exist only when someone *actually* perceives them. Rather, as he explains in section six of the Antinomy of Pure Reason, entitled "Transcendental Idealism as the Key to Solving the Cosmological Dialectic", the idea is the more general one that all empirical realities in the world are possible 'appearances-to-us' in the sense that they necessarily stand in some lawful spatiotemporal material and causal connections to our actual perceptions (i.e. in an 'empirical regress' of conditions):

> That there could be inhabitants of the moon, even though no human being has ever perceived them, must of course be admitted; but this means only that in the possible progress of experience we could encounter them; for everything is actual that stands in one context with a perception in accordance with the laws of the empirical progression. Thus they are real when they stand in an empirical connection with my real consciousness, although they are not therefore real in themselves, i.e., outside this progress of experience. (A493/B521)

Kant in fact now suggests that this critical solution of the Antinomies constitutes an *indirect proof of transcendental idealism*, in addition to the direct proof of that doctrine that he had given earlier in the Transcendental Aesthetic and which we shall explore in the next chapter. As an indirect proof or *reductio ad absurdum*, the argument begins with the opposed assumption that transcendental realism is true: that is, the assumption that the empirical objects that make their appearance to us are 'things in themselves'. As Kant then puts the matter:

> The proof would consist in this dilemma. If the world is a whole existing in itself, then it is either finite or infinite. Now the first as well as the second alternative is false (according to the proof offered above for the antithesis on the one side and the thesis on the other). Thus it is also false that the world (the sum total of all appearances) is a whole existing in itself. From which it follows that appearances in general are nothing outside our representations, which is just what we mean by their transcendental ideality. (A506–7/B534–5)

Both the intellectualist Theses and the empiricist Antitheses consider the appearances, the sensible objects of the spatiotemporal world, to be 'things in themselves' (transcendental realism). Both, in effect, apply the ideal *logical* postulate of reason to the world *constitutively* rather than merely *regulatively*. Both thus assume that the entire sum or series of appearances in itself must automatically conform to reason's legitimate logical pursuit of "a completeness in the series of premises that together presuppose no further premise" (A416/B444). This assumption or *transcendental illusion* then seems to support the conclusion of an unconditioned whole on both sides of the antinomial conflicts. Consequently these conflicts can only be resolved, Kant is arguing, by distinguishing between objects *considered as appearances to us in space and time* as opposed to being *considered as things in themselves*. The cosmos considered as an ever expansive domain of objects that make their appearances to us in space and time is always the thought of some infinite *empirical regress* in possible experience, and this conception does not warrant any conclusion concerning the cosmos as a *completed whole* or totality. Transcendental idealism is thus indirectly proved by being the only solution to the Antinomies that inevitably arise on transcendental realist assumptions, whether rationalist or empiricist in character.

One question that has been raised in relation to the present 'indirect proof' is whether or not Kant here *begs the question* in favour of transcendental idealism, that is, by already assuming the truth of that doctrine from the outset in his actual arguments in the Antinomies concerning the spatiotemporal 'appearances', as he calls them throughout the arguments for the Theses and Antitheses. It seems to me, however, that in the Antinomies Kant is using a conception of experienceable appearances that conforms to his *a priori* principles of understanding and sensibility as far as the necessarily *empirically conditioned* nature of such empirical objects or appearances is concerned; that is non-negotiable, for Kant (and surely rightly so). But *that* assumption by itself does not require the assumption of transcendental idealism in the actual arguments of the Antinomies, although Kant does of course argue (in the Transcendental Aesthetic, as we shall see in the next chapter) that transcendental idealism is in fact ultimately inseparable from those experiential principles. (For further discussion of this point see e.g. Allison [2004]; Buroker [2006]; Melnick [1989: ch. 2]; Wood [2010].)

Let us now close out our discussion of the Antinomies by briefly examining Kant's critical solution to the crucial Third Antinomy. This will appropriately bring us back to an issue that has been with us since the beginning of Chapter 1.

In the case of the first two Antinomies, Kant tells us, the "series of conditions are obviously all homogeneous to the extent that one looks solely at how far they **reach:** whether they conform to the idea [of reason], or are too big or too small for it" (A530/B558). But the third and fourth Antinomies are concerned with a "dynamical" or causal connection as opposed to a homogeneous or quantitative "mathematical" synthesis of appearances, and this turns out to be highly significant for the contrasting nature of Kant's solutions to the final two Antinomies. For in this case:

> the dynamic series of sensible conditions ... allows a further condition different in kind, one that is not part of the series but, as merely **intelligible**, lies outside the series; in this way reason can be given satisfaction and the unconditioned can be posited prior to appearances without confounding the series of appearances, which is always conditioned, and without any violation of the principles of understanding. (A531/B559)

The Third Antinomy concluded both that there *must* be (Thesis), and yet that there *cannot* be (Antithesis), a causality through freedom that is operative in nature. But here Kant's transcendental idealist distinction between the spatiotemporal phenomena in nature and purely intelligible noumena will ultimately bear its most important fruit.

For we can now resolve the Third Antinomy by considering our own freely willed actions in the world *in the twofold sense* that is required by transcendental idealism: namely, as phenomenal appearances in nature that are completely subject to causal determinism, and as purely intelligible 'noumena' or 'things in themselves' that satisfy the principles of pure reason. (For more on Kant on freedom, begin with Allison [1990] and Guyer [2006a: ch. 6].) With respect to free will and causal determinism, then, "**both**, each in a different relation, might be able to take place simultaneously in one and the same occurrence" (A536/B564). For in relation to the human being and its power of willing, "one can consider the **causality** of this being in two aspects, as **intelligible** in its **action** as a thing in itself, and as **sensible** in the **effects** of that action as an appearance in the world of sense" (A538/B566; recall our brief discussion in §1.2 of Kant on free will in relation to the 'two aspect' interpretation of transcendental idealism):

> Of the faculty of such a subject we would accordingly form an empirical and at the same time an intellectual concept of its causality, both of which apply to one and the same effect. Thinking of the faculty of an object of sense in this double aspect does not contradict any of the concepts we have to form of appearances and of a possible experience. (A539/B567)

On the one hand, we can conceive the human will and our voluntary actions 'from the outside' or scientifically, as it were, in terms of what Kant calls the *empirical character* of our faculty of volition. Conceived this way, all of our bodily movements and even all of the empirical psychological processes that produce them are simply occurrences in nature that are entirely determined by natural causal laws that ultimately stretch back before we were born. This is in accordance with the *a priori* principles of our experiential understanding, in particular the law of causality in time.

On the other hand, the very same volitions and intentional actions can also be conceived as pure intelligibles or 'things in themselves'. As such they are conceived to conform to the *a priori* principle of pure reason, hence as involving the purely intellectual thought of an absolutely unconditioned or *self-originating causation* of natural effects. It is true that we literally *cannot understand*, in the theoretical sense, what such an unconditioned causal condition might be like, and we thus have no real knowledge or theoretical cognition of *how* free will is possible. But because of the transcendental idealist distinction between appearances and things in themselves, it is for the first time, Kant argues, at least *thinkable as possibly true*, without any internal conflict of reason, that we do possess the power to absolutely originate our own actions in nature. By contrast, on the usual 'transcendental realist' assumption that all of the inner and outer empirical objects and states that make their appearance to us in the spatiotemporal universe are 'things in themselves', free will becomes impossible, unintelligible:

> Here I have only wanted to note that since the thoroughgoing connection of all appearances in one context of nature is an inexorable law, it necessarily would have to bring down all freedom if one were stubbornly to insist on the [transcendental] reality of appearances. Hence even those who follow the common opinion about this matter have never succeeded in uniting nature and freedom with one another. (A537/B565)

Hence Kant contends that both sides of the Third Antinomy are conceivably true: namely, that every human thought and action considered as an appearance in the spatiotemporal universe is in all relevant respects entirely causally determined, and yet those same thoughts and actions considered as intelligible 'things in themselves' through pure reason can be the products of an absolutely free will. The Fourth Antinomy argues for a similarly thinkable solution to the idea of an absolutely 'necessary being' as the 'ground' (i.e. unconditioned condition) of the empirically unending series of contingent beings in nature. Again, we have no real (theoretical) knowledge of how such noumenal beings are possible but, as we saw in Chapter 1, Kant goes on to argue in later works that practical reason and morality do require us to assume that we possess a free will, and here Kant claims to have demonstrated that there is no insuperable *objection* to that assumption. Hence for the first time, in Kant's view, we can finally reconcile unconditional freedom and morality with our understanding of nature as an inexhaustibly conditioned and scientifically lawful universe.

The Antinomies of Pure Reason and Hume's scepticism are both wake-up calls for human reason. And the Antinomies are only one part of Kant's overall "fiery test of critique". For the latter also includes direct diagnoses of the various fallacies that Kant argues are involved in all theoretical arguments for the existence of the soul (in the "Paralogisms of Pure Reason" chapter) and God (in the "Ideal of Pure Reason" chapter). We shall briefly discuss the Paralogisms at the end of Chapter 4 in relation to Kant's conception of the self in the Transcendental Deduction. And at the start of the concluding chapter we shall briefly discuss the Ideal in relation to the idea of God and the related role of the 'regulative maxims of reason' within the First *Critique*. The hope, however, is that the discussion of the Antinomies in this chapter has provided a reasonably detailed picture of what Kant, in the Transcendental Dialectic as a whole, intended to be a devastating *critique of pure reason* in all of pure reason's traditional and ever-seductive philosophical guises.

Many subsequent philosophers have found various aspects of Kant's critical arguments in the Transcendental Dialectic to be quite convincing. In this spirit Kant is among those philosophers, past and present, who have argued that philosophy as traditionally practised needs to undergo *radical criticism* and be *radically reformed* if philosophy is to be genuinely conducive to human knowledge and wisdom. When combined with Hume's sceptical arguments concerning the impossibility of any knowledge of necessary principles concerning matters of fact and existence in nature in general, one might well think at this point, as many 'critically reforming' philosophers have but Kant pointedly does not, that we should abandon metaphysics altogether, at least if it is conceived as demonstrating necessary and universal principles governing matters of fact and existence. Why shouldn't philosophers turn – again, as many have today – to something more like Hume's own conception of philosophy? Philosophy for Hume is essentially the patient and systematic empirical investigation, *a posteriori*, of what the contingent uniformities of inner and outer sense experience reveal to us about nature's ways, in particular focusing on the fascinating empirical regularities that lie waiting to be uncovered in our own human nature as thinking, feeling and acting beings (Hume's proposed 'science of human nature'). One might well ask, what would be so bad about seeing philosophy as consisting in just that sort of highly general and broadly naturalistic enterprise?

In the chapters to follow, however, we shall now examine Kant's contention that in addition to such valuable empirical, naturalistic and analytic inquiries as Hume and other naturalists allow us, there remains, contrary to Hume's view, an objectively valid theoretical *metaphysics of nature* that is based on pure *a priori* rather than empirical grounds. Kant's new grounds for such a metaphysics of nature will show how genuinely universal and necessary synthetic *a priori* principles are demonstrably true of our spatiotemporal universe. It turns out, then, that for Kant it is "the fiery test of critique" that first makes possible the genuinely successful metaphysics of nature that he had long been seeking.

It will not be a speculative metaphysics of purely intelligible noumenal beings, based on the illusion of knowledge that *transcends* the spatiotemporal limits of human experience. Rather, it will be an *immanent metaphysics* of the *a priori* principles that make any human experience of any world or nature possible in the first place. For the truth of the matter – or so Kant will argue – is that we can no more rest content with Hume's otherwise praiseworthy and moderate sceptical empiricism than we could rest content with the inspiring but illusory claims of traditional rational metaphysics. To adapt the remark from Kant that served as a motto for this chapter, it is such questions as *'How are synthetic a priori judgments possible?'* and, more particularly, *'How is our experience of the world itself possible?'* that will pursue us and require us to go beyond empiricism or, perhaps better, to go 'behind' scepticism, naturalism and empiricism by conducting an *a priori* transcendental examination of the presuppositions behind the very restrictions that worthy empiricists such as Hume would impose on us from the start. But what this might mean will only become clear when we have seen Kant's 'transcendental' strategy of argument and analysis put to work in the Transcendental Aesthetic and Transcendental Analytic of the First *Critique*.

CHAPTER 3

SPACE AND TIME AS FORMS OF HUMAN SENSIBILITY

> We can accordingly speak of space, extended beings, and so on, only from the human standpoint. If we depart from the subjective condition under which alone we can acquire outer intuition, namely that through which we may be affected by objects, then the representation of space signifies nothing at all. This predicate is attributed to things only insofar as they appear to us, i.e., are objects of sensibility.
>
> (Kant, *Critique of Pure Reason*, A26–7/B42–3)

Kant pulls no punches in the passage above. Certainly outside philosophy – for that matter, even inside philosophy – it must strike us as counter-intuitive to assert that spatial properties such as size, shape, location and distance are correctly attributed to, and hence possessed by, material bodies "only from the human standpoint". For when we human beings speak truly about or mathematically represent the fact, for example, that a certain planet's average distance from the sun is approximately 5,869,660,000 kilometres, what is thereby represented is a fact about the spatial layout and temporal history of the material universe. And that is a fact that obtained long before any human beings intruded on the scene. Kant's 'transcendental idealism and empirical realism', as we saw in Chapters 1 and 2, is supposed to be compatible with any and all such empirical discoveries about the vast and limitless 'age and size' of the material universe in space and time. In fact, Kant himself developed a well-known 'nebular hypothesis' about the physical birth of our solar system. So one difficult task that will confront us in relation to such passages as the one above, which is taken from Kant's Transcendental Aesthetic concerning space and time as forms of human sensibility, will be to try to figure out what Kant really means by his *transcendental idealism*.

This is, of course, a topic that we have already explored during the course of Chapters 1 and 2, and we shall encounter it again in later chapters. In the

SPACE AND TIME AS FORMS OF HUMAN SENSIBILITY

present context we shall have to try to figure out what Kant might mean by asserting that if we abstract from the subjective conditions that determine our human way of representing such spatiotemporal facts, "the representation of space signifies nothing at all". Why, for example, could not the forms of space and time *both* be essential to our human way of representing the world (if they are) *and* be the corresponding entirely mind-independent structures in which things 'in themselves' exist as well (a well-known objection to Kant's view that we shall consider later)? Addressing such questions will require examining at least a selection of Kant's arguments that space and time are *a priori* forms of our sensory intuition, and his further claim that as such forms of representation, space and time pertain *solely* to things conceived as 'appearances' rather than as 'things in themselves'. (In this chapter we shall focus primarily on space, with only occasional reference to Kant's parallel arguments concerning time. In Chapters 4 and 5 we shall further explore time as the *a priori* form of our 'inner sense'.)

Of course, there is a trivial sense in which 'the human standpoint' is the standpoint from which *we* human beings speak about and represent anything at all. An equally trivial truth results if the phrase "the representation of space" (or of time) refers only to our ways of *representing* space or time, rather than to the spatial and temporal facts about the objects or events that are thereby *represented*. Philosophers sometimes stumble over this '-ing/-ed' or 'act/object' ambiguity. Any non-Kantian, so-called 'transcendental realist' philosopher with her wits about her will grant the trivial truth that our mental and linguistic acts of represent*ing* the properties of objects – as opposed to the spatial and temporal properties of objects that are thereby successfully represent*ed* – can be understood only in relation to 'the human standpoint'. After all, it is we human beings who are doing the representing. But since Kant's controversial transcendental idealism about space and time is not supposed to consist of such trivial tautologies, what sort of claim is that thesis supposed to be? And how does Kant argue in direct support of that claim in the Transcendental Aesthetic (A19–49/B33–73)?

We shall begin by jumping right into Kant's notoriously brief but substantive analysis or **"metaphysical exposition"** of our concept of space (with brief references to the parallel case of time), and throughout I shall now assume familiarity with all the terms and distinctions already introduced in Chapters 1 and 2. At the outset, however, it will perhaps be helpful to recall that Kant makes a basic distinction in human cognition between sensory intuition and conceptual thinking, and within each of those between the *a priori* as opposed to *a posteriori* elements involved in our knowledge. Tables 3.1 and 3.2 review some of the key contrasts involved in those two distinctions. (Note that while Kant links '*a priori*' with '*form* contributed by the mind', other philosophers would deny this connection. Note also, as

Table 3.1 Intuitions and concepts.

Intuition	Concept
Faculty of sensibility	Faculty of understanding
Passive sensory receptivity	Active (spontaneous) discursive thinking
Singular reference to a *given* particular	General features shared by objects
Immediate: direct presentation of object	Mediate: via intuition + 'common marks'

Table 3.2 *A priori* and *a posteriori*.

A priori	*A posteriori*
Pure intuitions and pure concepts	Empirical intuitions and empirical concepts
Independent of sensation	Dependent on sensation
'Form' contributed by the mind	'Matter' contributed by the object

discussed in §1.1, that there are 'impure' as well as pure *a priori* propositions, so Table 3.2 is slightly misleading in that respect.)

One important complicating factor in the Transcendental Aesthetic and beyond will concern the fact, already mentioned in §1.2, that *both* sensory intuition and conceptual thinking are required in order for us to have any knowledge of objects: "intuitions without concepts are blind", as we saw Kant put the requirement for concepts in cognition (A51/B75). Some philosophers today contend, in fact, that when Kant's full story is taken into account, particularly in the Transcendental Analytic to be discussed in Chapters 4 and 5, one of his key insights is that our 'sensory intuitions' of objects are themselves really a certain kind of *conceptually* informed response to and direct presentation of given objects. In recent years John McDowell (1996), in part following Sellars, has been a notable defender of this view. On the other hand, recent interpreters such as Robert Hanna (2006, 2008) and Lucy Allais (2009) – and in another respect, Sellars here too! – argue that Kant's sensory intuitions are fundamentally *non-conceptual* representations of objects. So one should be aware that Kant's central distinction between concepts and sensory intuitions is a crucial but variably interpreted and controversial aspect of his view (cf. Wenzel [2005] for a discussion of this issue).

The 'aesthetic' in Kant's 'Transcendental Aesthetic' harks back to its Greek roots as a term designating *sensible* objects as opposed to (alleged) purely intelligible objects, as discussed in Chapters 1 and 2. In this section Kant attempts to isolate a distinguishable contribution that is made to our cognition of objects by our faculty of sensibility alone, in the form of space and time as pure *a priori* forms of human sensory intuition. The complicating problem of how Kant can say anything intelligible about sensory intuition *apart* from such intuitions being conceptualized has appropriately been called *the blindness problem* (cf. Falkenstein 1995). The point to note for now is that Kant wants to contend that a distinctive *a priori* form of spatio-temporal representation is contributed to our cognition of objects by our faculty of sensibility or sensory intuition, and that this contribution can be examined independently (and perhaps, in some sense, functions independently) of the equally ineliminable role played by conceptual thinking in our cognition of objects.

Kant's 'metaphysical expositions' of space and time are supposed to be 'metaphysical', in Kant's sense, in so far as they "exhibit" our concepts of space and time "**as given** *a priori*" rather than as being derived empirically from sense experiences (A23/B38). So Kant's initial aim is to determine just what sort of representation our representations of space and time are. Kant will argue that space and time are *pure intuitions*: they are pure *a priori* rather than empirically derived representations, and they are immediate sensory intuitions of space and time as singular individuals, rather than being general concepts of kinds or features of individuals. Kant's analysis of our 'concepts' of space and time will thus reveal that our representations of space and time, at least in certain fundamental respects, are sensory-intuitive representations rather than conceptual representations.

Kant will then appeal to these initial claims about the nature of our *representations* of space and time in arguing for his overall transcendental idealist conclusion. Space and time turn out *not* to be either 'things in themselves' or properties and relations of things in themselves. Rather, space and time just are pure forms of human sensory representation. Or as we might put it: (i) subjectively considered, space and time are the *a priori* forms of our human sensory represent*ings*; (ii) objectively considered, space and time are the structural relations necessarily exhibited by all represent*eds* in experience, that is, by all empirically real inner and outer objects; and (iii) considered as 'things in themselves' by pure reason, space and time are nothing at all.

After the four metaphysical expositions (as listed in the B-edition on space) we shall then examine Kant's 'transcendental exposition' of the concepts of space and time. A 'transcendental exposition', Kant indicates, is an "explanation of a concept as a principle from which insight into the possibility of other synthetic *a priori* cognitions can be gained" (B40–41). In the case of space this will concern the possibility of synthetic *a priori* propositions in geometry (the science of space), and similar arguments are intended to apply to time in relation to the possibility of a mathematical science of kinematics, that is, of motions in space as alterations through time (A31/B47–9).

On the basis of the combined metaphysical and transcendental expositions, Kant will conclude that space and time are neither things in themselves (in opposition, for example, to the Newtonian 'absolute' theory of space and time) nor properties, determinations or relations of things in themselves (in opposition, for example, to the Leibnizian 'relational' theories of space and time) (cf. A23/B37, A39ff./B56ff.). Rather, space and time are "the pure forms of all sensible intuition"; and as such "conditions of sensibility" they are *empirically real* yet *transcendentally ideal* (A39/B56). As Kant puts this conclusion in the case of space:

> Our expositions accordingly teach the **reality** (i.e., objective validity) of space in regard to everything that can come before us externally as an object, but at the same time the **ideality** of space in regard to things when they are considered in themselves through reason, i.e., without taking account of the constitution of our sensibility. We therefore assert the **empirical reality** of space (with respect to all possible outer experience), though to be sure its **transcendental ideality**, i.e., that it is nothing as soon as we leave aside the condition of the possibility of all experience, and take it as something that grounds the things in themselves. (A28/B44)

So let us see how Kant attempts to guide us into the arms of transcendental idealism by means of a philosophical analysis of our concepts of space and time.

3.1 SPACE AND TIME AS PURE FORMS OF SENSORY INTUITION

Kant opens the section on the metaphysical exposition of space with some important clarifications followed by some key questions. The clarifications concern the notions of 'inner sense' and 'outer sense':

> By means of outer sense (a property of our mind) we represent to ourselves objects as outside us [*ausser uns*], and all as in space. In space their shape, magnitude, and relation to one another is determined, or determinable. Inner sense, by means of which the mind intuits itself, or its inner state, gives, to be sure, no intuition of the soul itself, as an object; yet it is still a determinate form, under which the intuition of its inner state is alone possible, so that everything that belongs to the inner determinations is represented

> in relations of time. Time can no more be intuited externally than space can be intuited as something in us. (A22–3/B37)

The distinction between 'outer sense' and 'inner sense', as Kant and other philosophers have used such terms (compare Locke's 'ideas of sensation' vs. 'ideas of reflection', for instance), embodies a contrast between sensations that are due to the actions of external objects affecting our bodily sense organs and sensations that are due to the internal activity of our own minds or 'souls' (see e.g. Falkenstein 1995: 161–5). Thus by 'outside us' or 'external to us' (*ausser uns*), in some contexts, Kant seems to mean *distinct from us* in the more general sense of being something *other* than ourselves as experiencing subjects. His overall view will be that representing something as *outside us in space* is necessary if we are to represent anything as 'other than us' in this sense at all. (Allison [2004] and Guyer [1987] both emphasize this point; but see also Warren [1998], noted further below.) Kant's contention will be that space is the pure *a priori* form of outer sense (i.e. of intuition of objects other than ourselves), while time is the pure *a priori* form of inner sense (i.e. of intuition of states of our own 'inner' selves).

It should be noted that when more of Kant's full story is in place, in particular including the arguments of the Transcendental Analytic to be discussed in Chapters 4 and 5, the representation of time will be shown necessarily to include *all* empirically knowable objects, both inner and outer. Furthermore, while we do not represent our inner mental representations as spatial objects – we represent our own thoughts, for example, as temporally successive but not as having a certain size or shape or weight – Kant will later argue that our inner mental representings must themselves be represented as standing in certain necessary relations to the outer world of material objects in space. The inner and the outer will thus turn out to be inextricably linked, on Kant's overall view.

In this important introductory paragraph, Kant now proceeds to frame the key questions that he wants to raise concerning the nature of space and time:

> Now what are space and time? Are they actual entities? Are they only determinations or relations of things, yet ones that would pertain to them even if they were not intuited, or are they relations that only attach to the form of intuition alone, and thus to the subjective constitution of our mind, without which these predicates could not be ascribed to anything at all? (A23/B37–8)

Kant, as we know, will argue that space and time are "relations that only attach ... to the subjective constitution of our mind". For the Newtonians, by contrast, absolute space and absolute time are either actual entities themselves or perhaps they are 'determinations' or accidents of God's mind; in either case, space and time would be or pertain to 'things in themselves'. For the Leibnizians, by famous contrast, space and time are basically abstractions derived from the relations of sensory appearances, the true grounds of which are Leibniz's metaphysical 'monads' or simple substances as things in themselves (as discussed briefly in the Introduction). So Kant is here contrasting his transcendental idealist view of space and time with its two main transcendental realist competitors.

On anyone's view, space and time are going to be rather unique and comprehensive aspects of the empirical world. For on the one hand, it seems that *everything* that happens occurs at some time and (at least in the case of all 'outer' events) in some location or region of space. On the other hand, as Kant will emphasize throughout the *Critique*, there is a sense in which *we do not perceive space and time themselves*, but only the manifold material realities and psychological states that *occupy* space and are *ordered* in time. (Kant's term 'manifold', for future reference, basically refers to a plurality: a 'many-fold', as it were.) A frequent premise in later chapters, for instance, will be Kant's claim that "time itself cannot be perceived" (A181/B225). I can perceive the changes of the hands on a clock or the movements of the sun – but time itself?

Furthermore, there is an important sense (recently clarified and explored in detail by Falkenstein [1995]) in which the orderings and locations of objects, properties and events in space and time are not fully determined by any of the empirical features or intrinsic natures of those objects, properties or events. For example, there is a spectral ordering of colours on the colour scale such that orange falls between red and yellow, but the location and sequence of coloured objects in space and time cannot be determined from any such *empirical* ordering principle. So although spatial and temporal orderings are given with the empirical contents they structure, they are not *derivable from* any other ordering that is intrinsic to or supervenes on those empirical contents themselves.

In general, then, while all the antics of perceptible empirical objects take place *in* space and *over* time, space and time do not *themselves* appear to be sense-perceptible objects or properties in the same way. What, then, are they? Since at least the time of Plato's dialogue the *Timaeus*, philosophers have striven to understand the unique way in which space and time seem to be the 'invisible receptacles', as it were, in which everything in the cosmos is somehow contained.

Let us turn, then, to Kant's metaphysical exposition of the nature of our cognitive representations of space and time, focusing on the case of space. I shall discuss the first metaphysical exposition of space more extensively, and then the other three more briefly.

The metaphysical expositions: space and time as a priori *intuitions (A22–32/B37–48)*

The first two metaphysical expositions of the concept of space, and likewise for the concept of time, are supposed to show that space and time are pure *a priori* representations rather than *a posteriori* empirical representations. The other two metaphysical expositions (numbered (3) and (4) in the B-edition on space) are supposed to show that the representations of space and time are immediate and singular *intuitions* rather than general discursive concepts. Each of the four expositions is just a brief paragraph, but they are important, and they are filled out and debated extensively in the secondary literature on Kant. (In the A-edition there were five metaphysical expositions for both space and time. Expositions (1) and (2) stressed the *a priority* and (4) and (5) the *intuitional* nature of our representations of space and time, as just mentioned, while (3) showed how other synthetic *a priori* cognitions [e.g. in geometry, chronometry and kinematics] are possible only if space and time are indeed *a priori* intuitions. However, in the B-edition on space, (3) was omitted and rewritten as a separate 'transcendental exposition of space', to be discussed separately below.)

Kant's first metaphysical exposition of the concept of space runs as follows:

> (1) Space is not an empirical concept that has been drawn from outer experiences. For in order for certain sensations to be related to [*bezogen*] something outside me [*ausser mir*] (i.e. to something in another place in space from that in which I find myself), thus in order for me to represent them as outside and next to one another, thus not merely as different but as in different places, the representation of space must already be their ground. Thus the representation of space cannot be obtained from the relations of outer appearance through experience, but this outer experience is itself first possible only through this representation.   (A23/B38)

The first metaphysical exposition of time argues similarly for the conclusion that "time is not an empirical concept drawn from an experience" on the grounds that we can perceive or "represent that several things exist at one and the same time (simultaneously) or in different times (successively)" only if "the representation of time" is presupposed as their *a priori* ground (A30/B46). The gist of these passages might seem to be straightforward, but in fact Kant scholars have rightly emphasized that some digging needs to be done in order to see what Kant's argument might really be here (see e.g. Allison 2004: ch. 5; Buroker 2006: ch. 3; Falkenstein 1995: ch. 5; Gardner 1999, ch. 4; Guyer 1987: ch. 16; 2006a: 51–70; 2007; Rosenberg 2005: ch. 5; Warren 1998).

The passage concerning space contends that our cognitive representation of space is not an empirical representation derived from our outer sensory experiences of appearances in space, *a posteriori*. For in order for our sensations to refer to things located in space externally to us and distinct from one another at all, the representation of space must already be presupposed as the *a priori* ground that makes such outer experiences possible in the first place.

One reason that this argument is not so straightforward is that it might appear to embody a merely trivial truth, one that Kant's opponents could accept while denying Kant's conclusion that space must be an *a priori* representation. For such an opponent could certainly agree with the trivial claim that in order for us to represent anything as located in space, we must have the representation of space! That trivial tautology remains emptily true, they might say, no matter what the origin of our representation of space might be. The road would be left wide open for empiricists such as Locke or Hume, or a 'phenomenal relationist' about space such as Leibniz, to argue that we acquire our representation of space *a posteriori* from particular outer sense experiences, which is what Kant is attempting to deny. Let us briefly take Hume as an example of one such philosopher who attempts to account for our ideas of space and time on the basis of the empirical contents of particular sensory experiences.

Hume argued in *A Treatise of Human Nature* "*that the idea of space or extension is nothing but the idea of visible or tangible points in a certain order*" (*Treatise*, 1.2.5.1). Setting aside various issues about 'points' as perceptible *minima*, Hume's basic view is that our idea of spatial extension (distance, shape, etc.) is 'copied' from complex sense impressions of the layout of visible and tangible objects. To take an example of Hume's:

> The table before me is alone sufficient by its view to give me the idea of extension. This idea, then, is borrow'd from, and represents some impression, which this moment appears to the senses. But my senses convey to me only the impressions of colour'd points, dispos'd in a certain manner. If the eye is sensible of any thing farther, I desire it may be pointed out to me. But if it be impossible to shew any thing farther, we may conclude with certainty, that the idea of extension is nothing but a copy of these colour'd points, and of the manner of their appearance. (*Treatise*, 1.2.3.4)

Open your eyes and, according to Hume, you immediately have a complex sense impression of the layout or spread of the visible colours (i.e. the array of coloured objects) before you. Your idea of spatial extension is 'copied' from this complex impression. (Similarly, according to Hume, hearing five notes played in succession on a flute is sufficient to give us the idea of *time as a succession of ideas.*) Hume then attempts to show how basic principles of association and imagination can work upon these complex impressions and resulting ideas to produce all of our more 'abstract' beliefs about the structure of space.

Hume argues that many of our beliefs about space (and time) are based on "fictions" and "mistakes" of the imagination such that the relevant ideas are *not* traceable back to any sense impressions from which they were copied, and which are thus problematic. For example, it is widely believed that space is infinitely divisible; that there would be distance or spatial extension even in a vacuum, that is, even in the absence of any visible material bodies (and similarly, that there could be 'time without change', i.e. without any perceptible succession); that the *place* occupied by something seen is different from the thing occupying that place; and so on. To take a simple example, we do distinguish the *place* a thing occupies from the thing itself, but only because (on Hume's view) we know by past experience that other objects could replace or 'fill in' for the current object in relation to the surrounding objects. (Leibniz constructs space and time out of relations among appearances in a similar fashion. See the fifth letter of Leibniz's correspondence with Samuel Clarke, the defender of Newtonian absolute space [Alexander 1956: 55ff.]) Hume regards some of these beliefs to be more problematic than others, but his "science of human nature" aims to account for every aspect of our abstract ideas or representations of space and time on *a posteriori* grounds, that is, in terms of the complex sensory impressions and psychological principles mentioned above.

In relation to Kant's first metaphysical exposition, then, it seems open to Hume to reply, as above, that our 'outer' sensory experiences of visible and tangible objects do already involve or 'presuppose' the representation of space. He would insist, however, that this is simply because the idea of space is directly 'copied' *a posteriori* from our complex sense impressions of particular 'extensions' that consist of presented arrays of coloured and tangible 'objects' (or perceptible 'points', for Hume). Such complex impressions and corresponding ideas are then subsequently developed into our 'abstract ideas' of space (and time) by means of complex principles of imagination and association, in some cases involving various 'fictions' and 'mistakes' of the imagination.

(Note that Falkenstein's book *Kant's Intuitionism* [1995], offers extensive and interesting arguments in Kant's favour against any 'constructivist' empiricist positions that attempt – *unlike* Hume's account just given, I think – to derive the idea of space from impressions *without* presupposing that those initial impressions, appearances or objects are immediately presented as extended in a spatial array. Falkenstein argues, as mentioned earlier, that a major problem with such views is roughly speaking that no empirical principle of ordering such impressions can plausibly deliver the features of specifically *spatial* ordering. But here I am interested in empiricists such as Hume and perhaps Leibniz as well as many other 'transcendental realists' who would grant that our initial sensory impressions are of objects or appearances as extended or 'spread out' before us.)

In light of the *prima facie* plausibility and non-circularity of Hume's empiricist account, then, we should look for a less trivial reading of what Kant might be up to in his 'first exposition' of space. Henry Allison has argued that Kant is really making the following non-trivial claim: the representation of objects as 'outside us' *in space* is necessary for the possibility of our having any cognition of objects as 'outside us' or 'external to us' in the more general sense (noted earlier) of being *distinct from us* and from each other at all, that is, as mind-independent, individuated objects. But although I think Allison's account is insightful and Kantian in spirit, the actual text of Kant's first exposition clearly indicates that it is specifically the representation "of something *in another place in space* from that in which I find myself", and so on, that Kant is arguing is possible only if the representation of space is presupposed *a priori*. (This has been pointed out by Falkenstein and Warren in opposition to Allison's reading [Allison 2004: 100–104 and endnotes].) I also do not find plausible the objection that Hume's assumption that impressions can initially come in extended arrays is circular or that it clearly begs any questions against Kant.

Perhaps, however, Kant's (and Allison's) anti-empiricist point about space being an *a priori* presupposition of all outer experience can be read as essentially highlighting the following sort of claim. Contrary to what Hume says, it is not clear that the complex sense impression of a table or of 'visible and tangible points disposed in a certain manner' really is "sufficient" to account for the *representation of spatial extension*. This is for reasons, as Kant's text suggests, that have to do with the nature of the initial sensory presentation of the table as outside us in space and as distinct from other objects, that is, prior to any further 'constructions' or associative processes of imagination that might be appealed to by the empiricist in order to explain how our more abstract and comprehensive ideas of space and time are allegedly produced. Bearing in mind Hume's claim that our idea of space is ultimately derived from particular complex sense impressions of visible and tangible objects "disposed in a certain manner", consider the following interpretive remarks of Jay Rosenberg (some of these points bear on the other three metaphysical expositions of space, too):

> Kant argues that this sort of [empiricist] account cannot be correct. "Space is not an empirical concept that has been drawn from outer experiences" (A23/B38). You can't get to the concept of *space*

simply by piling up concepts of spatial characteristics. Concepts of spatial characteristics are *systematic*, and the center of focus of this systematicity is the concept of a three-dimensional spatial continuum. The systematic structure of the family of concepts of spatial characteristics, that is, *presupposes* the concept of the unitary individual, space. One can't think of a point, line, plane, or solid, except as a point, line, plane, or solid *in space*. But to be located in space at all is to be in one place *rather than another*, and so the *whole* of space is implicit in every spatial experience.
(Rosenberg 2005: 65)

Adapting these remarks to our present case, my immediate sensory experience of the particular 'extension' presented by the table already necessarily represents that extension as being systematically spatially related both to the current position of my body (the table is *over there* as viewed *from here*, i.e. from my *point of view*) and to the surrounding objects in space that contrast with the contours of the table. Our representation of space is thus essentially holistic and *perspectival*. Our immediate sensory presentation of objects in space does not have the *aggregative* or 'building-up' character that Hume's account suggests, even if we grant that his initial 'impressions' can present themselves as extended arrays.

If the Humean empiricist suggests in response that we can simply widen the initial complex sensory impression of objects or points disposed in a certain manner to include all the items we might care to mention (my body, the table, surrounding objects, etc.), it becomes only more evident that *any* spatial array of material contents will present itself from the start as a perspectively sensed region *within* a wider spatial framework of relations. In this sense a represented framework of spatial relations is necessarily epistemically prior to, rather than derived from, any particular sensed array of spatially extended contents. As we saw Kant state in conclusion in the first metaphysical exposition: "Thus the representation of space cannot be obtained from the relations of outer appearance through experience, but this outer experience is itself first possible only through this representation" (A23/B38). (Similar considerations can be mobilized in favour of the conclusion that our perspectival, unitary and systematic representation of objects as successive or simultaneous in time is not derived empirically from particular successions of perceptible contents, such as hearing five notes in succession on a flute.)

From this perspective we can at least very briefly indicate what Kant is up to in the other three metaphysical expositions concerning space. (Each of these expositions would merit as much discussion as the first one, but here we shall economize.) The second exposition of space runs as follows (and similarly for time):

> (2) Space is a necessary representation, *a priori*, that is the ground of all outer intuitions. One can never represent that there is no space, though one can very well think that there are no objects to be encountered in it. It is therefore to be regarded as the condition of the possibility of appearances, not as a determination dependent on them, and is an *a priori* representation that necessarily grounds outer appearances. (A24/B38–9)

The key asymmetry in the second sentence here is that while (i) we cannot represent outer objects or appearances without space, (ii) we can think of space as empty of any outer objects or appearances. In relation to (i), as we have seen, to sensorily represent any 'outer' appearance (distinct from the mind) is already to perspectivally represent that object or appearance as located within a wider framework of spatial relations. In relation to (ii), we are able to think (e.g. as geometers do) of the framework of three-dimensional spatial relations without representing any empirical objects contained within it. Furthermore, Kant seems to hold that it is possible for us to *conceive of* empty space, although on his view we can have no real cognition of empty space, and empty space cannot intelligibly be conceived to *exist* as a substantial entity on its own (cf. Falkenstein 1995: 203–16). Kant brings forth parallel considerations in relation to time: "In regard to appearances in general one cannot remove time, though one can very well take the appearances away from time. Time is therefore given *a priori*" (A31/B46).

The two points combined suggest that the representations of space and time are (i) universal and necessary for, and yet also (ii) an independent condition of, any possible experience of 'outer' or 'inner' sensible objects. Kant draws the conclusion that the representations of space and time are *a priori necessary conditions of the possibility* of any outer or inner appearances. Our representations of space and time are thus not dependent on, or derived from, relations among sensible objects, as Locke, Hume and Leibniz held. On the contrary, the representations of space and time are independent necessary conditions of our cognizing any mind-independent sensible objects in the first place.

Let us assume that metaphysical expositions (1) and (2) have shown that the representations of space and time are *pure a priori* rather than empirically derived representations. The considerations Kant now brings forth in metaphysical expositions (3) and (4) in relation to space (i.e. B39–40) are designed to show that this representation of space is an *intuition*, that is, an immediate sensory awareness of space as a particular or individual, rather than being a *concept* of some general kind or common feature of objects. The third exposition stresses that "one can only represent a single space, and if one speaks of many spaces, one understands by that only parts of one and the same unique space". (Similarly in relation to exposition (4) concerning time: "Different times are only parts of one and the same time" [A31–2/B47].) Particular spaces, extensions or regions are always presented or given in experience as surrounded by wider regions and as divisible into smaller regions of the same continuous and unbounded framework of spatial relations. Of course, we do not positively perceive the unboundedness, continuity, totality or infinite divisibility of space. (Recall our discussions of the first two Antinomies in the previous chapter.) But spatial regions and limits are sensorily present in our experience in such a way that any such limits are experienced as enlargeable and divisible, without 'gaps' (i.e. exhibiting continuity) and without any absolute boundary to further expansion or division.

From this we can perhaps already see the grounds for what Kant claims in metaphysical exposition (4) concerning space (and in the parallel exposition (5) concerning time): "Space is represented as an infinite **given** magnitude". In the case of conceptual representations, an in principle infinite number of individuals can *fall under* a general concept, such as red things exemplifying the general property of being red, or particular dogs instantiating the concept of that kind of animal. But space is sensorily present as (i.e. 'given' immediately as, not mediately 'conceived' via descriptive criteria as) continuously expansive and infinitely divisible into regions or parts *contained within* the same unitary space. In this sense the whole of space is prior to its parts. By contrast, concepts classify the kinds, relations and properties exhibited by multiple objects that are given as individuals not exhausted by those conceptual determinations (in this sense, 'parts prior to wholes'). Furthermore, neither the instances that can fall under a concept nor the definitional components of a concept are infinite parts of that conceptual representation in the way that the continuous parts of space are infinite parts *of* space and *in* space. Space is intuitively represented as exhibiting a continuous parts-of-a-single-whole mereology rather than an aggregate of objects-as-instances-of-concepts predicational structure.

Similar considerations are applied to the case of time: the "infinitude of time signifies nothing more than that every determinate magnitude of time is only possible through limitations of a single time grounding it"; therefore "the entire representation cannot be through concepts, for they contain only partial representations, but immediate intuition must ground them" (A32/B47–8).

Thus the four metaphysical expositions together contend that our representations of space and time are of unitary individuals having the following characteristics (here I also include Kant's *form–matter* distinction introduced earlier in the Transcendental Aesthetic):

- Space and time are *directly sensorily intuited as single, continuous, infinitely divisible and expansible wholes that are prior to their parts.*

(Metaphysical expositions (3) and (4) for space in the B-edition, expositions (4) and (5) for time.)
- And these unitary individuals, space and time, are *perspectival forms that are given prior to and independently of all the empirical contents or 'matter' of experience contained within them, and hence as a priori "conditions of the possibility of appearances"*. (Metaphysical expositions (1) and (2).)

Questions concerning how to interpret and evaluate each of Kant's all-too-brief metaphysical expositions abound in the secondary literature on Kant, including the question of how those expositions are supposed to bear on Kant's conclusion concerning the *transcendental ideality* of space and time. We shall comment on the latter issue in §3.2 below. First, however, we must turn to Kant's "transcendental exposition of space" (B40–41, replacing A24), which Kant believed to be decisive proof that space is transcendentally ideal, but which was rendered problematic by subsequent discoveries in logic, mathematics and physics in the nineteenth and twentieth centuries. Again the parallel considerations that pertain to time will be briefly noted.

Geometry and the transcendental exposition of space

In §2.1, we encountered the problem of synthetic *a priori* judgments in general. We saw that Hume's sceptical empiricism argues against the possibility of rationally justifying any universal and objectively necessary propositions about perceivable matters of fact in the world. In relation to Kant's 'transcendental exposition' of space, we saw in §1.1, that the term 'transcendental' pertains to "our mode of cognition of objects insofar as this is to be possible *a priori*" (A11/B25), that is, in so far as our judgments about reality *do* exhibit universality and objective necessity. Kant's 'metaphysical exposition' of our representations of space and time as *pure a priori sensory intuitions*, discussed above, will now form the basis for Kant's transcendental expositions of space and time (or metaphysical exposition (3) in the case of time). Kant tells us that in this case the exposition will be 'transcendental' in so far as it aims to explain "the possibility of other synthetic *a priori* cognitions". In the case of space Kant takes those synthetic *a priori* cognitions to be found in *geometry* as a science of space:

> Geometry is a science that determines the properties of space synthetically yet *a priori*. What then must the representation of space be for such a cognition of it to be possible? It must originally be intuition; for from a mere concept no propositions can be drawn

that go beyond the concept, which, however happens in geometry (Introduction V). But this intuition must be encountered in us *a priori*, i.e., prior to all perception of an object, thus it must be pure, not empirical intuition. For geometrical propositions are all apodictic, i.e., combined with consciousness of their necessity, e.g., space has only three dimensions; but such propositions cannot be empirical or judgments of experience, nor inferred from them (Introduction II). (B40–41)

Similarly in relation to time, Kant argues that the *a priori* intuition of time "grounds the possibility" of various "axioms of time": for example, that time necessarily "has only one dimension: different times are not simultaneous, but successive" (A31/B47). Kant also contends that certain universal and necessary propositions concerning the alterations and motions of objects in general (for example, that an object can both *have* and *not have* a certain property or location – namely, *at different times*) are cognizable only on the presupposition that time is an *a priori* intuition (cf. B48–9). Here I shall focus on the pure intuition of space as allegedly necessary for the possibility of synthetic *a priori* cognitions in geometry.

Classical Euclidean geometry, since it demonstrates the necessary properties of two-dimensional lines and figures and of three-dimensional solids, is a mathematical science of space consisting of *a priori* rather than merely empirical propositions. Furthermore, Kant argues, geometry rests on *synthetic* or ampliative (amplifying) cognitions, rather than on analytic propositions that merely clarify what is already contained in its basic concepts. As Kant clarifies these points later in the Aesthetic:

> Take the proposition that with two straight lines no space at all can be enclosed, thus no figure is possible, and try to derive it from the concept of straight lines and the number two .... All of your effort is in vain, and you see yourself forced to take refuge in intuition, as indeed geometry always does. You thus *give yourself an object in intuition*; but what kind is this, is it a pure *a priori* intuition or an empirical one? If it were the latter, then no universally valid, let alone apodictic proposition could ever come from it: for experience can never provide anything of this sort. You must therefore give your object *a priori* in intuition, and ground your synthetic proposition on this. (A47–8/B65, italics added)

Both the basic concepts and the proofs found in geometry thus involve what Kant calls the *a priori* **construction** of concepts" in pure intuition, which we shall see in later chapters also involves the *pure imagination*. By 'construction' Kant initially has in mind the sort of geometrical procedure by which, considered merely empirically, we literally construct geometrical figures and proofs with a ruler and compass. Considered transcendentally, we can 'draw' or cognize the possibility of such figures in pure imagination, that is, in an *a priori* intuition of space. For example, in pure intuition we can construct in the mind a figure that ideally instantiates the conceptual definition of a *circle* as the set of points on a plane that are all equidistant from a given point. We construct such a circle by, as it were, 'rotating' a given line segment as radius from a given point. (See Euclid's Postulate 3, as well as Kant's remark: "Now in mathematics a postulate is the practical proposition that contains nothing except *the synthesis through which we first give ourselves an object and generate its concept*, e.g., to describe a circle with a given line from a given point on a plane" [A235/B287, italics added].) For more on the *a priori* construction of concepts, the reader is encouraged to read Kant's discussion of the relationship between philosophy, as based on concepts, and mathematics, as based on pure sensory intuitions, in the first section of the "Discipline of Pure Reason" chapter of the Transcendental Doctrine of Method at the end of the *Critique* (A713–21/B741–9; a helpful introduction to the "Discipline" section can be found in Buroker [2006: 290–98]).

Recall the 'box' of options regarding *a priori* vs. *a posteriori* knowledge and synthetic vs. analytic propositions discussed in §2.2. Grasping the concept of a circle, according to Kant, thus requires *constructing* that concept in pure intuition and not merely rehearsing or analysing the conceptual contents found in the abstract definition or in a general description. Hence geometrical cognitions, even of this most simple kind, are not merely 'analytic *a priori*' conceptual truths. Furthermore, empirical circles perceived by means of the senses do not exhibit the universality and necessity of the relations that are exhibited by that concept in pure intuition (see A47–8/B65, quoted above). Hence, geometrical concepts and cognitions are not merely 'synthetic *a posteriori*' truths of experience either. Thus the pure geometrical concepts of two- and three-dimensional objects in space must be based on *synthetic a priori pure intuitions*. The metaphysical exposition has shown (or attempted to show) that space is a pure *a priori* intuition; the transcendental exposition is now contending that this explains the possibility of certain synthetic *a priori* cognitions in geometry.

The same sorts of 'pure *a priori* constructions' can be illustrated by means of Euclid's *proof* procedures. Consider the first proposition that is proved in Euclid's geometry. A perfect equilateral triangle can be constructed from a given line segment (AB) using the above mentioned postulate concerning the construction of a circle, as illustrated in Figure 3.1. Basically, the procedure is to construct two circles using the radii from each endpoint (A and B) of a given line segment. The circles will intersect at some point C, thus ultimately

SPACE AND TIME AS FORMS OF HUMAN SENSIBILITY

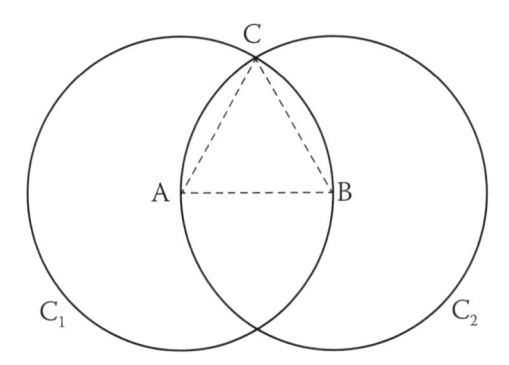

Figure 3.1 Proving the first proposition in Euclid's geometry.

showing that the radii that form the three sides of the constructed triangle are necessarily equal.

Kant's claim is that the *spatial objects and relations* described by such *a priori* mathematical constructions must be represented in singular and immediate intuitions (i.e. not just by general conceptual descriptions) that are given *a priori* (i.e. not merely given *a posteriori* through the senses, lacking genuine necessity and universality). Accordingly, Kant now concludes his 'transcendental exposition' by answering the question, "What then must the representation of space be for such a cognition [i.e. of geometry] to be possible?"

> Now how can an outer intuition inhabit the mind that precedes the objects themselves, and in which the concept of the latter can be determined *a priori*? Obviously not otherwise than insofar as it *has its seat merely in the subject, as its formal constitution for being affected by objects* and thereby acquiring **immediate representation**, i.e., **intuition**, of them, thus only as the form of outer **sense** in general.
>
> Thus our explanation alone makes the **possibility** of geometry as a synthetic *a priori* cognition comprehensible.
>
> (B40–41, italics added)

The synthetic *a priori* nature of the geometry of space can thus be explained only if the representation of space – that is, both our represent*ing* of space and the necessary geometrical structure of the 'constructed' objects thus represent*ed* – is a *pure form of intuition* that "has its seat" in our human cognitive sensory capacity and "its formal constitution for being affected by objects".

The next important claim made by Kant is that *if space pertained to 'things in themselves', then we could only learn about the properties of space by means of the senses*, that is, empirically (*a posteriori*). (See Kant's clarification of this point at A46–9/B64–6.) For the only way we human beings can learn about the nature of mind-independent objects is by being directly or indirectly affected by them through the senses. But any such reliance on empirical data, conceived as produced in us by 'things in themselves', would fail to explain the *a priori* necessity exhibited by the geometry of space as just discussed. Kant makes this point in his "Conclusions from the Above Concepts" (A26ff./B42ff.), which includes the passage with which we started this chapter ("We can accordingly speak of space ... only from the human standpoint"). In this section Kant finally explicitly draws his *transcendental idealist* (but also *empirical realist*) conclusions from the above metaphysical and transcendental expositions. (Recall that the general nature of Kant's transcendental idealism and empirical realism was discussed in §1.2.) He begins with the following two summary conclusions concerning space (with parallel conclusions drawn in the case of time):

> (a) Space represents no property at all of any things in themselves nor any relation of them to each other, i.e., no determination of them that attaches to objects themselves and that would remain even if one were to abstract from all subjective conditions of intuition. For neither absolute nor relative determinations can be intuited prior to the existence of the things to which they pertain, thus be intuited *a priori*.
> (b) Space is nothing other than merely the form of all appearances of outer sense, i.e., the subjective condition of sensibility, under which alone outer intuition is possible for us. Now since the receptivity of the subject to be affected by objects necessarily precedes all intuitions of these objects, it can be understood how the form of all appearances can be given in the mind prior to all actual perceptions, thus *a priori*, and how as a pure intuition, in which all objects must be determined, it can contain principles of their relations prior to all experience. (A26/B42)

Space is thus a formal structure of objects considered solely *as appearances* to us (as well as to any beings who may share our spatial form of sensory intuition). Space does not pertain to objects considered as 'things in themselves' through pure reason. Since the appearances are empirical objects in so far as they conform to space as our form of sensorily intuiting any objects whatsoever, Kant concludes that only on this transcendental idealist view can the synthetic *a priori* nature of geometry be shown to be applicable to the objects of experience.

What should we make of Kant's various arguments and conclusions in the Transcendental Aesthetic concerning space and time as pure *a priori* intuitions, and concerning the transcendental ideality and empirical reality of space and time?

3.2 ASSESSING KANT'S TRANSCENDENTAL IDEALISM CONCERNING SPACE AND TIME

Kant's transcendental idealist conception of space and time has been a hotly disputed aspect of his philosophy. As we saw in §1.2, in relation to the 'two aspects' (or perhaps 'two standpoints') versus 'two worlds' interpretations of his transcendental idealism, these disputes concern not only how to interpret and evaluate the arguments that we have just briefly canvassed above, but also how to understand the transcendental idealist thesis itself. Even among those philosophers who think that Kant's *Critique of Pure Reason* contains a wealth of insights concerning certain *a priori* sources of human cognition and concerning the experiential limits of human knowledge (we shall encounter many such insights in the following two chapters as well), there are some otherwise sympathetic interpreters who entirely reject Kant's transcendental idealism, that is, his conclusion that we have knowledge only of objects as 'appearances' not as 'things in themselves'. Among recent English-language commentators, for instance, philosophers such as Strawson (1966), Guyer (1987), Rae Langton (1998), Ralph Walker (1999), and others have attempted to defend Kant's more valuable insights by detaching them from what they argue is Kant's invalidly inferred, highly implausible and perhaps deeply incoherent transcendental idealist conception of space and time. (For a full display of the alleged incoherencies in Kant's transcendental idealism according to one classic 'two-world' interpretation, see Strawson [1966: pt 4].)

On the other hand, there are those who continue to defend central aspects of Kant's transcendental idealism, either as originally conceived or as modified and adapted in various respects. In this section let us take a very brief look at a selection of issues raised by, and some further reactions to, Kant's arguments concerning space and time in the Transcendental Aesthetic. (For an excellent overview and helpful analysis of the literature on Kant's transcendental idealism, see Ameriks [2003: chs 2, 3].)

Kant's 'argument from geometry' viewed in retrospect

Let us first consider the question of how Kant's transcendental exposition, or his 'argument from geometry' as it is commonly known, should be viewed in light of the revolutionary developments that have taken place in logic, mathematics and physics since the time of Kant's writings in the eighteenth century. In the final section we shall then briefly consider what might remain plausible in Kant's general transcendental idealist conception of space and time.

In the nineteenth century, mathematicians, building on centuries of previous labours, finally constructed fully consistent *non-Euclidean geometries*. Roughly put, these are geometries the basic axioms of which contradict certain intuitive axioms of the classical Euclidean geometry that Kant understandably took for granted. Most notably, Euclid's fifth postulate, known as the parallels postulate, is equivalent to the intuitive idea that, given a line and a point not on that line, there can be one and only one line through that point that does not intersect the given line however far they are extended (Figure 3.2).

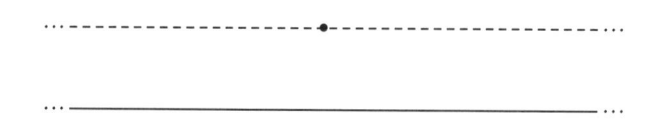

Figure 3.2 Euclid's fifth postulate.

Consistent non-Euclidean geometries were developed, however, based on the seemingly counter-intuitive assumption that there could be infinitely many such lines (*hyperbolic* geometries), or that there could be no such line at all (*elliptical* geometries). In early-twentieth-century physics Albert Einstein then proposed, in the theory of relativity, that it is in fact one of these 'counter-intuitive' non-Euclidean geometries that actually correctly represents the physical space–time of our universe, a theory that was then strikingly experimentally confirmed by Arthur Eddington in 1919. So it would seem that far from Euclidean geometry embodying synthetic *a priori* truths about space, as Kant assumed, the space of our physical world is in fact an elliptic or spherical (Riemannian) non-Euclidean space. It is as if the space (or space–time) of our world is curved like the surface of a globe (i.e. with no space 'inside' the globe), so that the sum of the angles of a triangle drawn on that sphere is *more* than 180 degrees, the shortest distance between two points is a *curved* line (a geodesic), and so on.

An influential group of mid-twentieth-century philosophers known as the 'logical empiricists' and 'logical positivists' consequently argued that, on the one hand, there are in fact many different internally consistent *pure geometries*. These are merely formal axiomatized systems, each with its set of internally consistent deductive consequences that are provable merely 'analytic *a priori*'. On the other hand, they argued, the correct *applied geometry* or physics of empirical reality turns out to be a non-Euclidean geometry, and this is something that is known only 'synthetic *a posteriori*' by means of Einstein's physical theory and by experimental testing. These developments seemed to many (but not all) philosophers to show that Kant's view of space as synthetic *a priori* was both substantively mistaken and methodologically misguided. Philosophers, it was argued, should restrict themselves to the two (seemingly) unproblematic 'boxes' or kinds of knowledge that have long been accepted by empiricists: namely, analytic *a priori* and synthetic *a posteriori* cognitions (recall §2.1). For those two boxes alone are sufficient to account for the nature of our representations of space and time in both science and philosophy, on this relatively widespread view of the matter.

It is not clear that the issue is so straightforward, however, and a variety of different defences of aspects of Kant's view, even on this particular matter, have been and continue to be put forward. Some authors argue, for example, that Kant's account of space as three-dimensional and Euclidean is arguably correct as an account *of the perspectival space of our perceptual experience* as opposed to whatever might be the case with the various 'spaces' invented in pure mathematics or with the scientific-theoretical space–time of the physicists. However, whatever the merits (or demerits) of such an approach to perceptual experience might be, it should be noted that most such attempts to drive a wedge between so-called 'perceptual space' or 'visual space' on the one hand and 'scientific space' or 'physical space' on the other, are in danger of running sharply against not only the letter but the spirit of Kant's own views. For according to Kant, the continuous three-dimensional space of the 'appearances' is supposed to *include* all of the matter that is to be met with in the spatiotemporal universe studied by physics; it is not supposed to be a merely 'perceptual space' that is somehow distinguishable from the empirically real space of the theoretical physicists. Rather, it is the *latter* that must be recognized as perspectival in nature through and through, if Kant is right. (For two interesting discussions of Kant in relation to 'visual space' and 'perceptual space' from the 1960s, see Bennett [1966: ch. 2], and Strawson [1966: pt 5]. For an interesting recent attempt to defend Kant's view of space as necessarily Euclidean in all possible *humanly experienceable* worlds, see Hanna [2001: ch. 5].)

Some philosophers, such as the neo-Kantian philosopher Ernst Cassirer (1874–1945), the analytic philosopher Wilfrid Sellars (1912–89) and, more recently, Michael Friedman in his analyses both of Kant and of subsequent developments in both neo-Kantianism and logical positivism (see e.g. Friedman 2001), have argued that Kant's views might express a fundamental truth at a different level of philosophical analysis, despite his particular arguments being conceptually dependent, in specific and important ways, on the superseded mathematical sciences of his time. Such philosophers thus grant that Kant's substantive views about the transcendental ideality of space and time as synthetic *a priori* forms of intuition were, for specific reasons, tightly linked to the mathematics and natural science of his day. (See in particular Friedman [1992] on how Kant's views on 'construction in intuition' in Euclidean geometry were superseded by Frege's later revolutionary development of a formal logic of polyadic relations.) However, they also contend that Kant's views on these matters nonetheless do contain important and enduring insights about the necessary presupposition of *substantive a priori 'framework principles' or 'coordination principles'* in all empirical and scientific knowledge. The idea is that there must be *some* such substantive *a priori* principles – admittedly different *a priori* principles constituting different scientific-conceptual frameworks over time – that make possible the coordination and coherent application of *any* mathematical system to any humanly knowable physical world. These conceptions of a kind of relativized and fallibilist 'synthetic (or perhaps better, *broadly* analytic) *a priori*' are another interesting way, only vaguely gestured at in what I have said here, in which some philosophers have attempted to defend the spirit of Kant's analysis in light of subsequent revolutionary developments in mathematics and natural science. (In the following two chapters we shall encounter further ways in which it might be argued that a Kantian '*a priori* metaphysics of physics' might be defensible in general despite the tight connections between some of Kant's specific views and the subsequently superseded physics of his day.)

Debating Kant's transcendental idealism

Let us turn now from the specific issue of the fate of Kant's views in relation to subsequent developments in mathematics and physics to questions concerning how to interpret and evaluate Kant's transcendental idealist conception of space and time in the Transcendental Aesthetic itself. We shall also have further occasion to reflect on Kant's transcendental idealism before the end of this book.

One of the most influential works on Kant's transcendental idealism in recent decades has been Allison's *Kant's Transcendental Idealism* (1983, rev. edn 2004; for earlier related views, see Bird [1962, 2006a]; Matthews [(1969) 1982]; Prauss [1974]). According to Allison's broadly 'two-aspect' as opposed to 'two-world' or 'two-object' interpretation (see §1.2), Kant's transcendental:

> idealism is not an ontological thesis about how things 'really are' (non-spatial and non-temporal), when seen from a God's eye view. It is rather a critical thesis about the conditions of the cognition

of things viewed from the 'human standpoint', which is the only
standpoint available to us.   (Allison 2004: 132)

Allison calls such *a priori* human cognitive conditions *epistemic conditions*. Such *a priori* epistemic conditions are necessary for the possibility of our experience of objects, rather than being *ontological* conditions that are allegedly necessary for the existence of things considered 'in themselves', and also rather than being merely empirically mind-dependent *psychological* conditions on our experience of objects. Allison also contends that Kant's main argument for the transcendental ideality of space does not rely on the controversial argument from geometry, thus safeguarding Kant's conclusion from the subsequent developments in geometry discussed above. Rather, according to Allison and other commentators, the grounds for Kant's 'formal' or transcendental idealism depend primarily on the opening 'metaphysical expositions' of our representations of space and time as *pure a priori intuitions*.

Kant's conclusions in the metaphysical exposition of space, as we saw in §3.1, were that the spatial form of all possible sensible objects of experience is necessarily represented as a single, continuous, perspectival space; and that this three-dimensional perspectival structure is immediately given as a whole independently of whatever *empirical* matters or sensible objects are thereby represented as structured by that form. Recall also that space as a 'pure form of sensory intuition' can thus legitimately refer (depending on the context) either to the pure form of our sensory intuit*ing* of objects or to the correlative form of the sensory intuit*eds* or objects that are thereby represented. In both respects, if Kant is right, the representation of space requires ineliminable reference to our mode, our human way, of sensorily representing things. Allison argues that on the basis of these claims Kant draws the two further conclusions that we highlighted above (i.e. A26/B42, (a) and (b), quoted at the end of the previous section): namely, that space as the content of such a representation (i) *cannot* be a determination (either intrinsic or relational) of things in themselves, and (ii) *can only* be a form of human sensibility (there being no other alternative account, Kant argues, that can explain the *a priori* nature of our sensory intuition of objects in space).

The following is one crucial but disputed claim involved in Allison's interpretation of how Kant makes the inference to the transcendental idealist conclusion that space is necessarily *only* a form of our sensibility and *not* a form of 'things in themselves'. Allison contends:

> [T]here is a contradiction involved in the assumption that the representation of something [i.e. space] that supposedly functions

> as a condition of the possibility of the experience of objects could have its source in the experience of these very objects. This is contradictory because it entails that experience is possible apart from something that is stipulated to be a condition of its possibility. Thus, if the representation of space plays the role it is claimed to in the Metaphysical Exposition, it must be *a priori* and, as such, have its ground in the cognizing subject rather than in the nature of the objects as they are in themselves. (Allison 2004: 125)

The idea is that since the representation of space, as a pure intuition, is an *a priori* 'epistemic condition' that makes our experience of any objects possible in the first place, such a condition *cannot be derived from* an experience of (and thus have its 'ground' in) those same objects: as Allison concludes above, "it must … have its ground in the cognizing subject rather than in the nature of the objects as they are in themselves".

Allison's interpretation and defence of Kant's transcendental idealism has been influential but has also been sharply criticized. Among Guyer's many objections to Allison's defence of Kant's transcendental idealism, he objects to Allison's specific claim just quoted, as follows. One could, Guyer argues, reply to Allison that "a necessary condition of knowledge may reflect the structure of *both* the epistemic subject and the object of knowledge, rather than of the former *instead* of the latter" (Guyer [1987: 340]; for a response, see Allison [1996: ch. 1]). Guyer's objection here essentially states a version of the famous *neglected alternative objection* to Kant's transcendental idealism, originally due to Adolf Trendelenburg in the 1860s (cf. Bird 2006c). Roughly put, even if we grant that the representation of space is a pure form of human sensibility, why couldn't both that be true and *space itself* be a correspondingly revealed structure of things as they are in themselves?

In his reply to that famous and long-standing objection to Kant, Allison argues that since Kant's metaphysical exposition shows that empirical space, as the represented content of a pure *a priori* form of our sensibility, is a mind-dependent and (in Falkenstein's sense mentioned earlier) 'presentational' ordering, as opposed to an intrinsic or 'qualitative' ordering of contents, it follows that no entirely mind-independent, *non*-presentational features of 'things in themselves' could even intelligibly be conceived as 'corresponding' to space as such a form of presentational sensibility (see Allison 2004: 129–32). If this is right, then space can *only* be a form of sensibility, and 'things in themselves' are thinkable (in a way that is empty of any positive content) only as *non-spatial* (and *non-temporal*). (In the literature Kant's controversial claim that objects conceived as 'things in themselves' are non-spatial and non-temporal is often called Kant's *non-spatiotemporality thesis*; see Falkenstein [1995: ch. 9], and Buroker [1981] for further discussion.)

I shall not pursue further exploration of the important ongoing debate between Allison and Guyer on the nature of Kant's transcendental idealism here. There is, however, another related line of thought that commentators, including Allison, have used to spell out how Kant's metaphysical exposition of space might support at least something closely resembling Kant's own transcendental idealist conclusion.

We saw that in the metaphysical exposition of space Kant contends that the *a priori* intuition of space represents sensible objects as occupying distinct spatial locations within a single system of spatial relations experienced from the perspective or point of view of the experiencer. The space of our experience is thus an ineliminably *perspectival* or 'point-of-view-ish' structure that orients objects with respect to *here*, and as *above or below, to the left or right of, behind or in front of* one another. Similar points hold with respect to events in time experienced as *past, present or future* in relation to the 'moving' *now* of the experiencer. Terms such as 'here' and 'now' are called *indexicals* by philosophers and linguists. So among Kant's contentions in the metaphysical exposition is that space, as the *a priori* perspectival form of our sensory intuition of objects, exhibits an 'indexicality' (left–right, here–there, etc.) that is a necessary condition of our experiencing any objects that are distinct from our particular intuitings and distinct from each other. Furthermore, the claim is that this *a priori* contribution of sensibility is distinguishable from any *conceptual* contributions to our experience of objects.

Various considerations can be cited in support of Kant's contention here that the perspectivality and indexicality of space is an *a priori* condition that is necessary for the possibility of *individuating* objects (see e.g. Koch 1990; Rosenberg 2005: 84–5; Strawson 1959: chs 1–2). For example, if I give a merely *general conceptual* description of all the properties that are true of the table in front of me – however detailed – it remains *conceivable* that all of those conceived general properties could be found instantiated in an *exactly similar table* existing elsewhere. In the face of that possibility, however, a key factor that distinguishes or 'individuates' *this* table *here* from any other qualitatively identical table is precisely its being sensorily intuited *by me here* and *now*.

In the 'Amphiboly' section of the First *Critique* (an Appendix to the Transcendental Analytic) Kant uses the example of two numerically distinct yet qualitatively identical raindrops for a similar (anti-Leibnizian) purpose. If we consider two exactly similar drops of rain 'as things in themselves', that is, considered through pure thought alone, then they would have no distinguishing feature or property. Only if we consider them as objects that must make their *appearance to us* in a single spatial framework that is in principle systematically coordinated to an origin of experience *here and now*, can such intrinsically similar objects be individuated as *two* drops of rain (see A263ff./B319ff.). In relation to issues concerning post-Kantian scientific developments, briefly commented on above and earlier in §2.2, it is arguable on this basis that any *non*-indexical, scientific-theoretical conception of space or space–time must *also ultimately presuppose* or implicitly depend on the *experiential* individuating framework of space and time as forms of sensory intuition.

In the *Prolegomena to any Future Metaphysics* (1783; 81–2=4:285–6), Kant ingeniously attempted to provide further support for his transcendental idealist conclusion about space in the *Critique* by analysing the example of *incongruent counterparts*, such as exactly similar left and right hands. (See Buroker [1981], Van Cleve & Frederick [1991] and Van Cleve [1999: ch. 4] for in-depth discussion and further references.) Kant explains the concept of an incongruent counterpart in the following passage from his earlier, pre-Critical work concerning "Directions in Space" (1768), in which he had used such examples to argue against Leibniz's relational view of space and (at that time) in favour of Newton's absolute conception (the latter was subsequently rejected in Kant's later writings, except as preserved as a 'regulative idea' in his *Metaphysical Foundations of Natural Science*, ch. 4):

> [T]he most common and clearest example is furnished by the limbs of the human body …. The right hand is similar and equal to the left hand. And if one looks at one of them on its own, examining the proportion and the position of its parts to each other, and scrutinising the magnitude of the whole, then a complete *description* of the one must apply in all respects to the other, as well. I shall call a body which is exactly equal and similar to another, but which cannot be enclosed in the same limits as that other, its *incongruent counterpart*.
> (Kant, "Concerning the Ultimate Ground of the Differentiation of Directions in Space" [1768], in Kant, *Theoretical Philosophy, 1755–1770*, 369–70=2:381–2, first italics added)

Despite the fact that incongruent counterparts such as left and right hands, or the mirror-image of a hand, for example, are exactly similar in every intrinsic spatial respect, a glove for the one hand, as we all know, will not fit the other hand. The identically proportioned hands have different *spatial orientations* or 'directions'. Conceived as 'things in themselves' through pure understanding or reason alone, however, the two objects each possess all of the same intrinsic spatial properties and all the same properties or relations of relative distance in relation to other surrounding bodies, and so on. Roughly put, Kant argues that Leibniz's relational account of space thus cannot appeal to any (non-indexical, non-perspectival) differentiating properties to distinguish the incongruent counterparts. And we have already seen that the metaphysical exposition of space in the *Critique* also eliminates Newtonian absolute space, conceived as an imperceptible, contentless, yet somehow substantial 'thing in itself' (see A39/B56), as a possible alternative way of explaining how such sensible objects are situated within a wider space that is directly experienced as a whole-prior-to-its-parts.

Kant concludes that we "can therefore make the difference between similar and equal but nonetheless incongruent things (for example, oppositely spiraled snails) intelligible through no concept alone, but only through the relation to right-hand and left-hand, which refers immediately to intuition" (*Prolegomena*, 4:286). For reasons discussed above, this is arguably further confirmation of Kant's view that space is a pure form of perspectival intuition, and as such space cannot (if this argument has succeeded) intelligibly be conceived as a thing in itself or a property or set of relations of objects conceived as things in themselves.

Kant's contention is thus that a fundamental *sensory-intuitive principle of plurality*, in the form of space and time as the pure *a priori* forms of our perspectival sensory intuition of objects, can thus be argued to be a necessary condition of our experience of objects distinct from us and from each other. In sensory experience such pluralities or 'manifolds' are *given* to us as appearances (not as 'things in themselves'), and our essentially general concepts are applied to such sensory manifolds in our cognition of particular empirically real objects of experience. (We shall probe these issues further in the next chapter, for example in relation to the problems arising from the fact that sensory intuitions without concepts are 'blind'.)

There are other ways of attempting to support or to further spell out aspects of Kant's conception of, and arguments for, transcendental idealism. Of particular interest, for example, is Kant's contention that "everything in our cognition that belongs to intuition ... contains *nothing but mere relations*, of places in one intuition (extension), alteration of places (motion), and laws in accordance with which this alteration is determined (moving forces)", and that *"through mere relations no thing [Sache] in itself is cognized"* (B66–7, italics added). "It is certainly startling to hear", Kant writes later in the anti-Leibnizian Amphiboly section, "that a thing should consist entirely of relations, but such a thing is also mere appearance, and cannot be thought at all through pure categories; it itself consists in the mere relation of something in general to the senses" (A284–5/B340–41; cf. also "Some Remarks on Ludwig Heinrich Jakob's *Examination of Mendelssohn's Morning Hours*", in Kant, *Anthropology, History, and Education*, 180–81=8:153–4). For present purposes, however, I shall assume that a sense has now been sufficiently conveyed in this chapter of how some philosophers continue to find insights in Kant's Transcendental Aesthetic and his transcendental idealism about space

KANT'S *CRITIQUE OF PURE REASON*

and time, while also recognizing that this central doctrine is one of the most criticized aspects of his philosophy.

3.3 THE PROBLEM OF AFFECTION AND 'THINGS IN THEMSELVES'

There is, however, another important class of objections to Kant's transcendental idealism that needs to be addressed in some detail. These objections have to do with what has been called the *problem of affection* in Kant, which is closely related to Kant's claims concerning the *unknowability* of 'things in themselves'. We saw Kant assert at the start of the Transcendental Aesthetic that the direct cognition of any object requires intuition, and that for us this "takes place only insofar as the object is given to us; but this in turn, is possible only if it *affects* the mind in a certain way" through sensibility (A19/B33, italics added). The 'problem of affection' refers to certain difficulties that have been raised in relation to Kant's conception of this *affection relation*, problems that some have argued threaten the coherence of Kant's transcendental idealism from the ground up. (For helpful discussions of the classic German sources of this particular objection, as well as for their own much discussed attempts to defend Kant's view, see Allison [2004: 64–73], and Bird [2006a: 122–6 & ch. 23]. For recent criticisms of the views of Bird and Allison, along with their replies to those criticisms, see Baiasu & Grier [2011] and Wood *et al.* [2007]. For an earlier pathbreaking account in German, see Prauss [1974]. For sophisticated recent interpretations from metaphysical perspectives that are opposed to the views of Bird, Prauss and Allison, see Ameriks [2003, 2006], Guyer [1987], Langton [1998] and Van Cleve [1999]. For an interesting recent 'one-world' account that properly rejects "any interpretation of transcendental idealism that mentalizes appearances", but which also attempts to preserve a substantive ontological role for 'things in themselves', see Allais [2004: 681].)

The problem of affection has traditionally been raised by thinking through the question: how should we construe the 'objects' that Kant says 'affect our sensibility'? (i) Are they the objects considered as sensible 'appearances' – for example, the ordinary material objects that are located in space? (For present purposes I shall focus on the objects of outer sense, although parallel complex considerations arise in relation to one's own mental events as the objects of inner sense, i.e. to the appearances that arise as a result of the mind's own "self-affection"; cf. B66–9, B152–8.) If so then the 'affection' involved would presumably simply be the ordinary empirical causal affection of our senses by outer material objects, involving motion, light waves and so on. (ii) Or does Kant hold, rather, that the objects that *really* affect our faculty of sensibility are the objects considered non-spatiotemporally as 'things in themselves' through pure reason? (iii) Or is it *both*, so that Kant was envisaging that a kind of 'double affection' is involved, with two 'processes' going on simultaneously, one of them an ordinary 'empirical affection' and the other a timeless, non-spatial 'noumenal affection', as it were? Problems have been raised with all three 'choices'.

With respect to (i), however, I think it should by now be clear that Kant's view certainly does involve the *empirical* notion of affection as an ordinary causal relation between empirical objects as appearances and our own affective sensory and intellectual representational responses to those spatiotemporal objects. In particular there is a two-way or *mutual interdependence* involved in Kant's *empirical realism*. On the one hand, our cognition of any object requires that it (i.e. the empirical object) be 'given' to us in experience. We do not 'create' such objects but are rather dependent on some sensible object's being 'given' to our sensibility, and this is one sense in which talk of 'appearances' presupposes some *thing* or object that appears. On the other hand, for our experiential cognition to succeed in being of an *object* at all in the first place requires that such objects are represented in conformity with our own *a priori* forms of sensibility and understanding. This is Kant's 'Copernican' turn and his transcendental idealism, which do entail that those same empirically real spatiotemporal objects must themselves be recognized, from the transcendental philosophical perspective, as 'representations in us', that is, as knowable only as they are represented *by* us under those *a priori* forms. The transcendental sense of 'appearances' reflects this ineliminable relation to our own *a priori* forms of sensible and intellectual representation, as was discussed earlier. But only mistaken interpretations of Kant's philosophy will conclude from this that this account by itself renders problematic the sorts of ordinary causal-empirical affections involved in (i).

With respect to (iii) and the evaluation of the idea that Kant's view involves a theory of 'double affection', this depends entirely on the sort of answer one gives to the prior difficult question concerning (ii). This is the question of what we should make of Kant's various references to *unknowable 'things in themselves'* (and also to 'noumena' and to 'the transcendental object', although I shall emphasize the distinctions between these three concepts only when necessary) *as affecting our sensibility*. In this vein Kant also writes of things in themselves as the 'ground' or 'non-sensible cause' of our sensory representations and thus also of the sensible appearances or empirical objects that we experience. (See Collins [1999] for the view that Kant is committed to the existence of 'things in themselves' but not 'noumena'; but see Bird [2006a: 535ff.] for recognition of this distinction but also for criticism of Collins's inference to the existence of things in themselves.)

Already in the B-Preface, for example, we have seen Kant assert in relation to objects as appearances "that even if we cannot **cognize** these same objects as things in themselves, we at least must be able to **think** them as things in themselves. For otherwise there would follow the absurd proposition that there is *an appearance without anything that appears*" (Bxxvi–vii, italics added). This passage indicates that we must at least be able to *think* of objects as 'things in themselves', for the reason that the idea of an appearance (in the relevant sense) *without something that appears* would be absurd. This by itself has to some readers seemed to entail that in addition to the objects as appearances that affect us empirically, Kant also held that we can know that there also *exist* non-spatial, non-temporal 'things in themselves' as the non-sensible ground of the appearances (whereas Bird and Allison reject this latter interpretive inference). Other passages do indeed assert that things in themselves must be conceived as the "non-sensible" (i.e. non-spatiotemporal) "cause" of our sensible representations, and as the intelligible "ground" (*Grund*) of the appearances (e.g. A537/B565), as illustrated by the following passage concerning the "transcendental object" (from Section VI of the Antinomies, "Transcendental Idealism as the Key to Solving the Cosmological Dialectic"):

> The sensible faculty of intuition is really only a receptivity for being affected in a certain way with representations …. The non-sensible cause of these representations is entirely unknown to us, and therefore we cannot intuit it as an object; for such an object would have to be represented neither in space nor in time …, without which conditions we cannot think any intuition. Meanwhile we can call the merely intelligible cause of appearances in general the transcendental object, merely so that we may have something corresponding to sensibility as a receptivity. (A494/B522)

On some ways of interpreting Kant's view (e.g. on the traditional 'two-world' interpretations discussed above and in §1.2), these and similar passages have understandably been thought to support the sort of metaphysical picture that has resulted in the 'problem of affection' being seen as irresolvable for Kant. For it looks as if Kant is saying that in addition to the empirical causality through which objects are 'given' to our sensibility and are knowable as 'appearances', there is *also* a corresponding non-spatial and timeless relation of causality or affection between 'things in themselves' and our faculty of sensibility. Even if coherent sense could be made of that problematic metaphysical picture itself (which most defenders of this sort of interpretation of Kant themselves argue cannot be done), a further question is how Kant could be entitled to make any such assertions at all concerning the allegedly 'really real' "non-sensible cause of these representations", since Kant stresses throughout that 'things in themselves' or "the merely intelligible cause of appearances" are *unknowable* by us.

Our category of causality, for example – and hence, it would seem, our only coherent conception of 'affection' – gives us knowledge only of relations among appearances. All that the *Critique of Pure Reason* establishes, as Kant later explains in the Preface to the Second *Critique*, the *Critique of Practical Reason* (139–42=5:4–6), is our reason's necessary recognition of the logically consistent *thinkability* of 'things in themselves' in relation to appearances. Things in themselves must be thinkable (while not being knowable) if reason itself is to remain internally consistent overall; but nonetheless we are not able to establish the *real possibility* of anything outside the empirical realm of appearances in nature. In the Second *Critique* Kant goes on to argue that there is an *a priori* "fact of reason" concerning the pure *practical* reality of our moral obligations that requires us to make the further allowable assumption that we *do* in reality (i.e. 'practical reality') have free will in a sense that cannot be accounted for in terms of the law-governed appearances in nature, but which is at least coherently thinkable (as we saw in relation to the Third Antinomy in Chapter 2). How to further clarify the distinction between the irreducible framework or standpoint of 'pure practical reason' or morality, as opposed to the standpoint of the empirical cognition of objects in nature, thus turns out to be crucial to the assessment of *the only cognitively contentful role* that Kant assigns to the unavoidable idea of 'things in themselves'. For this one would have to look more deeply at the Third Antinomy again, and then pursue the rest of Kant's Critical Philosophy in its practical dimensions subsequent to the First *Critique*. For it is thus *solely* the practical reality of freedom that, as Kant tells us, "establishes by means of a fact what could [in the First *Critique*] only be *thought*" (*Practical Reason* 141=5:6).

Kant does characteristically, in many places, make such assertions as that:

> if we view the objects of the senses as mere appearances, as is fitting, then we thereby admit at the very same time that a thing in itself underlies them, although we are not acquainted with this thing as it may be constituted in itself, but only with its appearance, i.e., with the way in which our senses are affected by this unknown something. (*Prolegomena*, 107=4:314–15)

But the crucial question concerns the overall best interpretation of such passages, since in at least one primary sense the most that the First *Critique* allows us with respect to 'things in themselves' is the conception of *noumena* in the "merely negative sense", a conception that remains (in Kant's sense) "*problematic*, i.e., the representation of a thing of which we can say *neither that it is possible nor that it is impossible*" (A286–7/B342–3, italics added).

Clearly, on any reading of Kant, some rather subtle distinctions must be involved if Kant's views in this area are to be rendered internally consistent, which, as we saw earlier, some commentators such as Strawson, Guyer and Langton, among others, argue cannot be done in relation to Kant's transcendental idealism. And it is issues such as these that famously led Kant's contemporary, the philosopher Friedrich H. Jacobi (1743–1819), to conclude in relation to Kant's system of transcendental idealism that "*without* the presupposition [of the thing in itself] I cannot enter the system, and with that presupposition I cannot remain in it" (Jacobi [1787] 1968: 304; cf. Allison 2004: 8, 64–7). That is, Kant's system requires 'things in themselves' to be what really correspond to, and are the 'non-sensible cause' of, our sensible representations as 'appearances'; but Kant's 'critical restriction' of our knowledge to sensible phenomena then renders this apparently metaphysical role for things in themselves incoherent or incomprehensible from within that system. This is the heart of the traditional problem of affection.

As indicated earlier, however, other commentators continue to defend alternative interpretations of Kant's conception of 'things in themselves' and of 'the transcendental object' and so on, in ways that suggest that it is only by misinterpreting passages such as those highlighted above that the metaphysical obscurities and alleged difficulties have been thought to arise for Kant's view.

We should perhaps begin again by first recalling Kant's continual emphasis on our sensory-intuitive *passivity* in relation to the empirical objects that we experience. This holds not only empirically, based on *a posteriori* case-by-case evidence, but also at the transcendental philosophical level through its thinkable contrast with the bare idea of a possible 'intellectual intuition' (belonging, say, to a divine being) that would literally *create* the objects or the world that it intuits or knows. In at least this sense it is definitive of the kinds of cognitive beings that we are that we do not create the 'appearances' or empirical objects of which we come to have knowledge. Rather, we are *dependent* for the cognition of such appearances-to-us on the *existence of some thing* that thus appears, a thing that is in at least this minimal sense the 'ground' of the appearances-to-us. The key question then becomes, once again: what can we say about the things that thus make their appearance to our senses in this sense?

Consider again the passage from Bxxvi–vii noted above: that is, the absurdity of an *appearance without anything that appears* [*daß Erscheinung ohne etwas wäre, was da erscheint*]. To this passage others could be added, such as Kant's claim that "it follows naturally from the concept of an appearance in general that something must correspond to it which is not in itself appearance" and "from this arises the concept of a *noumenon*" (A251–2). As noted above, in such passages Kant does assert that we must at least be able to *think* or conceive of the objects that appear to us, as 'things in themselves'. In fact, we *inevitably do* conceive of these empirical objects or conditioned appearances as directly entailing ("**sight unseen**" [A500/B528], as we saw Kant put it earlier) the existence of things in themselves as their ultimately real cause or explanatory ground. We saw this in §2.3, on the Antinomies, in connection with the *a priori* transcendental 'principle of pure reason'. Our natural and unavoidable but demonstrably problematic thought is that there exists an 'unconditioned' condition or totality of conditions that is required as the ultimately necessary explanation or 'ground' of all the conditioned appearances or objects that we encounter in experience.

As was clear from that discussion, Kant regards such thoughts or ideas as *illusory* if they are regarded 'constitutively' as providing a cognition of the nature or existence of such objects as 'things in themselves' (cf. Kant on the concept of noumena in the 'positive' sense, with the corresponding notion of a possible 'non-sensible' or 'intellectual intuition' of such putative intelligible beings; B306–8). Rather, such ideas of reason have genuine cognitive significance for us only when interpreted either as *regulative maxims* governing the conduct of our empirical inquiries within experience (we shall discuss this role again in Chapter 5 and in the concluding chapter), or as *practical postulates* that are necessary solely from the purely practical or moral point of view, as noted above. Neither of the latter kinds of indispensable ideas or thoughts entails the theoretical presupposition or cognition of the real existence of the 'noumenal objects' or 'things in themselves' that would correspond to those ideas. Such maxims, postulates and ideals of pure reason are allowable, on Kant's view, because they are at least non-contradictory and are in principle not *dis*provable from the point of view of genuine theoretical cognition, while also playing the indispensable regulative and practical roles just noted.

In particular in the Antinomies we saw Kant argue that the 'naturalist' or 'empiricist' attempt to assert the entirely sufficient and exclusive existence of the universe of appearances or empirical objects in space and time would be equally 'dogmatic' and unjustified. It is in fact a crucial function of the contrasting concept of noumena in the 'negative' or limiting sense that the necessary *thought* of such unknowable things in themselves plays the role, not only of representing the critical restriction of our knowledge to the appearances in nature, but simultaneously of blocking the equally unwarranted dogmatic claim that those empirical objects might reasonably be *asserted to exhaust all of reality*. The denial of the latter putative knowledge is part of what opens up the possibility of a rational faith based solely on our moral freedom, for Kant. Apart from the latter, morality-based assumption of free will, then, our reason "sees around itself a space for the cognition of things in themselves, although it can never have determinate concepts of those things and is limited to appearances alone" (*Prolegomena*, 4:352).

So while we must indeed think or conceive of things in themselves or noumena as the 'non-sensible cause' of our sensible representations, and as the 'ground' of the objects as appearances that we cognize in experience, this inevitable and indispensible thought is consistently treated as 'problematic' in Kant's strong sense (A254–6/B310–11). Note further that in the passage quoted above concerning the 'non-sensible cause' of the representations with which our sensibility is affected, Kant had stated: "Meanwhile, we can call the merely intelligible cause of appearances in general *the transcendental object*, merely so that we may have something corresponding to sensibility as a *receptivity*" (A494/B522, italics added). Here the 'merely intelligible' (but necessary) thought of a 'transcendental object' as 'something' that corresponds to our passive sensory receptivity, and which is thought as the cause of appearances 'in general', also plays a pivotal role in Kant's view. For taken *one* way, we do inevitably think of such a transcendental object as a 'thing in itself', in the several 'problematic' ways just discussed. But taken *another* way, Kant also indicates (e.g. in the transcendental deduction in A) that this concept of a transcendental object as the 'correlate of' or 'corresponding to' our sensible receptivity plays its indeterminate but indispensable role *entirely within* the domain of our cognition of empirical objects as appearances:

> The pure concept of this transcendental object (which in all of our cognitions is really always one and the same = X) is that which in all of our empirical concepts in general can provide relation to an object, i.e., objective reality. Now this concept cannot contain any determinate intuition at all, and therefore concerns nothing but that unity which must be encountered in a manifold of cognition insofar as it stands in relation to an object. This relation, however, is nothing other than the necessary unity of consciousness, thus also of the synthesis of the manifold through a common function of the mind for combining it in one representation. (A109)

Understanding what this passage might mean will require the work of our next chapter on the Transcendental Deduction. Basically, however, Kant is referring to what I called above, in relation to the notion of 'empirical affection' and Kant's empirical realism, the *mutual interdependence* between our *a priori* forms of representation (and in fact the very possibility of our "unity of consciousness") and the empirically mind-independent "objective reality" of the objects *as appearances* that affect us, and of which we can have straightforward theoretical cognition. Here the necessary thoughts discussed above of our essential passivity and of the necessary relation of our sensible representations to a 'transcendental object' or to 'things in general' takes a form that is conceived differently from the thought of an unknowable 'thing in itself' (which we have also seen to be inevitable for us). While the thought of a transcendental object in this cognition-yielding sense does not itself, as Kant puts it, "contain any *determinate* intuition at all" and so is 'non-sensible' in that sense, it nonetheless refers in an indeterminate but empirically determinable way to the sorts of categorially judged 'things that appear' that are the sensible objects of our experience. It is only in *this* shape that any cognition is provided by the necessary thought, common also to our thought of 'objects in general' and of 'things in themselves', that our sensible representations of appearances must be 'caused by' or 'grounded in' a 'something' that 'affects us' and 'of which' they are the appearances. (The proliferation of 'scare quotes' here is intended to remind us of the systematic ambiguities to which Kant's employment of such terms is self-consciously subject, as has just been argued.)

These are certainly difficult and controversial issues of Kant interpretation, topics that require any reader of Kant to investigate further with respect to both the primary sources and the secondary commentaries. Here I shall add just one last point concerning the *unknowability* of things in themselves in light of the above discussion, and particularly in relation to Kant's practical or moral philosophy as articulated in the Second *Critique*, the *Critique of Practical Reason*.

As we have seen, in his moral theory Kant makes especially clear that "it is really the concept of freedom that, among all the ideas of pure speculative reason" – in contrast to the idea of God, for example – "alone provides such a great extension in the field of the supersensible" (that is, in the field of non-sensible 'things in themselves'), "though only with respect to practical cognition" (*Practical Reason*, 222=5:103). Thus "of all the intelligible absolutely nothing [is cognized] except freedom (by means of the moral law), and even this only insofar as it is a presupposition inseparable from that law" (*Practical Reason*, 197=5:70). Kant argues that reason's idea of freedom is contentfully thinkable and cognizable from a purely practical perspective despite not being cognizable or even comprehensible from a theoretical or scientific perspective. Reason's idea of freedom involves our thinking in accordance with the pure, *unschematized* (roughly, non-spatiotemporal) category of causality, as the *mere thought* of an existential dependence of one thing on another (cf. Chapter 5 on the Schematism). Furthermore, our moral freedom, as we have seen, is itself a presupposition of what Kant calls a *fact of reason* concerning the will: "for so we may call a determination of the will that is unavoidable even though it does not rest upon empirical principles" (*Practical Reason*, 184=5:55). With respect to the *"ideas of reason"* pertaining to God, freedom and immortality, which have occupied our attention since the beginning of Chapter 1 and which, as we saw, represented for Kant the highest aims of speculative metaphysics, Kant concludes that:

> our concern with these ideas is not for the sake of theoretical cognition of their objects but only with whether they have objects at all. Pure practical reason provides this reality, and theoretical reason has nothing further to do in this than merely *to think* those objects through categories, and this, as we have elsewhere clearly shown, can be done quite well without needing intuition (whether sensible or supersensible) because the categories have their seat and origin in the pure understanding solely as the faculty of thinking, independently of and prior to any intuition, and they always signify only an object in general, *in whatever way it may be given to us*. Now, insofar as the categories are to be applied to these ideas, it is not possible to give them any object in intuition; but *that an object really exists*, so that a category as a mere form of thought is here not empty but has significance, is sufficiently assured them by an object that practical reason presents beyond doubt in the concept of the highest good, namely the *reality of the concepts* that are required for the possibility of the highest good, without, however, effecting by this increment the least extension of cognition in accordance with theoretical principles. [These are the] ideas of God, of an intelligible world (the [moral] kingdom of God), and of immortality. (*Practical Reason*, 249–50=5:136)

In conclusion, we have seen that there is a somewhat imposing set of distinctions that one needs to keep in mind as one attempts to come to grips with Kant's complex views on such questions as: what are the objects that are 'given' to us by 'affecting' our sensibility? What does Kant mean when he refers to a 'something' that 'grounds' the appearances? What are the various relationships between those issues and questions concerning the multifarious roles that the concepts of 'appearance', 'things in themselves', 'noumena' and the 'transcendental object' play within Kant's philosophy? And what does Kant really mean when he says that the *only* cognition we can really have of 'things in themselves' is a *practical cognition* that is based solely on the objective validity of pure practical reason's indispensable presupposition of the ideas of freedom and sensibly unconditioned morality?

In this section I have outlined some of the distinctions that must be mobilized in any sympathetic attempt to understand Kant's views on these difficult but intriguing matters that lie at the core of his philosophy. With respect to the nature and even the very existence of 'things in themselves', by our rational nature we will always be led to ask such questions and to attempt to offer affirmative answers to them. But Kant has argued that we shall never be able to offer any *intelligible* answers to such questions except by finally turning away, once and for all, from all theoretical speculation in this domain and attending solely to the 'practical' reality of our moral obligations and the freedom that they presuppose, as well as to the consequent rational needs, aspirations, and hopes that those moral obligations are supposed to entail. Here, however, I shall let Kant have the last word on what he takes the First *Critique* to have shown in relation to these topics:

> In this manner our previous proposition, which is the result of the entire *Critique*, remains: 'that reason, through all its *a priori* principles, never teaches us about anything more than objects of possible experience alone, and of these, nothing more than what can be cognized in experience'; but this limitation does not prevent reason from carrying us up to the objective *boundary* of experience – namely, to the *relation* to something that cannot itself be an object of experience, but which must nonetheless be the highest ground of all experience – without, however, teaching us anything about this ground in itself, but only in relation reason's own complete use in the field of possible experience, as directed to the highest ends. This is, however, all of the benefit that can reasonably even be wished for here, and there is cause to be satisfied with it.
> (*Prolegomena*, 150=4:361–2)

CHAPTER 4

THE CATEGORIES OF UNDERSTANDING AND THE THINKING SELF

> To sum this up: the business of the senses is to intuit; that of the understanding, to think. To think, however, is to unite representations in a consciousness. (*Prolegomena*, 98=4:304)

> Now there are only two ways in which a necessary agreement of experience with the concepts of its objects can be thought: either the experience makes these concepts possible or these concepts make the experience possible. (B166–7)

> Thus as exaggerated and contradictory as it may sound to say that the understanding is itself the source of the laws of nature, and thus of the formal unity of nature, such an assertion is nevertheless correct and appropriate to the object, namely experience. (A127)

4.1 CONCEPTUAL THINKING: THE CATEGORIES AS *A PRIORI* FORMS OF UNDERSTANDING

The need for a transcendental deduction of the categories

In the previous chapter we examined Kant's novel contention in the Transcendental Aesthetic that even our most basic *sensory* capacities already presuppose certain pure *a priori* dimensions of human cognition that are not themselves derived from sensation *a posteriori*. These are the universal frameworks of space and of time as pure forms of our outer and inner sensory intuition. According to Kant, we human beings can have knowledge of objects only if they are *given* to us, directly or indirectly, by affecting our receptive faculty of sensibility. The resulting sensory intuitions of objects are immediate and singular presentations of particular objects, such as a visual intuition of the Eiffel Tower from a certain perspective or point of view. Kant's main conclusions in the Transcendental Aesthetic were:

- we can be sensorily presented with particular objects only as appearing within a continuous three-dimensional space and a single comprehensive time-order as pure intuitions;
- this is possible only if those spatiotemporal structures pertain solely to objects as 'appearances to us' rather than as 'things in themselves' (transcendental idealism); and
- only in this way can we account for the possibility of synthetic *a priori* cognitions in pure mathematics (for example, in geometry).

Assuming, for the sake of exploring Kant's upcoming arguments, that he has established the above controversial claims concerning space and time, where does this now leave us with respect to the remaining central problems addressed by the *Critique of Pure Reason*?

As we saw in Chapter 2, Hume's powerful sceptical challenge, framed by Kant in terms of the possibility of synthetic *a priori* judgments, applies not only to the possibility of pure mathematics but also to any supposed rational basis for certain of our most basic and (as Hume himself emphasizes) indispensable assumptions about the lawfulness and intelligibility of the world. Such putatively rational assumptions about the necessary structure of empirical reality include the following key principles among others:

- necessarily, every experienceable event or happening has some determining cause or other (the *principle of causality*);
- necessarily, throughout all experienceable changes in the world, substance (in particular matter) persists and does not entirely pass out of existence (the principle of the *persistence of substance*); and
- our experiences are not limited to our own subjective perceptions but necessarily provide knowledge of an objective and shared empirical reality (the rejection of 'empirical idealism' and of doubts about the external world).

These assumptions, as 'every ... must ...' principles characterized by universality and necessity, are ostensibly objective and synthetic *a priori* principles. If they are such principles, then the source of their validity would have to be entirely independent of the contingencies of sense experience, as we have already seen. But Hume's compelling sceptical arguments, as we also saw, led him to the conclusion that these principles at bottom have their origin solely in our sense experiences as worked up by our often conflicting natural instincts and our associative imagination. However useful and unavoidable such *a posteriori* principles of human nature may be, they do not have their ultimate origin in reason in a way that rationally certifies their objective validity *a priori*.

What Kant calls a *transcendental deduction* – with the term 'deduction' here being used in a special way – will be an attempt to display the rational warrant or ground for these sorts of synthetic *a priori* principles of human *understanding* (rather than of mere human *sensibility*), by demonstrating their *objective validity* in relation to all possible objects of human experience. (For a selection of recent helpful analyses of the Transcendental Deduction, see e.g. Allison [2004: ch. 7]; Dicker [2004: ch. 4]; Guyer [2006a: 80–95]; Kitcher [1990: chs 3–6]; Landy [2010]; Rosenberg [2005: chs 2, 4–5]; Van Cleve [1999: ch. 7].) The following famous passage will be worth having before us in full:

> Jurists, when they speak of entitlements and claims, distinguish in a legal matter between the questions about what is lawful [or right] (*quid juris*) and that which concerns the fact (*quid facti*), and since they demand proof of both, they call the first, that which is to establish the entitlement or the legal claim, the **deduction**. We make use of a multitude of empirical concepts without objection from anyone, and take ourselves to be justified in granting them a sense and supposed signification even without any deduction, because we always have experience ready at hand to prove their objective validity. But there are also concepts that have been usurped, such as **fortune** and **fate,** which circulate with almost universal indulgence, but that are occasionally called upon to establish their claim by the question *quid juris*, and then there is not a little embarrassment about their deduction because one can adduce no clear legal ground for an entitlement to their use either from experience or from reason.
>
> Among the many concepts, however, that constitute the very mixed fabric of human cognition, there are some that are also destined for pure use *a priori* (completely independently of all experience), and these always require a deduction of their entitlement, since proofs from experience are not sufficient for the lawfulness of such a use, and yet one must know how these concepts can be related to objects that they do not derive from any experience. I therefore call the explanation of the way in which concepts can relate to objects *a priori* their **transcendental deduction**, and distinguish this from the **empirical** deduction, which shows how a concept is acquired through experience and reflection on it, and therefore concerns not the lawfulness but the fact from which the possession has arisen. (A84–5/B116–17)

For shorthand I shall refer to this as the *'quid juris'* passage.

Consider again the table of five 'Sceptical challenges' that I used in Chapter 2 (Table 2.2) in order to illustrate Hume's general form of sceptical challenge to our knowledge of the external world, induction, causal necessity, the self and 'other minds'. In each case 'Hume's fork' led us to ask whether the disputed concept or claim concerns something that can be either (i) observed or intuited directly by means of the senses (i.e. a synthetic *a posteriori* 'matter of fact'), or (ii) logically demonstrated or proved such that its denial would entail an internal logical contradiction or conceptual incoherence (i.e. analytic *a priori* 'relations of ideas'). In short, the question that both sceptics and empiricists legitimately raise in relation to all supposed *a priori* concepts and principles that are allegedly embodied in our most basic beliefs and assumptions about reality is the question of what Kant above calls our "legal ground for an entitlement to their use either from experience or from reason". On Hume's view, we possess neither an *a posteriori* empirical warrant nor an *a priori* rational entitlement to apply to the objects of our experience the sorts of *a priori* concepts and principles listed above. Throughout the upcoming Transcendental Analytic, by contrast, Kant will attempt to demonstrate our rational entitlement to apply such synthetic *a priori* principles of understanding to all possible empirical objects of our sensory experience.

A word of caution, however, before we begin. Whenever in this chapter and the next one various references are made to 'the mind-independent object', 'the objects themselves', the 'objective world of matter' and so on, none of those references will be to objects considered as (unknowable) 'things in themselves'. In this chapter we shall be talking exclusively – as Kant himself generally does throughout his discussions of the "Principles of Pure Understanding" – about the objective empirical world of outer material objects and inner psychological realities. That is, our concern will be with the 'phenomenal world' of objects as they make their 'appearances' to us and are represented by us in space and time. We shall not be talking about pure reason's inevitable but deeply problematic idea of purely intelligible 'noumena' or 'things in themselves' as the unknown 'ground' of appearances, except where this is explicitly indicated (in particular at the end of Chapter 5).

Returning to the task at hand, Kant explains in the section that contains the *quid juris* passage (B-edition, §13) that the problems now raised in relation to the pure concepts and synthetic *a priori* principles of understanding are subtly different from those that were resolved to Kant's satisfaction in the Transcendental Aesthetic in relation to sensibility (Chapter 3 above). The synthetic *a priori* principles of sensibility concerned what must be true of objects in so far as they are directly intuited or sensed; and the result was that the possibility of such sensory encounters presupposes that space and time are pure forms of our intuition rather than forms that pertain to 'things in themselves". The *a priori* principles of understanding, by contrast, will concern claims about the objective existence of objects of possible experience in so far as they are *thought about* or *judged* rather than merely sensed. What Kant will argue, however, is that the very possibility of our making any judgments about objects of experience has crucial implications for the necessary form that our sensory experiences of objects must take.

Let us again take as our example the synthetic *a priori* principle of causality, which will be defended by Kant in the "Second Analogy of Experience". The principle of causality requires that for any given "happening" or event in experience (call it *B*; an explosion, for instance), there must have existed some prior kind of event (call it *A*) such that events of kind *A* are universally and necessarily followed by events of kind *B*. Reserving detailed discussion of the principle of causality for the next chapter, the important point for now is that although in this case the inferred prior event *A* must be an object of *possible experience* – it must be a spatiotemporal phenomenon – our justified belief in the existence of such an empirical event does not require that anyone ever actually discovers or directly sensorily encounters that particular event. If the causal principle is objectively valid, then we know that *some* such prior event necessarily occurred in objective empirical reality in space and time, but we are (allegedly) able to know this whether or not that particular cause is ever actually discovered or observed by anyone. Kant must show that our inference to some such empirical cause for each observed event is a *rationally warranted* form of conditional judgment or inference in general, whether or not we happen to sensorily encounter that cause.

But Hume's incisive sceptical question in relation to such inferences, as we know, was this: how are we rationally entitled to make any such claims about the existence of empirical matters of fact (i) that we have not directly experienced *a posteriori*, and (ii) the non-existence of which is at least logically possible (i.e. thinkable *a priori*, without internal conceptual contradiction or incoherence – e.g. a world where events 'just happen', without causes)? That we *do in fact* make such causal inferences beyond what we have directly experienced is a point that Hume happily emphasizes, while arguing that nonetheless we can display no rational entitlement or origin in reason for such deep-seated natural inferences. Hume's 'science of human nature' then seeks to explain our habit of making such inferences based on *a posteriori* empirical observations of human nature. That is, Hume seeks to explain such inferences naturalistically in terms of the complex, experience-produced and instinct-grounded expectations that are natural to us as human animals. Kant's previous arguments in relation to space and time as the pure forms of all our direct sensory intuition do not address *this* sort of challenge to our supposed synthetic *a priori* cognition of nature's empirical lawfulness in general.

Furthermore, on Kant's account in the Aesthetic it was seen to be crucial that we can always directly *give ourselves*, that is, 'construct' or 'constitute' in pure spatiotemporal intuition, the relevant synthetic *a priori* mathematical structures and forms to which all the objects of our empirical intuition or sense perception must conform. By contrast, Kant will later emphasize that the *a priori* laws governing the *existence* of appearances as objects of possible experience (for example, as causally inferred but not directly observed) cannot be 'constructed' *a priori* in the way that the mathematical structures of pure sensibility can be so constructed. What Kant will call the "dynamical" as opposed to "mathematical" principles of pure understanding, such as the principles of causality and substantial persistence, "have the peculiarity that they do not concern the appearances and the synthesis of their empirical intuition, but merely their **existence** and their **relation** to one another with regard to this their existence", and "this existence cannot be constructed" *a priori* (A178–9/B220–22). In fact, it is because the *a priori* principles of pure understanding concern our thoughts about the existence of possible objects of experience, rather than the mere form of our sensibility, that we are especially tempted to apply such principles of pure understanding *beyond* the realm of possible experience in space and time (A87–8/B120–21), in an extension that we have seen the *Critique of Pure Reason* is designed to show is unwarranted.

So the fundamental question concerning the source of our entitlement to make causal inferences and other *a priori* existence claims about empirical objects or 'appearances' is clearly a different kettle of fish from what was addressed in the Transcendental Aesthetic in relation to immediate sensibility.

The interdependence of concepts and intuitions in cognition

A further reason that Kant gives in §13 for the difference between the upcoming Transcendental Deduction of the categories and the previous conclusions concerning space and time is particularly interesting but more difficult to interpret. The further reason Kant gives for the difference is that, in the case of sensibility, "objects can indeed appear to us without necessarily having to be related to functions of the understanding, and therefore without the understanding containing their *a priori* conditions"; that is, "[a]ppearances would nonetheless offer objects to our intuition, for intuition by no means requires the functions of thinking" (A89–90/B122–3). Commentators disagree on whether Kant himself accepts or rejects the possibility that is described here (for a full discussion, see Allais [2009]; Westphal [2004]). The apparent thought is that sensory intuition alone, without the contribution to experience of the *a priori* categories or pure concepts of understanding, would nonetheless still present objects to our sensory intuition.

The reason that this sort of claim in Kant requires careful interpretation is that, as we have already briefly seen in §1.2, Kant famously holds that "Thoughts without content are empty, intuitions without concepts are blind" (A51/B75). Let us consider the latter half of this well-known dictum first: the claim concerning the 'blindness' of 'intuitions without concepts'.

The blindness metaphor surely suggests that there is at least a primary sense, for Kant, in which sensory intuition cannot provide cognition of objects for us in the absence of conceptualization. And indeed, when Kant subsequently discusses the thought of our possibly having sensory intuitions of appearances in the absence of the objectively valid applicability of *a priori* conceptual rules (e.g. A100–101, 111–12, 121–2; B195; B681–2), he emphasizes that in such scenarios there would be no cognition of appearances as objects of our experience. Without the contribution of pure *a priori* concepts (the categories), for example:

> it would be possible for a swarm of appearances to fill up our soul without experience ever being able to arise from it. But in that case all relation of cognition to objects would also disappear, since the appearances would lack connection in accordance with universal and necessary laws, and would thus be intuition without thought, but never cognition, and would therefore be as good as nothing for us. (A111)

(Kant's closing remark here that such appearances "would ... be as good as nothing for us" should later be compared with his claim in the Transcendental Deduction at B131–2, to be discussed in section §4.2 below, that representations in me "would be nothing for me" if they could not be accompanied by the 'I think' of self-conscious 'apperception' and conceptual recognition.) In such a scenario the "manifold of perceptions ... would then belong to no experience, and would consequently be without an object, and would be nothing but a blind play of representations, i.e., less than a dream" (A112; cf. A121–2). Accordingly, we shall find Kant arguing in the Transcendental Deduction that we can have no cognition of any object *as* an object of experience, in a crucial sense to be explored, without those experiences being informed by concepts (and hence by the logical forms of judgment).

But it seems to me that this argument is not necessarily intended by Kant to rule out various less demanding senses in which the sensory states of both humans and other animals can 'represent' objects in ways that do not require conceptualization. What is absolutely essential to Kant's view, however, is his contention that there is a principled distinction between the cognitive significance of the sensory experiences of beings such as we are, who are able to experience the world conceptually in a sense that involves the logical forms of judgment, and any beings or any forms of 'animal cognition' for which this is not the case. This is a difference, Kant will argue, that makes all the difference as far as our rational entitlement to apply synthetic *a priori* principles to the world is concerned.

With respect to the other half of Kant's famous dictum – that is, *thoughts without content are empty* – Kant primarily has in mind any concept that is supposed to relate to an object despite the fact that no possible object of sensory intuition can be given in experience corresponding to or instantiating that concept (cf. A95). It should be recalled, however, that on Kant's view thoughts that are thus 'empty' for theoretical cognition in the sense of lacking intuitional content or empirical application criteria need not for that reason be entirely *meaningless*, all things considered. As we know, practical reason's sense-transcending ideas of free will and moral obligation, along with the morally derivative, rational need-based 'postulates' of God and immortality, are ideas that have non-intuitional cognitive content, on Kant's view, but only from the practical standpoint of moral deliberation. Kant thus distinguishes between a broader and a narrower sense in which 'thought' can have meaningful 'content'.

For instance, after remarking with respect to objects as appearances in space and time that "even if we cannot **cognize** these same objects as things in themselves, we at least must be able to **think** them as things in themselves", Kant adds in a clarifying footnote:

> To **cognize** an object, it is required that I be able to prove its possibility (whether by the testimony of experience from its actuality or *a priori* through reason). But I can **think** whatever I like, as long as I do not contradict myself, i.e. as long as my concept is a possible thought ... But in order to ascribe objective validity to such a concept (real possibility, for the first sort of possibility was merely logical) something more is required. This 'more', however, need not be sought in theoretical sources of cognition; it may also lie in practical ones. (Bxxvi–vii)

As we saw at the end of Chapter 3 in relation to Kant's conception of unknowable 'things in themselves', it can often be a matter of considerable complexity to determine whether a thought or a concept that is, by Kant's own admission, *empirically empty* can nonetheless be regarded as having some legitimate use or 'content' for some purpose other than the theoretical cognition of objects. The important point for now is that it is solely the objective validity of our theoretical cognition of objects in space and time that is Kant's concern in the Transcendental Deduction.

Returning now to the *quid juris* passage quoted earlier, Kant clearly thinks that there are many concepts that people mistakenly assume either to have objective empirical content or to have some ground in reason for their objectively valid application to the objects of experience, when in fact such concepts fail to withstand the test of a properly critical scrutiny or 'critique' of their epistemic credentials. Recall Kant's remark that the concepts of "**fortune** and **fate**", for example, cause "not a little embarrassment about their deduction" (i.e. about the certification of their cognitive legitimacy or objective validity) in that "one can adduce no ground for an entitlement to their use either from experience or from reason" (A84–5/B116–17). Suppose, for instance, that someone says to you, "It was a matter of *fate* that we met at this party!" This was probably just an attempt to say something nice to you. Suppose, however, that being a philosopher you unwittingly extinguish all romantic possibilities by asking, "But what is fate anyway? Is fate some kind of real property belonging to physical objects? Or rather to 'mental objects'? Is fate a law determining the behaviour of all things, like gravity? You don't *really* believe in fate as a determining cause of events – *do* you?" Consequently alone and with time on your hands, you reflect further that there seems to be *no possible course of experience* that would go any way towards either refuting or confirming the claim that something happened 'due to fate' (or due to fortune, or by destiny, or because of God's divine providence, and so on). Any occurrence, or its direct opposite, will readily be ascribed to fate by the believer as and when required, with the result that no possible empirical outcome would serve to diminish the believer's conviction that whatever happens in the world happens because it was fated to happen. Such ideas, whatever their practical import may be, do not seem to have the determinate (theoretical) applicability to empirical reality that they often pretend to have.

Having clarified the senses in which thoughts without content are empty and intuitions without concepts are blind, we can now return to the crucial case of the categories as pure *a priori* concepts of understanding. We have seen that Kant agrees with Hume that universal and necessary *a priori* concepts or categories, such as those of causality and substance, are not derived from sense experience. Nor, unlike the pure intuitions of space and time, are such categories *a priori* conditions of our mere sensibility. Rather, with such categories of thought we boldly lay claim to the necessary structure of all possible empirical objects that can ever make their appearance to us in space and time. But with what *right*, in the sense of what source of entitlement or origin either in reason or in experience, do we thus take ourselves to be warranted in applying such *a priori* concepts to empirical objects? For example, what grounds can we possibly have for assuming that our application to the brute empirical world of the synthetic *a priori* principle that 'every event must have some cause' is really any better off than our arbitrary imposition on the world of such objectively dubious thought-entities as the judgment that such-and-such happened 'due to fate'?

As Kant frames the general issue at stake in the Transcendental Deduction, "a difficulty is revealed here that we did not encounter in the field of sensibility, namely how **subjective conditions of thinking** should have **objective validity**, i.e., yield conditions of the possibility of all cognition of objects" (A89–90/B122). Kant had, in fact, pressed essentially this same question nine years prior to the publication of the First *Critique*, in a famous letter to Marcus Herz of 21 February 1772. In this letter Kant discussed his ongoing plans for what eventually became the *Critique*, under the projected title of *The Limits of Sensibility and Reason* (for more on this letter, see Gardner [1999: 27–30]):

> As I thought through the theoretical part, ... I noticed that I still lacked something essential, something that in my long metaphysical studies I, as well as others, had failed to consider and which in fact constitutes the key to the whole secret of metaphysics, hitherto still hidden from itself. I asked myself this question: What is the ground of the relation of that in us which we call 'representation' to the object? ... [T]he pure concepts of the understanding must not be abstracted from sense perceptions, nor must they express the reception of representations through the senses; but though they must have their origin in the nature of the soul, they are neither caused by the object nor do they bring the object itself into being [i.e. as practical volitions].
> (Kant, Letter to Marcus Herz,
> 21 February 1772, in *Correspondence*, 133=10:130)

Kant proceeds to remark that in his own earlier Inaugural Dissertation of 1770, a very important but still 'pre-Critical' work entitled *On the Form and Principles of the Sensible and the Intelligible World*, he had "silently passed over" this crucial "question of how a representation that refers to an object without being in any way affected by it can be possible". Similarly, the central question for Kant's Transcendental Deduction is once again: how can putatively synthetic *a priori* principles, such as that 'necessarily, every event has some cause' or 'necessarily, throughout all changes matter persists', be certified to have objectively valid application to empirical objects when no amount of sensory experience of objects in general, as Hume had shown, can rationally warrant such an application? It is not without good reason that Kant stresses that "the reader must be convinced of the unavoidable necessity of such a transcendental deduction before he has taken a single step in the field of pure reason" (A88/B121). On to the first step, then!

The 'Clue' or 'guiding thread': the Metaphysical Deduction of the categories

What has come to be known as Kant's 'Metaphysical Deduction' of the categories takes place in the first chapter of the "Analytic of Concepts" entitled: "On the Clue [or 'Guiding Thread': *Leitfaden*] to the Discovery of all Pure Concepts of Understanding" (A66–83/B91–116). In this important section Kant takes his first step towards an eventual transcendental deduction of our rational entitlement to apply *a priori* categories of understanding to the objects of possible sense experience. Kant himself later sums up the results of the Metaphysical Deduction and the Transcendental Deduction as follows: "In the **metaphysical deduction** the origin of the *a priori* categories in general was established through their complete coincidence with the universal logical functions of thinking"; and then "in the **transcendental deduction** … their possibility as *a priori* cognitions of objects of an intuition in general was exhibited (§§20, 21)", and in particular "the possibility of cognizing *a priori* **through categories** whatever objects **may come before our senses**" (B159, §26). (The 'in particular' here reflects two stages in Kant's argument in the Transcendental Deduction in its second B-edition version, known as the 'B-Deduction').

The aim of the Metaphysical Deduction is thus to establish the "origin" (B159) or "birthplace" (A66/B90) of the twelve pure concepts or categories of human understanding as lying *a priori* in the *universal logical functions of all thinking about objects in general*. Kant lays out the logical functions of judgment and the corresponding categories of understanding in two separate tables (A70–80/B95–106), and these will also provide the basis for his eventual classification of the 'principles of pure understanding' to be defended throughout the rest of the Transcendental Analytic. So it might be helpful to lay out all of these together in one table (Table 4.1; cf. *Prolegomena*, 96–7=4:302–3).

What Kant will argue for overall is that the fact that our judgments about objects have certain universal and necessary features – in particular, certain logical functions and forms – provides a clue to the discovery of why certain corresponding *a priori* categories and principles embodying those logical forms necessarily *apply to* all possible objects of sense experience, despite the fact that such concepts and principles are *not derivable from* any sense experiences. That is how Kant will attempt to reveal "the key to the whole secret of metaphysics, hitherto still hidden from itself": that is, to answer

Table 4.1 The functions of judgment, the categories and the principles of understanding.

	Forms of judgment	Categories of understanding	Principles of pure understanding
Quantity	Universal Particular Singular	Unity Plurality Totality	**Axioms of intuition** All intuitions are extensive magnitudes
Quality	Affirmative Negative Infinite	Reality Negation Limitation	**Anticipations of perception** In all appearances the real, as object of sensation, has intensive magnitude
Relation	Categorical Hypothetical Disjunctive	Substance Cause/effect Community	**Analogies of experience** 1. Law of persistence of substance 2. Law of cause and effect 3. Law of simultaneous interaction
Modality	Problematic Assertoric Apodictic	Possibility Existence Necessity	**Postulates of empirical thinking** 1. Formal *possibility* in experience 2. Material *actuality* in experience 3. Material *necessity* in existence

the question of how representations that originate *a priori* in the mind can nonetheless be necessary for the cognition of empirical objects that exist independently of the mind.

While Kant's full justification for these 'tables' will only become clear at the end of his treatment of the synthetic *a priori* principles of human understanding in the Transcendental Analytic (Chapter 5 below), there has recently been some excellent scholarship done on the exact nature and purpose of Kant's initial Metaphysical Deduction or 'Clue' to the discovery of the categories. (See in particular Longuenesse [1998, 2005]; Reich [1992]; Wolff [1995]; and for recent introductory treatments, see Guyer [2006a: 72ff.]; Rosenberg [2005: ch. 4]; Savile [2005: ch. 3].) These recent commentaries have fruitfully addressed many of the long-standing questions that have been raised about Kant's metaphysical deduction and his tables of judgment and the categories, some examples of which are the following.

What is the formal or rational basis for the structure and content of Kant's initial table of the functions of judgment, for instance, beyond Kant's own seemingly arbitrary and unsystematic remark in the *Prolegomena* that he had simply "cast about" and "found" the "already finished ... work of the logicians" (*Prolegomena*, 115–16=4:323–4)? And what is the justification for

Kant's claim to the completeness of this table, that is, that all and only these twelve functions of judgment, as grouped above, "exhaustively exhibit the functions of unity in judgments" (A69/B94)? Furthermore, to what degree has Kant's classification of the logical functions or forms of judgment been rendered obsolete by the later revolutions in formal logic inaugurated by Gottlob Frege and Bertrand Russell among many others (see e.g. Dicker 2004: 57–9; Strawson 1966: 74–82)? And beyond those questions concerning the logical functions of judgment there are further questions concerning how those logical forms are really supposed to provide a 'clue' or a guide to the discovery of twelve corresponding indispensable pure concepts of objects (the categories). The recent commentaries mentioned above have helped to clarify both the grounds for many of Kant's particular claims in relation to his tables as well as his general strategy in the Metaphysical Deduction. Here I shall only attempt to convey some of the overall aims and key insights in Kant's 'Clue' to the discovery of the categories.

In thinking about the sources of our knowledge of the world it is tempting to begin, as empiricists do, with what we take in from the world through sensation. The attempt is then made by empiricist-leaning philosophers to understand our *understanding* of the world in terms of the various ways in which such sensory data is remembered, associated, generalized and applied. These natural psychological processes result in the formation of further such ideas or anticipatory imaginings and habitual expectations of what *will* be sensorily encountered as we navigate the world in common experience and in scientific inquiry. For many philosophers of the early modern period, including Hume, this general approach led to what has sometimes been called "the 'idea' idea" (not in Kant's sense of the 'ideas of reason', of course). Put in a conveniently idealized form, the 'idea' idea was that human *conceptual* thinking should thus similarly be understood, at bottom, as a form of combination and separation by means of association, imagination and reasoning of various 'ideas' or mental images that were originally recorded in the form of inner and outer sensory impressions. My 'idea' of a dog, on such a view, is a 'faded copy' or mental image of what was originally a direct sensory impression of a dog. Such particular ideas are subsequently made 'abstract' or 'general in their representation' by being associated not only with many other similar instances or impressions of dogs, but also with the regular application of the *word* 'dog' to such instances (see e.g. Hume on 'abstract ideas' in his *Treatise*, 1.1.7). Thinking, judging and understanding, on this widespread early modern view, were various forms of the contemplation and combination of separable idea-contents or 'terms' by means of association, imagination and reasoning.

One of Kant's most important philosophical contributions in the 'metaphysical deduction' was to defend an importantly different, and in my opinion far more adequate, approach to the nature of *concepts* than is possible on the above broadly empiricist conception of human understanding.

Suppose we begin by thinking about our understanding of the world, not in the first instance in terms of what we take in from the world due to our 'animal nature' as sensing and habit-forming beings, but rather as broadly rational beings capable of articulating our understandings *discursively* in conceptualized thoughts, in ways that (at least in mature form) are expressible overtly in discourse and in writing. What is perhaps most notable, from this perspective, is that our thoughts about and our knowledge of both 'inner' and 'outer' objects of sense experience are typically expressible in sentences, or more generally in judgments and propositions, about *what is the case* (or what must be the case, or what may be the case) in the world: that is, about 'how things stand' or are characterized or are related to one another. Kant argues that we should analyse human understanding first and foremost in terms of the most basic unities that are *understood*, and these are not 'ideas' in the empiricist's sense but rather articulable propositions expressible in judgments. As Aristotle had also emphasized, in human conceptual cognition we *predicate* something *of* something, in ways that for that very reason can be *true or false* of the objects and states of affairs we encounter in the world and in our own 'inner' reflections. We say *of human beings*, for instance, that they *are bipeds*, thereby taking a shot at truthfully representing and committing ourselves to what is the case in the world by predicating one concept of another in a judgment. Kant's insightful discussion in the 'Clue' or Metaphysical Deduction investigates some of the ways in which conceptual thinking is very different from the association of mental images in the mind, as well as some of the ways in which judgment or assertion is different from any mere concatenation of 'terms' or stringing together of words (cf. Brandom 2009: ch. 1).

In the Metaphysical Deduction Kant contends that "the cognition of every, at least human, understanding is a cognition through concepts"; and concepts rest "on functions", where by 'function' Kant tells us he understands "the unity of the action of ordering different representations under a common one" (A68/B93). The term 'unity', in general, refers to a 'one', just as the term 'manifold' refers to a 'many'. Here the "different representations" are the several concepts that, in an act of judgment, are to be subsumed or otherwise combined with one another in *one unified thought* about some actual or possible object or objects of cognition (and ultimately, if there is to be real theoretical cognition, of some objects of possible sensory *intuition*). Concepts are thus "predicates of possible judgments" in the strong sense that "the understanding can make no other use of these concepts than that of judging by means of them" (A68/B93). And since judgments are "functions of unity among our representations", we can thus "trace all actions of

Table 4.2 The logical forms of judgment.

Quantity		Quality	
Universal	*All F is G*	Affirmative	*F is G*
Particular	*Some F is G*	Negative	*F is not G*
Singular	*This F is G*	Infinite	*F is non-G*
Relation		Modality	
Categorical	*All F is G*	Problematic	*Possibly, F is G*
Hypothetical	*If F is G, then H is I*	Assertoric	*F is G*
Disjunctive	*Either F is G, or else F is H*	Apodictic	*Necessarily, F is G*

the understanding back to judgments, so that the **understanding** in general can be represented as a **faculty for judging**" (A69/B94). In the table of the logical functions of judgment (i.e. the 'Forms of judgment' column in Table 4.1 above), Kant accordingly seeks to specify the general logical forms in which conceptual contents are subsumable or otherwise combinable with one another in having unified thoughts about objects, logical forms that may be symbolized as shown in Table 4.2 (where *F*, *G*, etc., stand for general concepts).

So, for example, the thought that '*Dogs* are *animals*' (*F* are *G*) has the form of a (i) universal, (ii) affirmative, (iii) categorical and (iv) assertoric judgment. It has the right sort of logical form to make an assertion or 'take a shot at the truth', as I put it above, about some object or objects of cognition. (Note that although 'dogs' occurs in the subject position here, it functions as a general concept because it can also occur in predicate position and subsume other representations *under* it: for example, 'this beagle is a dog'.)

Now on Kant's view what he calls *general logic* abstracts "from all content of cognition, i.e. from any relation of it to the object, and considers only the logical form in the relation of cognitions to one another, i.e. the form of thinking in general" (A55/B79). But *transcendental logic* for Kant is a science that "would determine the origin, the domain, and the objective validity" of all pure *a priori* concepts and "laws of the understanding and reason, but solely insofar as they are related to objects *a priori*" (A57/B81–2). As we know, the term 'transcendental' for Kant concerns the possibility of *a priori* cognition. In this case, if understanding is a form of thinking unified predicative thoughts that take a shot at the truth, as explained above, then such thoughts will come in the form of judgments. But supposing, in addition, that there is to be a 'pure', non-empirical understanding or *a priori* conceptual cognition of some real objects of sensory intuition, as envisaged in Kant's transcendental logic (but as denied by Hume), then such thoughts, unified in conformity with the above logical forms of judgment, would in particular have to be combinations of pure concepts of objects of sensory intuition that are objectively valid *a priori*. And since, as we know, no *a priori* cognitions can be derived from or 'wait upon' any contingent sensory information that is delivered to us in the form of empirical intuitions *a posteriori*, such *a priori* combinations of pure concepts of intuitable objects must therefore somehow concern the latter as objects of *pure intuition* (space and time) rather than of empirical intuition *per se*. The "Clue to the Discovery of all Pure Concepts of Understanding" (A76/B102) is thus that such *a priori* categories would have to represent ways in which concepts of any objects of intuition (for us, spatiotemporal intuition) can be logically combined in objectively valid thoughts or judgments about such objects. And that is just what the twelve *categories*, when Kant's full story is in, turn out to be.

The following much discussed passage expresses the heart of Kant's Metaphysical Deduction or Clue to the discovery of the categories, and also foreshadows the strategy of the upcoming Transcendental Deduction that will attempt to display our *entitlement* to apply such pure categories to all possible objects of sensory experience (for insightful explorations of the significance of this passage, see McDowell [2009: 29ff., 70, 94, 109, 148, 260–61, 265–6, 271]):

> The same function that gives unity to the different representations **in a judgment** also gives unity to the mere synthesis of different representations **in an intuition**, which expressed generally, is called the pure concept of understanding. The same understanding, therefore, and indeed by means of the very same actions through which it brings the logical form of a judgment into concepts by means of the analytical unity, also brings a transcendental content into its representations by means of the synthetic unity of the manifold in intuition in general, on account of which they are called pure concepts of the understanding that pertain to objects *a priori*; this can never be accomplished by universal logic.
> (A79/B104–5)

That is, the same combinatory logical functions that make it possible for us to unify multiple concepts within single thoughts, in judgment, are what will also make it possible for us to know *a priori* that any cognition of objects of our sensory intuition must also conform to *a priori* principles of 'synthesis' or combination as well. "By **synthesis**" (or 'putting-together') Kant understands "the action of putting different representations together with each other and comprehending their manifoldness in one cognition" (A77/B103). The categories "pertain to objects *a priori*" by representing "the synthetic unity of the manifold in intuition in general": that is, by being the rules of conceptual combination of 'manys-into-ones', as we might put it, that first make it possible for us to comprehend any given sensory 'many' as the cognition of 'one' unified intuitable object or objective state of affairs in space and time.

In his further comments on what such a categorial 'synthesis' of representations involves (A77–9/B103–4), Kant begins to move into territory that is more properly treated in the Transcendental Deduction of the categories, to which we shall now turn. Note, however, that having identified in the Metaphysical Deduction the source and origin of the twelve pure concepts or categories, in the upcoming Transcendental Deduction Kant will now address the question of our capacity and entitlement to apply those categories to experience in terms of the very general question: with what right do we apply *any a priori concepts* to objects of sensory intuition in general and to the objects of our senses in particular? The twelve categories individually will not be the focus of Kant's attention until after the general source of their legitimacy has been successfully accounted for in the Transcendental Deduction. Both the Metaphysical and Transcendental Deductions fall within that part of the Transcendental Analytic entitled "Book I: Analytic of Concepts". The various justifications for the specific applications to objects of the particular categories that fall within each of the four groups distinguished above will subsequently be treated in "Book II: Analytic of Principles", to be discussed in Chapter 5 below. Only then shall we be in a position to know exactly why it is, for example, that the 'hypothetical' and 'categorical' forms of judgment and corresponding categories of causality and substance are really necessary for the possibility of representing specific kinds of 'synthetic unity' in the manifold of our sensory intuitions.

With the 'leading thread' or 'Clue' in hand, then, we can now turn directly to Kant's deep and difficult (but I think, deeply insightful) Transcendental Deduction of the Pure Concepts of Understanding.

4.2 THE TRANSCENDENTAL DEDUCTION OF THE CATEGORIES

Kant's central task in the Transcendental Deduction, as we have seen, is to explain how it is that we are entitled to apply *a priori* concepts to the empirical objects that we encounter *a posteriori* in experience. In the Metaphysical Deduction Kant argued that the twelve logical forms of judgment have provided a clue to the origin of twelve corresponding *a priori* concepts or categories as pure forms of understanding: the categories are the pure forms in which we can have unified thoughts about any objects of sensory intuition whatsoever. Kant is, if nothing else, a master at finding the most general formulation of a problem, and this is part of what makes his writing both so difficult and yet so compelling. The high level of abstraction at which Kant will now explore the topic of the Transcendental Deduction will involve such questions as: how is it possible in general for the stream of our thoughts and sensations to represent an 'object' conceived as existing independently of those representations? What would it take to be able to prove the objective validity of any *a priori* concept of such an object of our thoughts and experiences?

In attempting to answer such extremely general questions Kant will argue that the very concept of an experienced object of our cognition requires or presupposes the objective validity of certain conceptual representations that have an *a priori* origin in our thinking itself, rather than being derived empirically from our experience of the world. Kant explains in his "Transition" to the Transcendental Deduction (i.e. §14 in B) that such an *a priori* concept would be "determinant of the object *a priori* if it is possible through it alone to **cognize something as an object**" (A92/B125). The conclusion towards which Kant is aiming will accordingly be that:

> the objective validity of the categories, as *a priori* concepts, rests on the fact that through them alone is experience possible (as far as the form of thinking is concerned). For they then are related necessarily and *a priori* to objects of experience, since only by means of them can any object of experience be thought at all …
>
> The transcendental deduction of all *a priori* concepts therefore has a principle toward which the entire investigation must be directed, namely this: that they must be recognized as *a priori* conditions of the possibility of experiences. … Concepts that supply the objective ground of the possibility of experience are necessary just for that reason.   (A93–4/B126; cf. A158/B197)

If Kant is right, then the empiricist's appeal to sense experience as the sole origin of our knowledge of matters of fact in the world would unwittingly presuppose the objective validity of just those sorts of universal and necessary *a priori* concepts and principles upon which Hume had attempted to cast doubt. That is the exciting and controversial claim that we are now to explore in the rest of this chapter and in the next one. Given the results of Kant's 'Clue' discussed above, the *a priori* concepts that make experience possible will then subsequently be identified with the twelve categories. Finally, the full justification and explanation of each category's application to experience will await the "Principles" section of the *Critique* to be discussed in the next chapter. So let us now attempt to figure out what it is that Kant argues is involved in the possibility of our having any cognition of an object of any experience whatsoever, knowing in advance that his answer will be that such experience requires the objectively valid application of *a priori* concepts to the objects of our experience.

Before diving into this pool, it is important to recall again that Kant replaced the second and third sections of the first A edition version of the Transcendental Deduction (A95–130) with an entirely new version in B that he then divided into sections numbered §15 to §27 (B129–69). There are insights in what is now usually called the A-Deduction that are not contained in its B-Deduction replacement, and vice versa, so for our purposes I shall be drawing on passages from both versions when helpful. Even by Kant's standards the Transcendental Deduction is a notoriously complex text that is open to a myriad of interpretations. The brief analysis to follow in the rest of this chapter is just one way of attempting to spell out two main lines of argument that can be found in both versions of the Transcendental Deduction.

The concept of an object of possible experience

In order for beings such as we are to have any cognition of an object, our senses must be affected by such objects as they make their appearances to us in ways that have been discussed in previous chapters. In the A-Deduction in particular, Kant offers a complex phenomenological and conceptual analysis of what he calls the *threefold synthesis* that is involved in our sensory "apprehension of the representations, as modifications of the mind in intuition; of the reproduction of them in the imagination, and of their recognition in the concept" (A97). Consider:

(1) visually apprehending a given red apple (sensory apprehension).
(2) imagining a red apple, or imagining unseen parts or aspects of a red apple.
(3) thinking of a red apple, having the general concept of an apple and of being red.

Kant's contention will be that all three of these cognitive abilities – roughly, sensing, imagining and thinking – must be possessed by anyone having the simple sensory experience described in (1), *if* this is to constitute the perception of a red apple *as* a red apple – or more generally, the experience of an object *as* an object of one's experience. (What the 'as' means here should become clearer as we proceed.) These "three subjective sources of cognition", as Kant puts it, make possible "all experience as an empirical product of understanding" (A97–8). In what follows I shall attempt to convey some crucial aspects of Kant's argument that there is more to perceiving an object than meets the eye, so to speak. After this analysis we shall then examine the pivotal role of judgment and self-consciousness (or 'apperception') in Kant's justification of the categories as *a priori* concepts of objects. Thus we shall follow Kant in basically approaching the same issues from two different directions, the former of which explores much of what Kant sometimes called the "subjective deduction", the latter the "objective deduction" of the categories (cf. the A-Preface, Axvi–xviii). I begin, then, with the "threefold synthesis".

With respect to Kant's views on the sensory apprehension of objects, we know from Chapter 3 that if we abstract away from all of the *a posteriori* empirical elements in our sensory experiences of objects or appearances there remain the pure intuitions of space and time as *a priori* forms of sensibility. Furthermore, since all objects, whether 'inner' or 'outer', are experienced or apprehended successively in time, throughout the Transcendental Analytic Kant focuses primarily on our cognition of the *temporal* characteristics of the objects that we conceive as corresponding to our sensory apprehensions (cf. A98–9) although, as we shall see, the representation of space and of objects in space is equally essential to Kant's overall argument. One of the key starting-points for Kant's analysis, particularly as expounded in the A-Deduction, is accordingly that all our experiences of objects undeniably (even for Hume) involve *temporally successive sensory experiencings or apprehensions* on the part of the experiencer. This is a point that Kant will repeatedly emphasize as a phenomenological starting-point throughout the rest of the Transcendental Analytic: "Our **apprehension** of the manifold of appearance is always successive, and is therefore always changing", as he later puts it in the important "Analogies of Experience" section (A182/B225).

At A99, however, Kant immediately makes a crucial distinction in relation to all sensory apprehension:

> Every intuition contains a manifold in itself, which however would not be represented as such if the mind did not distinguish the time in the succession of impressions on one another; for **as contained in one moment** no representation can ever be anything other than absolute unity. Now in order for **unity** of intuition to come from this manifold (as, say, in the representation of space) it is necessary first to run through and then to take together this manifoldness, which action I call the **synthesis of apprehension**, since it is aimed directly at the intuition, which to be sure provides a manifold but can never effect this as such, and indeed as contained **in one representation**, without the occurrence of such a synthesis.   (A99)

Kant immediately adds that such a synthesis must be exercised not only empirically but also *a priori*, in that the representation of space and time themselves requires a "**pure** synthesis of apprehension" (A100). The important general distinction in the passage, which applies to both pure and empirical intuitions, concerns the difference between a *manifold of representations*, on the one hand, and the *representation of a manifold* on the other. Put crudely, there is a difference between a manifold or succession of awarenesses, such as this:

> an awareness of A, and then an awareness of B, and then an awareness of C

as opposed to the awareness of something *as a manifold*, that is, as a plurality of items that are grasped together as one unity ("as contained **in one representation**"), such as

> a single awareness of A–*and*–B–*and*–C together:
> - as parts of or changes in a single unified object; or
> - as three events following each other in time (an objective succession); or
> - as three observations of the coexisting parts of a single object;
> - and so on.

Only the latter are examples of the awareness of a manifold *represented as such* a manifold, and Kant's claim is that such an apprehension requires a "synthesis" or combination whereby the many are represented as one object (or as one complex, or as a succession), that is, as A–*and*–B–*and*–C. This key distinction will be seen to have significant consequences as the argument proceeds.

Jumping ahead to the "synthesis of reproduction in the imagination", Kant provides examples in the following passage to illustrate a further synthesis or combination of representations that he contends is required in order to account for how the key distinction just noted is possible. Again, it is important to note how Kant's examples focus on the sorts of spatial and temporal magnitudes that, as discussed earlier in the Aesthetic, we can 'construct' or present to ourselves *a priori* in pure sensory intuition as well as perceptually apprehending them as properties of given empirical objects (a line, a length of time, a number, etc.):

> Now it is obvious that if I draw a line in thought, or think of the time from one noon to the next, or even want to represent a certain number to myself, I must necessarily first grasp one of these manifold representations after another in my thoughts. But if I were always to lose the preceding representations (the first parts

of the line, the preceding parts of time, or the successively represented units) from my thoughts and not reproduce them when I proceed to the following ones, then no whole representation and none of the previously mentioned thoughts, not even the purest and most fundamental representations of space and time, could ever arise. (A102)

"The synthesis of apprehension", Kant concludes, "is therefore inseparably combined with the synthesis of reproduction", a product of "the transcendental faculty of imagination" (A102). "*Imagination*", Kant explains at B151, "is the faculty for representing an object even **without its presence** in intuition". By this, Kant means that the imagination is our ability to directly present in an intuition (of imagination) a sensory content that is not presently being passively apprehended by outer or inner sensory intuition (e.g. the unseen backside of a seen book). We do this by forming either a sensory "**image**" (A120) or an '*a priori* schema' that includes that sensible content (more on 'pure schemata' in Chapter 5). One of Kant's most important claims is that the imagination of *presently unsensed* parts of objects of our experience, as sensorily represented in either a (conceptualized) image or a 'pure schema' of the object, is in fact necessary even for the possibility of our perceiving any *presently perceived* object *as* an object of our experience at all.

Note that not only the 'reproductive' imagination but also what Kant calls a pure "**productive synthesis of the imagination**" must "take place *a priori*; for the **reproductive** synthesis rests on conditions of experience" (A118; cf. A118–25, B151–2). We shall have more to say about the productive imagination later on, after we examine Kant's views on conceptual understanding below and in Chapter 5 (particularly in relation to the 'Schematism' chapter). As Kant will explain, "the transcendental synthesis of the [productive] **imagination**", insofar as it is "an exercise of spontaneity", is really "an effect of the understanding on sensibility" (B151–2); and so a proper understanding of its role – and also of what Kant calls the objective "**affinity**" of appearances (A113–14, A122; cf. Westphal, 2004) – really requires a grasp of aspects of Kant's view to be discussed below. At any rate, Kant stresses the crucial role of the transcendental imagination in relation to perceptual cognition in general in the following footnote:

> No psychologist has yet thought that the imagination is a necessary ingredient of perception itself. This is so partly because this faculty has been limited to reproduction, and partly because it has been believed that the senses do not merely afford us impressions but also put them together, and produce images of objects, for which without doubt something more than the receptivity

of impressions is required, namely a function of the synthesis of
them. (A120)

Having argued that a synthesis of imagination is required for our sensory apprehension of any object of experience as such an object, Kant now finally comes to the role of conceptual thinking in the 'threefold synthesis'. "Without consciousness that that which we think is the very same" – for example, the same house or day or line – "as what we thought a moment before, all reproduction in the series of representations would be in vain" (A103); and a "concept", Kant tells us, just "is this **one** consciousness that unifies the manifold that has been successively intuited, and then also reproduced, into one representation" (A103). The concept of "an object of representations" in general, according to Kant's analysis, is the concept of "an object corresponding to and therefore also distinct from the cognition" (A104). Furthermore – and this is the tricky bit – this corresponding object is conceived as that which determines that our experience or cognition *of* it has the particular content that it does. The concept of an object of experience thus includes the following idea: it is because it is a house that I am seeing, or a line that I am drawing in thought, that my seeing or 'drawing' has the represented content that it does.

What Kant is addressing here is what philosophers call the 'intentional content' or the 'objective purport' of an experience or thought. *Intentionality* in this technical sense concerns what something is *of* or *about* or *represents*, and in this case it concerns the conceptual-representational content that Kant is arguing is necessary for the possibility of any experience of an object as an object of experience at all. In the present context Kant connects the ideas of objective purport and conceptual content with the idea of a certain non-arbitrariness or necessity – in fact, as we shall see, it is a *rule-governedness* – in the ways in which the representations (i.e. the represent*ed* contents) must be conceived as related to one another, and to ourselves, in order for our representings to constitute the cognition of an object (whether as a particular kind of object or, more importantly, as an object of possible experience in general):

> We find, however, that our thought of the relation of all cognition to its object carries something of necessity with it, since namely the latter is regarded as that which is opposed to our cognitions being determined at pleasure or arbitrarily rather than being determined *a priori*, since insofar as they are to relate to an object our cognitions must also necessarily agree with each other in relation to it, i.e., they must have that unity that constitutes the concept of an object. (A104–5)

We shall see more on this point presently. It is important to be clear at the outset, however, that although we thus conceive the object to be that which determines our experience of it to be (in that respect) the way that it is, on Kant's view we cannot, as it were, 'reach out behind' the objects or 'appearances' as we experience them, in order to find out how such objects are 'as things in themselves' (for example, in an 'intellectual intuition' or from a God's-eye point of view as conceived on the 'transcendental realist' model discussed in earlier chapters). For "outside of our cognition we have nothing that we could set over against this cognition as corresponding to it" (A104).

That is, in our present attempt to make sense of and justify our concept of mind-independent objectivity or objective validity (and thus answer the *quid juris* question), we are strictly limited to the sorts of representations and 'appearances' that are directly intuitable by us in sense experience. But how is that possible? (Recall Kant's letter to Herz, discussed in §4.1.) The key question at this stage of Kant's analysis is therefore this: how then do we conceive that any particular succession of our experiences is the way that it is *because* it is the cognition of an object that is distinct from and determinative of those experiencings, and yet do so without making any leaps beyond the realm of 'appearances' that are directly experienceable by us in general? In other words, how do we conceive what are essentially 'appearances-to-us' to be objects that exist objectively on their own, independently of our representations of them?

Kant's answer, as I read him, is this. When we apply any general concept to experience, such as the concept of a house or a line, what we are applying, as Kant tells us, is a *rule*, and in the case of *a priori* concepts and principles in particular, he calls it a *law* (A113). Rules, as we know, sort matters into can's and cannot's, must's or may's, ought's and ought not's, and so on. (How exactly rules do this, as Ludwig Wittgenstein taught us in the twentieth century, is itself not an easy matter to sort out.) Concepts, for Kant, are rules or laws concerning what can and cannot happen, what must and must not happen, within any experience that can succeed in being an experience of *that* kind of object (whether a particular kind of object or as an object of experience in general). As Kant puts it, "this **unity of rule** determines every manifold" (A105). Conceptual rules or norms play this role by 'binding down' our representations in the sense of committing us to combine our actual and possible representations of the object only in ways that accord with the rules implicit in the concept of that kind of object.

To apply the concept of a house to some experience, for example, is implicitly to 'lay down the rule', as it were, that any past or subsequent or alternative possible experiences of this same object, by oneself or by anyone else, must have had, or will have, or would have had only certain kinds of represented experiential contents and not others. The "object for our intuitions", as Kant puts it, is "nothing more than the something for which the concept expresses such a necessity of synthesis" (A106). Or as he states it in the B-Deduction: "An **object** ... is that in the concept of which the manifold of a given intuition is **united**" (B137).

Having conceived a given object of experience to be a house, for instance, then (other things being equal) one is then committed by that conceptual rule to drawing subsequent inferences and performing actions in ways that are consistent with the various implicit assumptions that this conceptual content entails about how houses can and cannot behave or function within possible experience ('house rules', as it were). For example, a house is conceived to be the sort of object that will not – cannot – in the next moment be experienced to transform into a bird; a house cannot have come into existence only two seconds ago when I turned to look at it; a house has a presently unobserved inside and a back that I or anyone else *would* see if only we were appropriately situated; and so on. Of course, I could be mistaken in applying the concept of a house to this particular experience for various familiar reasons. But this is as it should be, since applying a concept is making a *judgment* about how matters stand, and as such it is the taking of an explanatory shot at the truth about some state of affairs in the 'inner' or 'outer' world of experience. The key point is that it is the object as thus conceived in this rule-governed way that is thereby conceived to be responsible for (rather than, as 'phenomenalist' interpretations of Kant have mistakenly assumed, being *reducible to*) various facts and counterfactual truths concerning my actual and possible apprehensions of that object. Later in the Second Analogy Kant expresses this key point – that is, his claim concerning the sort of rule-governed necessity that is involved in the general concept of an object of experience that is both distinct from and yet determinative of our own representings or experiencings of it – as follows:

> appearance, in contradistinction to the representations of apprehension, can thereby only be represented as the object that is distinct from them if it stands under a rule that distinguishes it from every other apprehension, and makes one way of combining the manifold necessary. That in the appearance which contains the condition of this necessary rule of apprehension is the object.
> (A191/B236)

Ironically, then, it is the conformity of the objects of experience, throughout all their possible appearances, to the conceptual rules and judgments that *we* apply to them – here is Kant's 'Copernican turn' once again! – that first makes possible our representation of those objects *as existing objectively*, that is, as empirical objects that exist independently of and determinative of our particular sensory apprehensions of them. Sellars, who was much influenced by Kant, once expressed a similarly 'Copernican' point of view: *"instead of coming to have a concept of something because we have noticed that sort of thing, to have the ability to notice a sort of thing is already to have the concept of that sort of thing, and cannot account for it"* (Sellars [1956] 1991: §45).

In my view the account given above is roughly how Kant attempts to explain the objective purport of our concepts of objects of experience without appealing to anything other than the contents of our own possible experiences themselves. We achieve this by conceiving the direct objects of our sensory intuitions or experiences to be bound by the very same rules of possibility and necessity that *general conceptual* content itself consists in, on this view of the conceptual or intentional content of our thoughts and judgments. This aspect of Kant's Copernican turn takes some getting used to. It is our application of conceptual rules *to* experience in judgments, according to Kant, that first makes possible the particular modes of coherence that, as a result of that application, we are now able simply to 'find in' those same sense experiences by, as it were, just opening our eyes and *looking*: that is, by having *direct conceptualized sensory intuitions* of the objects that are presented to us in experience. I hope the analysis given above has gone some way towards putting flesh on the bare bones of the crucial passage from the Metaphysical Deduction that was discussed above in §4.1: "The same function that gives unity to the different representations **in a judgment** also gives unity to the mere synthesis of different representations **in an intuition,** which, expressed generally, is called the pure concept of understanding" (A79/B104–5). And as we shall see in Chapter 5, this striking feature is especially true of the twelve *a priori* categories and pure principles of understanding, such as the principle of cause and effect – which "is called a **principle**", Kant later tells us, "because it has the special property that it first makes possible its [own] ground of proof, namely experience, and must always be presupposed in this" (A737/B765).

This highly original conception of objectivity and of intentionality or representational content in general would have been enough by itself to secure the lasting philosophical significance of Kant's Transcendental Deduction. Remarkably enough, however, Kant in fact embedded the entire analysis of the concept of an object of experience given above within an even more striking argument concerning the necessary structure of human self-consciousness or 'apperception', to which I now turn. Here again brevity will require that we focus on just a few key moves in Kant's argument, in this case primarily in the B-Deduction rather than the A-Deduction.

The unity of the 'I think' and the objective validity of the categories

In the analysis above Kant has argued that the concept of an object of experience requires a "threefold synthesis" of sensory apprehension, imagination and conceptual recognition in which, all taken together, experienceable spatiotemporal objects are conceptually apprehended in our sense perceptions according to rules or laws that determine which sorts of sequences and combinations of experienceable content are necessary and possible for the object. Where does this analysis leave us in relation to Kant's fundamental *quid juris* question, discussed earlier, concerning our entitlement to apply *a priori* concepts and principles to the objects of sensory experience?

What Kant's analysis has so far suggested is that something as seemingly simple as the perspectival sensory apprehension of a given object – an immediate sensory experience of the sort that a sceptic or an empiricist might be tempted to take for granted as a self-standing, subjectively 'given' starting-point – in fact already requires or presupposes the sorts of conceptual recognition of objective necessities and restricted possibilities in the object of which sceptics and empiricists are suspicious (for reasons we examined in connection with Hume's sceptical 'fork' argument in Chapter 2). Kant's analysis has so far contended that this entire wider package – that is, from the sensory apprehension of a given object in time to the rule-governed or lawful conceptual representation in judgments of empirically mind-independent objects – must stand or fall together as an interconnected whole. What Kant now attempts to show is that it is impossible for us to coherently deny that this package or framework as a whole is objectively valid, thus answering the original *quid juris* challenge discussed earlier.

Near the beginning of the B-Deduction (§16) Kant lays out certain fundamental claims about the necessary structure of our conscious experience that I have not addressed so far, in relation to what he calls the *transcendental unity of apperception* or self-consciousness:

> The **I think** must **be able** to accompany all my representations; for otherwise something would be represented in me that could not be thought at all, which is as much as to say that the representation would either be impossible or else at least would be nothing for me. ... Thus all manifold of intuition has a necessary relation to the **I think** in the same subject in which this manifold is to be encountered. (B131–2)

Kant describes this "representation **I think**" as an "act of **spontaneity**" or understanding as opposed to a passive reception of sensibility: a "**pure**" (non-empirical), "**original**" (i.e. non-derivative) "**apperception**" or awareness *of* one's own perceptions *as* one's own. He calls it a "**transcendental** unity of self-consciousness" because of "the possibility of *a priori* cognition arising from it" (B132), as he will now attempt to show.

What should we make of Kant's initial claim that the "I think must be able to accompany all of my representations" or else they "would be nothing for me"? For the 'I think' to *actually* accompany one of my 'representations' would presumably be for me to explicitly represent, in an act of thought, that a certain representation – a thinking, an experiencing, and so on – is or was thought *by me*. I might have the meta-thought, for example, that 'Yesterday I had the thought that he was leaving'. Or more compactly and abstractly, using the present tense neutrally to cover the past, present or future: '*I think* (i.e. I have the thought) that *p*' (where '*p*' might be 'it is raining'), or 'I perceive *A*' (where '*A*' might be 'a house'). Note that Kant is careful to say only that I "must *be able*" to think or represent, in this way, that my own thoughts and other mental representations are my own, not that I must always actually do so whenever I am thinking about something. Note also that in one sense, of course, the utterance or thought 'I think that *p*' might itself just be a first-order judging or a thinking (by me) that *p*. But Kant has in mind something else by the claim that the 'I think' must be able to accompany any representation that is to be consciously significant for me: namely, that in this cognitive domain I must in principle be able to have the *self-ascribing thought* that such a thinking or representing is mine.

The accompanying 'I think' is thus a thought that has as its intentional object one or more of my own 'inner' thoughts or representations, *thought of as my own*. In a later letter to Herz on 26 May 1789, Kant contrasts this form of potentially self-conscious cognition with typical non-human animal cognition as follows: in the case of non-human animals the "data of sense", he suggests, "could still (if I imagine myself to be an animal) carry on their play in an orderly fashion, as representations connected according to empirical laws of association, and thus even have an influence on my feeling and desire, without my being aware of them" – that is, without my being even potentially aware of them *as my experiences* (Kant, *Correspondence*, 314=11:52).

Kant's opening claim concerning the 'I think' thus indicates that the kind of cognition he is addressing is our potentially self-conscious cognition of the world as experienced 'from the inside', or from the 'first-person perspective', as it is often put. Minimally, each of us is undeniably aware *that we have thoughts* and experiences, whatever the correct account of such awareness might ultimately consist in. Hume famously argued, of course, that at a basic level our real idea of what philosophers call 'the enduring self' or 'the soul' is just the idea of a certain *bundle* of particular associated inner perceptions, emotions, ideas and so on (cf. Hume, *Treatise*, 1.4.6). But this shows that Hume's own rock-bottom starting-point appeals to our awareness of our perceptions as diversely succeeding one another in our consciousness. If so, then not even Hume would be in a position to deny the very minimal claim that he is aware of his particular perceptions through time as such, however sceptical he might be with respect to any *philosophical* account of what sort of thing 'he' ultimately is; or of what this inner awareness or 'idea' itself ultimately consists in; or of what can or cannot be rationally *inferred from* the stream of perceptions of which he is thus aware. (We should recall this latter point, however, when we come to discuss Kant's 'Refutation of (Empirical) Idealism' at the end of Chapter 5.)

Kant in fact holds that, when properly understood, this opening claim about the 'I think' amounts to a *logically analytic* proposition that ultimately expresses what he calls "the **analytical** unity of apperception" (B133): "this principle of the necessary unity of apperception is, to be sure, itself identical, thus an analytical proposition" (B135), he tells us, for "it says nothing more than that all **my** representations in any given intuition must stand under the condition under which alone I can ascribe them to the identical self as **my** representations" (B138; cf. A364, B407–8). There are really two thoughts involved in this 'analytic unity of apperception'. The first is the minimal point concerning what I will call *the 'I think' ability* as explained above. That is, I must in principle be able to think, in relation to each of *my* representations severally (call them *A* and *B*), a thought that can be represented as follows:

'I think *A*, and I think *B*.'   [The **'I think' ability**]

But what Kant's further remarks just noted make clear (e.g. "I can ascribe them to the identical self as **my** representations"), is that the 'I think' ability involves the self-ascribing thought that it is *the same I* who thinks each of my representations (cf. Rosenberg 2005: 124):

'I, who think *A*, = I, who think *B*.'   [The **analytic unity of apperception**]

So Kant's opening claim, as filled out above and as restricted to the domain of those inner experiences of which I can potentially be consciously aware, is the merely analytically true claim that I must be capable of thinking of each of my thoughts as mine, where 'my' and 'mine' are thereby *thought of* or represented as ascriptions to one's same thinking self. It is merely logically (i.e. analytically) true, understood in this sense, that I think of each of *my* thoughts, *A* and *B*, as belonging to me, that is, to the self-same 'I' that is thereby *thought as* the same one thinking self.

But *what is* this self-same *I*? Nothing in the above entails any knowledge of the *nature* of the self in any of the kinds of ways traditionally defended in the history of philosophy from Plato and Aristotle to Descartes and Locke. Neither, however, can we coherently rest with the scepticism of Hume regarding the self, essentially for reasons already discussed. These points should become clear in what follows.

First, it is important for the next stage of Kant's argument to keep in mind that the single, unitary self so conceived or thought is merely the analytic or logical unity of the representation, 'I think', across the possible self-ascription of all my own potentially conscious representations. The analytic unity of the 'I think' in this sense is *not* – as it is in Descartes' philosophy, for instance – a cognition of the nature of the self or the subject of thoughts as any kind of *object* or substance at all, whether 'material' (a body) or 'immaterial' (a soul or 'spirit'). Rather, it is simply the mere thought or representation of oneself as the self-same subject of one's own thoughts. Later in the Paralogisms, which we shall briefly explore further below, Kant strongly emphasizes the *emptiness* of the 'I think' as a purely logical or formal unity of apperception. Referring to what he will argue are the rational metaphysicians' fallacy-ridden attempts to prove the existence of the self as an identical, immaterial substance or soul (the 'doctrine of the soul'), Kant implicitly contrasts what he thinks is the genuine, purely formal role played in human cognition by the 'I think', as follows:

> At the ground of this doctrine we can place nothing but the simple and in content for itself wholly empty representation **I**, of which one cannot even say that it is a concept, but a mere consciousness that accompanies every concept. Through this I, or He, or It (the thing), which thinks, nothing further is represented than a transcendental subject of thoughts = x, which is recognized only through the thoughts that are its predicates, and about which, in abstraction, we can never have even the least concept; because of which we therefore turn in a constant circle, since we must always already avail ourselves of the representation of it at all times in order to judge anything about it; we cannot separate ourselves from this inconvenience, because the consciousness in itself is not even a representation distinguishing a particular object, but rather *a form of representation* in general, insofar as it is to be called a cognition; for of it alone can I say that through it I think anything.   (A345–6/B404, italics added; cf. Sellars [1972] 2002)

Second, however, it is equally important to bear in mind that the *mere 'I think' ability*, as represented above concerning my ability to represent each of my thoughts severally or any of my thoughts singly ('I think A, and I think B'), is by itself *insufficient* to account for the thought that it was shown to contain above: that is, for the thought that 'I, who think A, = I, who think B'

(the analytic unity of apperception). For if the 'I think' were merely a thought that could accompany each of our thoughts or isolated consciousnesses separately, *nothing* would thereby be added to the stream of thoughts in inner sense, that is, to the representations *A*, *B*, *C*, ..., themselves. We would be left with what Kant (in this context) calls mere "empirical apperception" or non-self-conscious "inner sense" (in fact, we would be left with merely non-human animal cognition, as discussed above). As Kant puts it: "I would have as multicolored, diverse a self as I have representations of which I am conscious" (B134). Or again:

> The consciousness of oneself in accordance with the determinations of our state in internal perception is merely empirical, forever variable; it can provide no standing or abiding self in this stream of inner appearances, and is customarily called **inner sense** or **empirical apperception**. That which should **necessarily** be represented as numerically identical cannot be thought of as such through empirical data. (A107)

Inner sense is our capacity to be affected by our own mental states and mental activities in such a way as to give rise to our inner apprehension or awareness of them as ordered in time. There is a sense, then, in which our mental lives would thus be present to us *empirically*, as apprehended from the inside, only as a stream or 'bundle' of thoughts, perceptions and feelings of much the sort that Hume reports finding inside himself when he introspects and fails to discover, in addition to this stream, what philosophers call 'the self' or soul (*Treatise*, 1.4.6.3). (It will turn out that the latter awareness of *our* inner states *as* inner states – and thus 'empirical apperception' as it normally occurs *for us* – is only possible for potentially self-conscious beings, for reasons about to be discussed.)

For these reasons none of the traditional approaches – neither metaphysical or rationalist, nor sceptical or empiricist – can successfully account for the mere content of our representation of 'the self-same I' that Kant has just argued is contained in the necessary form of our potentially self-conscious experience (beginning with the basic 'I think' ability). The stage is set for the final step in Kant's argument (as I have been reconstructing that argument here, at any rate).

For although the 'I think' is thus, as we have just seen, merely "a form of representation" (A345–6/B404, quoted above) rather than the representation or cognition of the self as any kind of object or thing or substance, Kant now proceeds to argue that the above "**analytical** unity of apperception is only possible under the presupposition of some **synthetic** one": for "it is only because I can combine a manifold of given representations **in one**

consciousness that it is possible for me to represent the **identity of the consciousness in these representations** itself" (B133–4). That is, in order for it to be possible that the form of my potentially self-conscious thinking is as it is represented in the analytic unity of apperception (namely, 'I, who think A = I, who think B'), it must be possible for me, *a priori*, to think *logically synthetic* unified thoughts of the general form:

'I think: (A and B)'.   [The **synthetic unity of apperception**]

As anticipated, the crucial considerations Kant now advances to support this claim join up smoothly with the sorts of considerations discussed earlier in relation to the 'threefold synthesis' involved in the *concept of an object* of experience in general. In this case, however, we begin 'from above', as Kant sometimes puts it, in relation to the *logical* structure of our thoughts and judgments, rather than 'from below' in relation to sensory apprehension and reproductive imagination (cf. A119–20).

Consider, for example, the difference between the following:

(a) an I has a manifold of thoughts
(b) an I thinks of a manifold

There is a difference between a succession of thoughts, A and B, taking place *in* a thinking subject, as opposed to a unified thought *by* that subject *of A and B*. For example, there is a difference between a consciousness of lightning ('I think A') being followed by a conscious anticipation of thunder ('and then I think B'), as opposed to a single consciousness that combines those two thoughts in the judgment *that lightning is followed by thunder* ('I think: A is followed by B', or 'I think: Bs follow As', etc.). We have encountered this difference before, of course. It is the difference made by the logical forms of *judgment*, as embodied in the categories of understanding, as the *a priori* logical forms in which thoughts can be combined into unified 'judgeables' or propositional contents that are capable of being true or false of the (inner or outer) world. Kant discusses this point clearly in §19 of the B-Deduction, which is entitled: "The Logical Form of all Judgments Consists in the Objective Unity of the Apperception of the Concepts Contained Therein" (B140). The "copula **is**" (for example, in the judgment *that A is B*), Kant explains, serves "to distinguish the objective unity of given representations from the subjective":

> Only in this way does there arise from this relation **a judgment**, i.e., a relation that is **objectively valid**, and that is sufficiently distinguished from the relation of these same representations in which there would be only subjective validity, e.g., in accordance with laws of association. In accordance with the latter I could only say 'If I carry a body, I feel a pressure of weight', but not 'It, the

body, **is** heavy', which would be to say that these two representations are combined in the object, i.e., regardless of any difference in the condition of the subject, and are not merely found together in perception (however often as that might be repeated). (B142)

The key move in Kant's argument is accordingly the following. We have seen that the 'I think', considered by itself, is *not* the cognition of the self as a unified object or substance (a thinking being or soul) in which our various thoughts could be cognized to inhere, in contrast to the intuited objects of 'outer sense' that are indeed cognized as the intuited logical subjects of predicated properties. We have also seen that the mere 'I think', if considered merely as able to accompany each of our representations severally but not *as combined*, would give us only the sort of associative, animal consciousness involved in what "is customarily called **inner sense** or **empirical apperception**" (A107), which fails to provide any recognition of experiences *as* such, or of changing objects as unities. Kant's striking contention, now, is that the mere thought or representation of the unity of our thinking selves – the mere analytic unity of the 'I think' as able to accompany all of one's own representations representable as one's own – is itself made possible as a form of representation only because of one's ability to think logically unified thoughts in accordance with the categories: for example, 'I think: *if A then B*', or 'I think *that A is B*' and so on. Such judgments conceptually represent (in the rule-governed way discussed earlier) the relevant spatiotemporally intuited contents *A* and *B as combined objectively*, that is, in the objective world of empirical objects thereby conceived as existing independently of our own subjectively successive thoughts and apprehensions of them. For as also discussed earlier in relation to the 'threefold synthesis', the only available contents to be combined by such objective judgments are the pure and empirical contents of our inner and outer spatiotemporal sensory intuitions, for example, in the 'drawing of a line in thought' or in the sensory perception of a given house (cf. B162–3). It is in this way that Kant finally claims to have accounted for:

> the possibility of cognizing *a priori* **through categories** whatever objects **may come before our senses**, not as far as the form of their intuition but rather as far as the laws of their combination are concerned, thus the possibility of as it were prescribing the law to nature, and even making the latter possible. (B159–60)

We shall have much more to say about what is involved in our "prescribing the law to nature" throughout the course of the next chapter.

So the transcendental unity of apperception – the unity or 'oneness' of human self-consciousness – is, according to Kant, a "form of representation" (in particular, a certain unity in our thinking) rather than the cognition of the self as an object or substance (soul). But Kant's unique contention has been that this irreducible form of representation is an achievement of representational unity in our thinking and experiencing that stands together, in one systematic *a priori* conceptual package, with our ability to represent *a world of objects* that are related and combined in ways that are thus represented as *independent* of our own apprehensions of them. So whether one begins 'from below' with our sensory apprehensions or 'from above' with the 'I think' of apperception, Kant's conclusion is that the *possibility of experience*, when correctly analysed as presupposing a certain synthetic unity over time in the ways discussed above, entails that the following two theses *mutually* condition and imply one another:

The awareness of oneself as having thoughts and experiences (the *unity of apperception*). **One Unified 'I think'**	⇔	The objectively valid application of *a priori* concepts to the objects of experience. **One Objective World**

That is why the *a priori* categories of understanding must be objectively valid in the sense required for an adequate response to the *quid juris* question from which we started: put compactly, the categories are necessary for the possibility of our experiencing any objects as such. It also follows, Kant concludes, that the *a priori* categories are validly applicable *only* to the objects of our possible experience, which result is the *critical restriction* that lies at the heart of Kant's entire transcendental philosophy:

> We cannot **think** any object except through categories; we cannot **cognize** any object that is thought except through intuitions that correspond to those concepts. Now all our intuitions are sensible, and this cognition, so far as its object is given, is empirical. Empirical cognition, however, is experience. Consequently **no *a priori*** cognition is possible for us except solely of objects of possible experience. (B165–6)

Kant on apperception, the empirical self and the soul: the Paralogisms

As we have seen, it is crucial for appreciating the force of Kant's Transcendental Deduction to recognize that the arguments above concerning the transcendental unity of apperception tell us nothing about the nature or substantial identity of our thinking selves. The Transcendental Deduction appealed to our undeniable awareness of the succession of our own experiences and then analysed the consequences and presuppositions of such a synthetically unified form of representation in general. The unity of apperception thus concerns the logical or formal structure of our self-conscious thinking as represented to and by ourselves; it is a thought "that serves only to introduce all thinking as belonging to consciousness" (A341/B399). The consequences of this point for the nature and limits of our knowledge of our own thinking selves requires some further explanation with reference to Kant's "Paralogisms of Pure Reason" in the Transcendental Dialectic.

Kant's view overall will entail that one should distinguish between (at least) three different things that one might mean by 'self-knowledge':

(i) the passive, empirical apprehension of one's own various mental states in "inner sense" (i.e. "empirical apperception": A107, B132, B139–40, B153).
(ii) the "transcendental unity of apperception" (both analytic and synthetic unity) as thought in the purely formal representation, "I think".
(iii) the putative rational demonstration that one's thoughts necessarily belong to a single, persisting, immaterial substance or soul (Descartes' *res cogitans* or thinking thing).

We have now explored Kant's conceptions of (i) and (ii), empirical apperception and transcendental apperception. In relation to the alleged speculative metaphysical knowledge traditionally defended in (iii), however, in the Paralogisms Kant launches an incisive and original diagnosis of the fallacious inferences that he contends are involved in the traditional arguments for the conclusion that the thinking self is necessarily an identical persisting substance or soul. I shall attempt to sum up Kant's complex diagnosis briefly in what follows.

The category of *substance*, for Kant, is basically the concept of an object that is a non-derivative subject or 'unhad haver' of properties. As applied to empirical reality, as we shall see in Chapter 5 in relation to the *a priori* principle of the 'persistence of substance' in the "First Analogy of Experience", Kant argues that we must indeed conceive every change that we encounter in sense experience as the alteration of some identical substance or substances that persist through those changes. Now, we have seen in relation to the 'I think' of transcendental apperception that one does necessarily represent one's thoughts, *a priori*, as belonging to oneself as the identical thinking subject of those thoughts. On this basis alone, the speculative metaphysical 'rational psychologist' (from the Greek '*psykhe*' for soul) such as Descartes might then appear to have a compelling *a priori* argument ready to hand, one that Kant (B410–11) frames as follows:

[1] What cannot be thought otherwise than as subject does not exist otherwise than as subject, and is therefore substance.

[2] Now, a thinking being, considered merely as such, cannot be thought otherwise than as subject.
[3] Therefore it also exists only as such a thing, i.e., as substance.

However, Kant diagnoses a fallacy of equivocation in this and similar attempts to draw an *a priori* inference from our consciousness of ourselves as the unified subjects of our thoughts (as we have seen, this is knowable *a priori*, but it is not the representation of a kind of thing or object), to the existence of ourselves as substantial thinking things or souls (this is the representation of a kind of thing or object, but one that is not an object of intuition for us). The transcendental unity of apperception does indeed entail that we cannot *represent ourselves* as other than the single, unitary subjects or thinkers of our thoughts. For this reason it is true that the 'I think' *cannot* function as the representation of a merely *non-basic, derivative* unity. But this does not entail that we have any cognition of a persisting *object* or substance as the logical subject of its changing properties, as we do when we perceive a changing material substance in space. The 'paralogistic' fallacy confuses the 'I think' of transcendental apperception, which is merely a necessarily represented *unity in our thinking*, with the putative cognition of a *unified object* of our thinking, that is, of a real thinking substance as the identical subject of its ever-changing thoughts. This is to confuse the unity of a form of representation with the representation of a unified 'immaterial' thing.

So while it is true, for example, that one cannot account for the synthetic unities that are involved in thought and judgment without representing such thoughts as belonging to one's identical thinking self, this does not entail that one has a positive cognition of oneself as a non-successive, simple entity or substance. In fact, Kant suggests that our conception of ourselves as unitary conscious subjects is logically consistent with the bare thought or idea that, considered 'as things in themselves', what we represent (non-spatially) in inner sense as unified minds and what we represent in outer sense as material bodies in space could both – in the sense of 'could' that pertains to merely logical as opposed to real possibility, for Kant – turn out to be modes or aspects of some single, ontologically more basic 'noumenal' reality (A359–60). Or again, in a fascinating passage at A363–4 (including the footnote), Kant argues that since the "identity of the consciousness of Myself in different times is therefore only a formal condition of my thoughts and their connection" and "does not prove at all the numerical identity of my subject" as an object or substance, "a change can go on that does not allow it to keep its identity" – that is, conceived as a 'thing in itself' the so-called 'self' might ultimately be just a *series* or succession or bundle of distinct noumenal substances or 'monads', for example – "and this even though all the while the identical sounding 'I' is assigned to it" (A363). As long as a unified consciousness as a *form of representation* was inherited (i.e. represented) across such a series of noumenal beings, we would never know the difference from within the perspective of our conscious experience as we know it. But as we know, according to Kant such merely logical possibilities must remain entirely empty thoughts for us, and the traditional metaphysicians' attempts to demonstrate the existence of any such ultimate 'unconditioned conditions' or noumena will always embody a fallacious 'logic of illusion'.

The combination of the transcendental and empirical truths that we do know about ourselves, according to Kant, leads only to an *empirically dualist* and *metaphysically agnostic* distinction between our synthetically unified 'inner' mental states in time and outer material bodies in space (including, most importantly, our own bodies). In addition to its formal transcendental role, Kant explains that the 'I think', as actually thought or uttered by me, is "an empirical proposition" in so far as it thereby already (*pragmatically*, as some would put it) "contains within itself the proposition 'I exist'" (B422 n.), although this existential claim holds "merely in regard to my representations in time" (B420). These issues will be explored further in the next chapter in relation to Kant's "Refutation of [Empirical] Idealism".

We should also note, finally, that even the rationalist's fallaciously inferred idea of the self as an immaterial substance or soul, according to Kant, has a legitimate use as a merely *regulative idea of reason*. That is, by thinking of the self 'as if' it were a perfectly identical and simple immaterial soul, Kant argues, we guard against the empiricist's tendency towards the equally fallacious and dogmatic error of "**materialism**" (B420). For the materialists and naturalists, too, are in danger of missing the crucial transcendental point that the *irreducible representational role* of "the simple I" of apperception cannot be accounted for in terms of concepts pertaining to the spatial pluralities with which matter presents us.

In this chapter we have sketched one way of trying to make sense of Kant's complex argument in the Transcendental Deduction, but even this has required us to enter into a forest of complex details. So in closing we should take a brief step back and reflect on what it is that Kant may or may not have achieved by means of his famous Transcendental Deduction.

Assessing Kant's Transcendental Deduction

Kant's Transcendental Deduction has been the subject of particularly heated interpretive disputes in the secondary literature. One of the most frequently discussed interpretations and defences of Kant's central line of argument in the Transcendental Deduction (or 'the Deduction', as I shall frequently refer to it) was that offered by Strawson in *The Bounds of Sense* (1966: esp. pt 2, ch. II, "Objectivity and Unity"; for more on Strawson and Kant, cf. Glock [2003]; and see also Bird [1962] for important insights on the argument of the Deduction that antedated Strawson's). Strawson offered some particularly insightful reflections in defence of Kant's argument, examined above, that there is a necessary conceptual connection between (i) the possibility of the self-ascription of experiences by any thinking subject (the 'I think' of apperception), and (ii) the necessary *objectivity* of experience as represented in rule-determining concepts of mind-independent objects of experience. For example, in contrast to the radical empiricist's ground-level conception of the self as a 'bundle' or stream of perceptions or 'sense-data' (states of consciousness), Strawson interprets Kant's contrasting contention this way:

> What then is implied ... by the potentiality – which must be present in every experience – of awareness of oneself as having it? The very minimum that is implied, Kant must reply, is precisely what the hypothesis of the purely sense-datum 'experience' attempts to exclude. The minimum implied is that some at least of the concepts under which particular experienced items are recognized as falling should be such that the experiences themselves contain the basis for certain allied distinctions: individually, the distinction of a subjective component *within* a judgment of experience (as 'it seems to me as if this is a heavy stone' is distinguishable within 'this is a heavy stone'); collectively, the distinction *between* the subjective order and arrangement of a series of such experiences on the one hand and the objective order and arrangement of the items of which they are experiences on the other.
>
> ... The more fundamental point of the Kantian provisions is that the experiences of such a subject must themselves be so conceptualized as to determine a distinction between the subjective route of his experiences and the objective world through which it is a route. The history of a man, we might say, is – among much else – an embodiment of a temporally extended *point of view* on the world.   (Strawson 1966: 101, 104)

As we have seen, the potential awareness of ourselves as experiencers on the one hand, and our implicit conception of the objective, rule-governed independence of that world from our particular experiences of it on the other, turn out to be co-implicative representational capacities. That is, each form of representation is necessary for the possibility of the other, and so they stand or fall together.

Whatever concepts or rules are thus argued to be necessary for our being able to represent an objective world in this way will thereby be shown to have a unique status within our experience. For they would thus be shown to be necessary (*a priori*) for the very possibility of our having any particular experiences whatsoever, at least in the potentially self-aware sense of 'experience' that we have seen Kant carefully articulate and analyse. In the Metaphysical Deduction, Kant's 'Clue' identified these *a priori* concepts with the twelve categories that he contends correspond to the twelve most basic logical forms employed in our cognitive thoughts about objects in general. In the upcoming 'Analytic of Principles' or 'Transcendental Doctrine of Judgment' to be examined in the next chapter, however, Kant will attempt to demonstrate how and why the objectively valid representation of a mind-independent empirical world in general – which has just been *warranted* for us in general by the Transcendental Deduction – can itself be represented only if the twelve categories are employed in certain specific judgments or principles applied to all possible objects or appearances in space and time. In short, the Principles to be examined in the next chapter will show how objectively valid experience is possible only if certain synthetic *a priori* principles embodying the twelve categories are true of all possible objects of our experience.

Kant's upcoming investigations will thus assume that the transcendental deduction of the general objective validity of the categories has been successful. But has it been? Here I shall consider just one important general form of objection to Kant's strategy of transcendental argumentation as examined in this chapter and as further clarified by Strawson above. (For contemporary debates on the success, or not, of Kant's Transcendental Deduction, see Bieri *et al.* [1979], Förster [1989], Stern [1999].)

The objection put bluntly is this. Even if Kant has succeeded in showing that certain of our conceptions or ways of representing ourselves and the world are necessarily connected to or imply one another, the objection is that this would tell us *only how we must conceive matters relative to certain other of our conceptions*; it would not tell us how *the world* must be. For example, even if our being able to ascribe experiences to ourselves, or perhaps our capacity to make logically structured judgments, were successfully shown by Kant to be possible only if we also conceptually represent the empirical world in general as existing independently of our particular experiences of it, this would only demonstrate something about the ways in which our conceptions of the world or our representational capacities are related to one another. But as Russell ([1912] 1998: 49–50) and more recently Barry Stroud (1968) have objected to Kant and to Strawson respectively (for further discussion and references, cf. O'Shea [2006]; Westphal [2010]), this form of 'transcendental argument' in general would not prove anything about *how the world itself must be* – for example, that it must obey universal laws of nature – but rather only about *what we must believe* about the world relative to certain other of our (admittedly perhaps deep-seated) beliefs about ourselves and about the world. Not only (the objection continues) does this not tell us anything about how the world itself is or must be *per se*; from this perspective it also becomes less clear that Kant has really advanced matters at all beyond Hume's own naturalistic emphasis on the complex structure of our instinctive beliefs about the world, beliefs which are useful and unavoidable but which are not themselves directly *rationally warrantable*.

On this basis critics such as Russell and Stroud (and similarly Hegel before them) have further contended that in this light we can now understand why Kant felt he needed to defend what such critics regard as his thoroughly dubious doctrine of *transcendental idealism* in the first place. As they see it, Kant's unfortunate view that we cannot know objects 'as they are in themselves' but merely objects 'as appearances to us' would seem to provide just the sort of merely subjectively 'constructed', quasi-mental 'objects-as-mere-appearances' to which Kant's transcendental style of argument *would* successfully apply. But again, this would be much to the disappointment of our genuinely realist hopes to have shown something about our knowledge of how the world or reality itself either is or must be constituted.

This is an important and pervasive form of objection to Kant's general transcendental strategy for justifying our alleged *a priori* knowledge of the empirical world. There have been many different ways of attempting to respond on Kant's behalf or to modify his views in a way that preserves some of his core contentions. One common form of response begins by agreeing with the objector that Kant's doctrine of transcendental idealism, at least as traditionally interpreted along 'two-world' lines (see §1.2), ought to be rejected. But it is then often argued that a central core of Kant's analysis in the Transcendental Analytic nonetheless succeeds independently of that incoherent transcendental idealist doctrine by showing that there are certain concepts and principles that play a unique enabling role in explaining how our empirical knowledge is possible. Strawson and Guyer take this general approach to Kant, for example. Furthermore, in a later 1987 article entitled "Kant's New Foundations of Metaphysics", Strawson suggests that Kant's general argument that "there are highly general formal conditions which objects must satisfy in order to become possible objects of human knowledge" does succeed in showing that any "attempt to establish how things really are in total abstraction from those conditions will be doomed to failure" (1997: 232–3). This 'Copernican' outlook, Strawson argues, is broadly sustained in the views of the later Wittgenstein and of such leading figures of 'analytic' philosophy as Putnam, Quine, Donald Davidson and Michael Dummett (and we might add Sellars, Robert Brandom and John McDowell, too; cf. O'Shea 2006), while entirely rejecting Kant's (allegedly) incoherent doctrine of transcendental idealism.

Perhaps from this last perspective, however, one might alternatively come to question Strawson's own 'two-world' interpretation and consequent rejection of Kant's transcendental idealism itself (again see §1.2, as well as the final section of Chapter 3 on the 'problem of affection'). For along the above lines it might be contended that Kant's transcendental 'restriction' of our theoretical knowledge to objects as 'appearances' that conform to the *a priori* conditions of human sensibility and understanding does not really restrict us *from* any other kind of would-be superior kind of intelligible theoretical knowledge of so-called 'ultimate reality'. That latter speculative metaphysical hankering for an 'unconditioned' reality involves precisely the inevitable transcendental illusion of pure reason that Kant was centrally concerned to diagnose. Kant's aim was to *redirect* that inevitable urge of reason away from traditional speculative metaphysics and towards a proper recognition of the true *practical* or moral significance of reason's own self-generated ideals pertaining to unconditioned 'things in themselves', in particular as embodied in the indispensable assumption of our own free will and in pure practical reason's conception of the highest good (and hence, he argues, the 'practical postulates' of God and immortality, too).

Thus once one properly emphasizes (i) the extreme generality of Kant's premises, which would apply to any sensorily affected, minimally self-aware, concept-using being; and once, in so doing, one also emphasizes (ii) the resulting *emptiness* of content for us of any attempt to establish claims about so-called 'things in themselves' independently of the general formal conditions on human knowledge that Kant seeks to defend; then the idea becomes more plausible that Kant's empirical realism of the humanly knowable world is first-rate knowledge of the *real* world in its only intelligible theoretical form. The objections to Kant's transcendental idealism are, from this point of view, seen to be without any real fangs.

What Kant's transcendental idealism does properly restrict us from, on this latter view, is any attempt to understand our practical agency and our free actions, our selfhood and the validity of our moral claims and religious beliefs, on the model of a putative *theoretical cognition* of such 'objects', whether the latter are (mis)conceived as 'material' or as purely 'spiritual' objects. As Kant would have predicted, such theoretical models of human agency and of the nature of morality itself continue to be the constant temptation of scientists, philosophers and religious believers alike. Kant's stress on the unconditioned, purely intelligible, noumenal 'timelessness' of our free agency, on this arguably more charitable understanding of his transcendental idealism, does not involve a philosophical commitment to the existence of ourselves or of any other being as special objects or entities that exist *outside* of time and space as well as within them, although that *idea* or thought has certain legitimate, merely regulative uses within experience, Kant argues. It is the contention, rather, that the practical perspective of our intentional agency has an unconditional objective validity, and generates ideal rational hopes and aspirations, that cannot intelligibly be either validated or invalidated when viewed from the theoretical perspective of our unending scientific cognition of nature, including our own psychological nature. Kant's transcendental idealism, on this view of its nature, was primarily a sophisticated defence of the mutual irreducibility and the joint validity of precisely those two human conceptual standpoints on the nature of reality: the standpoint of our scientific theoretical cognition of objects in nature, and the standpoint of our free rational agency and moral ideals. I think there is much to be said for this general form of interpretation and defence of Kant's transcendental idealism

But no doubt to many philosophers the above remarks will not seem to have adequately responded to the objector's initial worry that in the Transcendental Deduction itself – however congenially his transcendental idealism is interpreted – Kant's conclusions about objectivity and about necessary rules governing objects and so on, are only shown to be necessary relative to the possibility of certain very general features of our own forms of experiencing and of verifying our claims about the world in general. For this reason the objector might continue to insist that Kant's so-called 'empirical realism' only succeeds in articulating certain conditions on what is *verifiable-by-us* about reality, rather than delivering any conclusions about the necessary structure of the empirical world itself. I am inclined to think, however, that for the reasons given above the objector at this point is pressing a worry that has been stripped of any clear meaning. Given the admittedly intractable nature of this last stand-off, however, it is not surprising that philosophical debates about 'realism and anti-realism' and about the limits of human knowledge, both in general and in relation to Kant, remain as heated today as they have ever been. My aim here has been to convey some of the senses in which Kant's unique transcendental approach to those problems continues to be a lively presence in those debates, and to suggest, however briefly, some of the lines along which his view might be defended.

Fortunately, we shall understand Kant's transcendental approach much better once we have explored the actual application of Kant's categorial principles of pure understanding throughout the next chapter. For it is in these *'application-deductions'*, as I shall call them, that we shall find specific arguments designed to show that the application to experience of each of the categories is necessary for the very possibility of our experiencing a world of objects in space and time. Only then will we understand what Kant really means when he says that his Transcendental Deduction has shown that, "as exaggerated and contradictory as it may sound", the "understanding is itself the source of the laws of nature" (A127).

CHAPTER 5

ONE LAWFUL NATURE

> All true metaphysics is drawn from the essence of the faculty of thinking itself.   (Kant, *MFNS*, 187=4:472)

> The fall of a stone, the motion of a sling, resolved into their elements and the forces manifested in them and treated mathematically, produced at last that clear and henceforth unchangeable insight into the structure of the world which, with continued observation, one can hope will always be extended while one need never fear having to retreat.
>   (Kant, *Practical Reason*, 270=5:163)

5.1 APPLYING CATEGORIES TO THE WORLD IN THE PRINCIPLES OF PURE UNDERSTANDING

Let us begin our explanation of Kant's Principles of Pure Understanding with a partial formulation of the result of the Transcendental Deduction in terms of the following conditional. This conditional expresses Kant's idea, discussed in the previous chapter, that the categories are shown to be objectively valid in so far as they are shown to be conditions that are necessary for the possibility of experience:

> Experience is possible *only if* the categories are objectively valid. (The Deduction)

With respect to the left-hand side of this conditional, in the previous chapter we saw that Kant's analysis of what is to be meant by 'experience' is conducted from several different directions, but in particular it involved *the concept of an object of sensory experience for a potentially self-aware experiencer.*

With respect to the right-hand side, we saw that the categories succeed in representing an objective world by being *rules or laws* that determine what is necessary and possible for the objects that are thereby represented.

On the assumption that he has established these results in the Deduction, Kant's primary task in the next sections of the First *Critique*, to be examined in this chapter, is to investigate how exactly the categories of understanding are *applied* to empirical objects or appearances in judgment. "If the understanding in general is explained as the faculty of rules, then the power of judgment is the faculty of **subsuming** under rules, i.e., of determining whether something stands under a given rule" (A132/B171). Because the categories are objectively valid *a priori* concepts, however, "the peculiar thing about transcendental philosophy is this: that in addition to the rule (or rather the general condition for rules), which is given in the pure concept of the understanding, it can at the same time indicate *a priori* the case to which the rules are to be applied" (A134/B174–5). Kant's remark that "the rule" given in a pure concept or category is really a "general condition for rules" will later be seen to reflect the fact that the categories and principles of pure understanding are *meta-conceptual*: they are concepts of kinds of concept or kinds of rule. That is, Kant's categorial principles, such as the principle of causality, will turn out to be second-order conceptual rules that normatively classify what it takes for any first-order empirical concept or rule – such as *x is burning* or *x exploded* or *x warms y* – to fulfil the representational role required by that particular *a priori* category (in this case, what it takes for a concept to be an objective *causal* concept).

Chapter 1 of the "Transcendental Doctrine of Judgment (or Analytic of Principles)" is "On the Schematism of the Pure Concepts of the Understanding" (A137/B176ff.), while Chapter 2 is on the "System of all Principles of Pure Understanding" (A148/B187ff.). The Schematism provides the most generic, comprehensive, yet nonetheless sensorily contentful rules for the application of both pure and empirical concepts to objects (A140–41/B179–80). Such schemata turn out to be *a priori* rules determining the intuitable *temporal* characteristics of sensible objects. The longer 'Principles' chapter includes the Axioms of Intuition, Anticipations of Perception, Analogies of Experience and Postulates of Empirical Thought (including the Refutation of Idealism). Here Kant provides what I have called 'application-deductions'. They are designed to prove that specific synthetic *a priori* principles that incorporate the temporally schematized categories are necessary for the possibility of our representing an objective, lawful world of empirical objects in time and space. Since Kant holds that our rational entitlement to the latter has already been secured by the Deduction, our entitlement to apply these synthetic *a priori* principles to experience will thereby also be established.

Schematizing the categories

Kant opens the Schematism with the following explanation, in which the idea that '*x* is homogeneous with *y*' means (at least) that '*x* shares something in common with *y*':

> In all subsumptions of an object under a concept the representations of the former must be **homogeneous** with the latter, i.e., the concept must contain that which is represented in the object that is to be subsumed under it, for that is just what is meant by the expression 'an object is contained under a concept'. Thus the empirical concept of a **plate** has homogeneity with the pure geometrical concept of a **circle**, for the roundness that is thought in the former can be intuited in the latter. (A137/B176)

Suppose one has an empirical cognition of a particular circular plate, in the perceptual judgment: 'This plate is circular'. In this case, Kant suggests, we can understand why the sense-perceived plate is correctly subsumed under the pure geometrical concept of a circle that is constructible in pure intuition. The conceived circularity that is predicated of or 'synthesized' with the empirical concept of the plate is also a directly intuitable feature of the plate. In this case the relevant empirical feature of the plate is one that is also 'constructible' in pure mathematical intuitive thought, in what Kant in the Deduction called the *pure productive imagination* (cf. A118–25, and the "figurative synthesis" of B151–2).

The general issue here is in effect a version of the old problem of the 'one and the many', of universals and particulars. In this case that problem takes the form: how is it possible for general concepts to be correctly applied to or subsume all and only the particular objects that 'fall under' those concepts? Concepts, as we know, are representations of general kinds and properties of objects, whereas a sensory intuition is the direct presentation of some particular object. Having briefly suggested above how pure geometrical concepts (e.g. of a circle) can be 'homogeneous with' and applied to empirically intuited objects, Kant also raises the question of how general empirical concepts, such as the concept of a dog, are applicable to particular perceived dogs. Looking up 'dog' in the *Oxford English Dictionary*, for example, we find: "A domesticated carnivorous mammal, **Canis familiaris** ..., which typically has a long snout, an acute sense of smell, non-retractile claws, and a barking, howling, or whining voice." In order to *apply* this general concept, however, one has to learn how to *perceptually recognize* that a particular object is a dog. The empiricist aspects of the thought of Locke, Berkeley and Hume compelled them to attempt to explain general conceptual meanings or 'abstract ideas', as they called them, in terms of associated particular image-like 'ideas' of objects. However, since any particular 'idea' of a dog, such as my current mental image of a black poodle, will possess features that are not applicable to dogs in general, those three philosophers struggled to explain how the particular 'ideas' that are copied from our sense impressions of particular dogs can become *general in their representation*, either through some process of abstracting away 'accidental' sensible features, or by the association of particular classes of resembling ideas (e.g. of instances of dogs) with particular words (the word 'dog'). Not an easy task.

Kant's conception of concepts as *rules*, as discussed in Chapter 4, gives him the resources for a more promising approach, although it must be admitted that this general problem remains thorny in Kant, too, and to this day (compare Wittgenstein on 'rule-following'). Kant suggests an answer to the problem in terms of what he calls "the schema of the imagination, as a rule for the determination of our intuition in accordance with a certain general concept" (A141/B180). Pure mathematical concepts, empirical concepts and the difficult case of the pure categories of understanding will all be *schematized* or schematically formulated by means of "the representation of a method" or "general procedure of the imagination for providing a concept with its image" (A140/B179–80). The schema of a concept of an object is thus not itself a particular mental image of an object, contrary to the basis of classical empiricist accounts. Rather, the schema is a general rule or recipe in accordance with which one can generate a perspectival, conceptually informed sensory image of such an object, thereby enabling one to *perceptually recognize* such objects when encountering them. Here one should recall Kant's striking conception in the Deduction of how "the imagination is a necessary ingredient of perception itself" (A120). The faculty of pure productive imagination is really a particular application to sensory intuition of our 'spontaneous' faculty of understanding: our ability to synthetically unify by means of conceptual rules (cf. B162 n.; A119). (For a famous alternative reading of both the A-Deduction and of the Schematism chapter in particular, one that emphasizes passages in which the transcendental imagination can be read as playing an even more fundamental role than the understanding, see Martin Heidegger's *Kant and the Problem of Metaphysics* [(1929) 1997].)

What is required for one to be able to perceptually recognize dogs is the flexible ability to specify the generic determinable concept of a dog (as a four-footed animal, within a certain size range, with a longish snout, able to bark, etc.) by forming or 'drawing in thought' a perspectival image of that appropriate spatial shape, as from a certain point of view, but "without being restricted to any single particular shape that experience offers me or any possible image that I can exhibit *in concreto*" (A141/B180). What this adds to the empiricists' account of the empirical association of past experienced particular images of objects – an important empirical story that is contained *within* Kant's account, too – is the *active* faculty of the pure productive imagination as bringing conceptual rules to bear on the cognitive construction of such perspectival sensory images. The schema is the concept of a kind of object consisting in a rule or recipe for forming appropriate rule-conforming, perspectival spatiotemporal images of such an object. On the one hand, it is the schema as a conceptual rule that guides the productive imagination in correcting for any unwarranted or 'accidental' specifics in the spatiotemporal image as an embodiment of that general rule (not all dogs are black; dogs are not hollow inside; dogs notoriously have backsides, etc.). On the other hand, the particular *images per se* that are thus formed from the sensory materials of experience under the guidance of the schematic rules of the imagination will in their particularity also be a function of one's past experience, and thus the resulting particular images should not be *identified* with the *schema* of imagination itself. In the following passage Kant recognizes that the actual cognitive processes involved in this process are not open to our pre-theoretical inspection, but nonetheless the combined pure and empirical functions of *association*, *imagination* and *understanding* are functionally specifiable cognitive capacities that are demonstrably necessary for the possibility of the resulting epistemic product:

> This schematism of our understanding with regard to appearances and their mere form is a hidden art in the depths of the human soul, whose true operations we can divine from nature and lay unveiled before our eyes only with difficulty. We can say only this much: the **image** is a product of the empirical faculty of productive imagination, the **schema** of sensible concepts (such as figures in space) is a product and as it were a monogram of pure *a priori* imagination, through which and in accordance with which the images first become possible, but which must be connected with the concept, to which they are in themselves never fully congruent, always only by means of the schema that they designate.
> (A141–2/B180–81)

Let us suppose that Kant's account as reconstructed has explained how both *empirical concepts* and *pure mathematical concepts* are 'homogeneous' with our sense experiences, in terms of schematic conceptual rules for the imaginative production of spatiotemporal intuitions and images of objects. Kant now argues that the question of the 'homogeneity' between the *pure categories* of understanding and the sensory objects to which they are applied demands its own unique solution. We can understand how something's being a circle or something's being a dog entails certain requirements and restrictions on the pure or empirical sensorily intuitable properties of such objects – on how they can and cannot 'look' and 'behave' in general, as it were. But as we know, Kant regards Hume as having correctly argued, for example, that the universal and necessary *causal* connection between two types of empirical event involves the concept of a *necessitation* between those types of observable events that is not itself a further observable or intuitable item. Crudely put, we do not 'see' the objective necessity itself, but only the uniformly repeated sequence or 'constant conjunction' of events of those two particular kinds. Nevertheless, Kant has argued in the Deduction that we are rationally entitled to *apply* such *a priori* categories to the objects of experience.

Kant's solution to the problem of the 'homogeneity' of such pure categories with brute sensory experience is roughly as follows. From the Aesthetic and the Deduction we know that (i) all possible sensible objects or appearances, whether inner or outer, necessarily take place *in time*; and yet we also know that (ii) time itself is the *pure a priori form* of all our sensory intuition in general, and as such time is necessarily synthetically unified in one apperceptive experience under the categories. In short, time has both pure and empirical aspects essential to its cognition:

> Now a transcendental time-determination is homogeneous with the **category** (which constitutes its unity) insofar as it is **universal** and rests on a rule *a priori*. But it is on the other hand homogeneous with the **appearance** insofar as **time** is contained in every empirical representation of the manifold. Hence an application of the category to appearances becomes possible by means of the transcendental time-determination which, as the schema of the concept of the understanding, mediates the subsumption of the latter under the former. (A138–9/B177–8)

In accordance with this proposal and with his architectonics, Kant proceeds to present temporal schemata for the four groups of categories, the discussion of which he sums up as follows: "The schemata are therefore nothing but *a priori* **time-determinations** in accordance with rules, and these concern, according to the order of the categories, the **time-series** [*Quantity*], the **content of time** [*Quality*], the **order of time** [*Relation*], and finally the **sum total of time** in regard to all possible objects [*Modality*]" (A145/B184–5). It will be more helpful, however, to reserve comment on these specific temporal schemata until we come to each of the various Principles of Pure Understanding in terms of which they are applied within experience. For here is where Kant finally attempts to argue for the specific synthetic *a priori* laws of 'time-determination' (the Axioms, Anticipations, Analogies and

Postulates) in terms of which the schematized categories are applied to our sensory experiences. The important general lesson to take away from the Schematism, in any event, is that "the schemata of sensibility first realize the categories", and "yet they likewise also restrict them, i.e. limit them to conditions that lie outside the understanding (namely, in sensibility). Hence the schema is really only the phenomenon, or the sensible concept of an object, in agreement with the category" (A146/B185–6). The pure *unschematized* categories, by contrast, have "only a logical significance [*Bedeutung*] of the mere unity of representation" merely for pure thought, but not for the representation of any *object* of our cognition (A147/B186–7). What is required in order for us to cognize any possible object of experience will now be the subject of Kant's Principles of Pure Understanding.

The 'mathematical' Axioms of Intuition and Anticipations of Perception

The second chapter of the Analytic of Principles is entitled the "System of all Principles of Pure Understanding" (A148/B187). Its first two brief sections, "On the Supreme Principle of all Analytic Judgments" and of "all Synthetic Judgments", respectively, provide some very helpful review of material already explored. This includes some particularly crisp articulations of the central conclusions of the Transcendental Deduction, such as this one: "The conditions of the possibility of experience in general are at the same time conditions of the possibility of the objects of experience, and on this account have objective validity in a synthetic judgment *a priori*" (A158/B197). However, it is the longer third section entitled the "Systematic Representation of all Synthetic Principles of Pure Understanding" that contains Kant's famous attempted proofs of such synthetic *a priori* principles as those of causality and the substantial persistence of matter.

On the assumption that Kant's transcendental deduction of the objective validity of the categories has been successful in its main purpose, we may take ourselves to be rationally entitled to apply the twelve *a priori* categories to the objects of sense experience in general. Kant will now attempt to demonstrate that four kinds of synthetic *a priori* principles of pure understanding (call them 'the Principles'), corresponding to the familiar four groups of categories, can be proven to have objectively valid application in relation to all possible 'appearances' or objects of our experience in time: namely, the Axioms of Intuition (*Quantity*), the Anticipations of Perception (*Quality*), the Analogies of Experience (*Relation*) and the Postulates of Empirical Thinking (*Modality*). Kant's contention will be that these *a priori* principles of 'time-determination' are objectively valid in so far as their application to the objects of our experience can be shown to be necessary for the possibility of our having any experience whatsoever of the various temporal features of experience under consideration in each case.

The rational warrant for judgments that fall under the Principles will thus lie in the fact that only as a result of such concept-applications can the sensible contents of our experience be related to one another, as Kant had put it in the B-Deduction, "*as combined in the object, i.e., regardless of any differences in the condition of the subject*" (B142, italics added). I have taken the liberty of characterizing the Principles as *application-deductions* in order to highlight the fact that the synthetic *a priori* conceptual time-determinations for which they argue, as we shall see, are required precisely in order to fulfil (and hence presume the general validity of) the general objectivity requirements previously established by the Deduction. For "these principles are nothing other than rules of the objective use of the categories" (A161/B200).

The general form taken by all of Kant's application-deductions in the Principles is roughly as follows. His arguments typically begin by highlighting certain purely formal features of our pure *a priori* intuition of time (and of space) that have already been investigated in the Aesthetic, the Deduction and the Schematism. Kant then explores the question of how it is possible – as we know from the Deduction it *must* be – for such purely formal features of our spatiotemporal intuition to be *empirically* represented in the objects or 'appearances' that we encounter in sense experience. For as we saw Kant argue in Chapter 4 above, the possibility of any potentially self-aware experience for sensory beings such as we are – whether such an experience is the mere 'drawing of a line in thought' (i.e. in pure spatiotemporal intuition) or the sensory apprehension of a given house – ultimately requires a 'threefold synthesis', taking place successively through time, of sensory apprehension, productive imagination and conceptual recognition, altogether constituting the conceptual representation of a mind-independent, rule-governed object of experience. A further crucial premise of all of Kant's arguments in the Principles, as it was in the Deduction, is that we do not perceive pure time or pure space *themselves* within experience, but rather only the various empirical realities that we sensorily apprehend *in* time and space. For as we know from the Aesthetic, space and time are relational 'forms' that structure everything that we experience, rather than being themselves peculiar empirical 'contents' given *a posteriori* in sense experience. On these bases, then, each of the Principles is argued to be necessary for the possibility of any objective empirical representation of the relevant *a priori* formal feature of time that is under consideration in the case of each Principle. The overall conclusion is that we are thus rationally entitled to apply those synthetic *a priori* principles to experience.

Kant's arguments in the Principles thus assume the validity of the general representational demands set by the Deduction, and then attempt to show that specific *a priori* categorial principles are required in order to fulfil those demands. The dependence of Kant's arguments in the Principles on premises that he takes himself to have already established in the Aesthetic and the Deduction is frequently left merely implicit in Kant's text and is thus left up to the reader to fill in where needed. In general there are two main questions to ask in relation to each Principle: (i) what is the relevant *a priori* feature of our synthetic intuitive representation of *time* peculiar to the case at hand; and (ii) why exactly is the application of a certain categorial *concept* supposed to be necessary in order to 'find' that feature – by thus representing it *a priori* – within the 'stuff' of our sensory experiences?

The principle of the Axioms of Intuition, as stated in the second 'B' edition, is that "**All intuitions are extensive magnitudes**" (B202; in A it was: "All appearances are, as regards their intuition, **extensive magnitudes**"). Kant will conclude that "this transcendental principle of the mathematics of appearances yields a great expansion of our *a priori* cognition. For it is this alone that makes pure mathematics in its complete precision applicable to objects of experience" (A165/B206). Let us briefly see what shape his argument takes in this case.

A magnitude, for Kant, is a determinate, measurable quantity of something apprehended in a possible experience. Roughly put, an *extensive* magnitude (as opposed to an *intensive* magnitude, to be discussed in the Anticipations) is a quantity that 'extends' across some stretch of time or some region of space, taking up more than a mere instant of time or point in space, and thus consisting of a multiplicity of distinguishable parts. (In fact, 'points' and 'instants' turn out to be merely ideal *limit* concepts or constructions, on Kant's view [A169–70/B211–12].) Kant's frequent references to the "homogeneous manifold" that is involved in any such cognition of a quantity or magnitude basically refers to the sameness-in-kind of the *units* by which we measure such quantities: for example, five minutes or ten miles. Kant's conclusion will be that everything that is empirically real must, as an object of possible sensory intuition, have some extensive magnitude or quantity in time and space (with the proviso that our own 'inner' mental states, as discussed at the end of the previous chapter, are not conceived as spatial items).

The "Proof" (B202) of the synthetic *a priori* principle that "**all intuitions are extensive magnitudes**" is clearly taken by Kant to follow rather directly from the considerations examined in the previous chapter in connection with the idea, as he puts it again here, that "I cannot represent to myself any line ... without drawing it in thought" (A162/B203). "On this successive synthesis of the productive imagination, in the generation of shapes, is grounded the mathematics of extension (geometry) with its axioms" (A163/B204). Since the *a priori* form of all our sensible experience is temporal succession, all possible self-conscious experience requires such a successive synthesis. We thus know *a priori* that our experience will at a minimum be characterized by the successive and synthetically unified apprehension of sensible contents, whatever they may be. The varying qualitative natures or "heterogeneity" of the apprehended realities is of no concern here (this will be addressed in the Anticipations), only the fact that there is a successively apprehended manifold of contents, which is recognizable *as* such a manifold of contents over time only due to our conceptualized consciousness of the combined unity of that manifold. Any potentially self-conscious temporal experience as such requires that the many contents in time – the most general 'schematized' units of experience, as it were – are 'aggregated' in the sense that they are conceptually recognized *as a manifold*. As Kant puts it:

> Since the mere intuition in all appearances is either space or time, every appearance as intuition is an extensive magnitude, as it can only be cognized through successive synthesis (from part to part) in apprehension. All appearances are accordingly already intuited as aggregates. (A163/B203–4)

It is only thereby that a "determinate time-magnitude is generated" (A163/B201). It is the successive "part to part" nature of the synthesis of apprehension that underlies Kant's claim in the Axioms that in this case the "representation of the parts makes possible the representation of the whole" (A162/B203), whereas in the Aesthetic his concern was to emphasize that all empirical cognition takes place within space and time as pure intuitions that present themselves as indefinitely extensive and continuous singular wholes.

Our application of various *empirical* concepts of magnitude (e.g. of so many *inches*) thus makes possible the quantification of appearances by supplying "homogeneous" units for the aggregation of experiential contents; and the most *schematic* representation of a temporal magnitude is composed out of "homogeneous" units of measured stretches of *time*. "The pure **schema of magnitude**", as Kant had put it in the Schematism chapter, "is **number**" understood in the following experientially applicable sense: "Thus number is nothing other than the unity of the synthesis of the manifold of a homogeneous intuition in general, because I generate time itself in the apprehension of the intuition" (A142–3/B182).

Kant's manner of argument in the Axioms of Intuition is likely to strike some mathematicians and logicians as implausible. Since mathematics is a formal and abstract discipline, it can be a tough pill to swallow to conceive the foundations of mathematics as depending on the representational requirements of a potentially self-conscious human experience across time. But there is no way around it: that is indeed the heart of Kant's view, a view that certainly has the virtue – one not exhibited by the views of mathematical 'platonists' – of attempting to demonstrate *how* it is possible that pure mathematics is necessarily applicable to the 'brute' empirical world of sense experience. Kant clarified his position on the relationship between time and mathematics in a letter responding to Johann Schultz on 25 November 1788:

> Time, as you correctly notice, has no influence on the properties of numbers (considered as pure determinations of magnitude), as it may have on the property of any alteration (considered as alteration of a quantum) that is itself possible only relative to a specific state of inner sense and its form (time); the science of numbers, notwithstanding succession, which every construction of magnitude requires, is a pure intellectual synthesis that we represent to ourselves in thoughts. But insofar as specific magnitudes (quanta) are to be determined in accordance with this, they must be given to us in such a way that we can apprehend their intuition successively; and thus this apprehension is subject to the time condition. So that when all is said and done, we cannot subject any object other than an object of a possible *sensible* intuition to quantitative, numerical assessment, and it thus remains a principle without exception that mathematics applies only to *sensibilia*.
> (Kant, *Correspondence*, 284–5=10:556–7)

In the spirit broadly of Aristotle rather than Plato, Kant thus holds that in so far as mathematical relations are to go beyond being mere empty thoughts without content, they must find *application* in the cognition of successively apprehended empirical objects. As he had in fact already emphasized back in the B-Deduction, "all mathematical concepts are not by themselves cognitions, except insofar as one presupposes that there are things that can be presented to us only in accordance with the form of that pure sensible intuition" (B147). The objective reality of pure mathematics is thus ultimately secured only in the light of a "transcendental logic" of temporal consciousness.

Again, since space and time are the *a priori* relational forms in which all empirical contents come, the principle governing the Axioms of Intuition, as will be the case with the other application-deductions, too, is that whatever holds *a priori* "in regard to the synthesis of the form of apprehension is also necessarily valid of the objects apprehended" (A166/B206). As we know, it is the Transcendental Deduction that has already provided the justification for this general form of inference.

The principle of the Anticipations of Perception, as stated in B, is this: **"In all appearances the real, which is an object of the sensation, has intensive**

magnitude, i.e., a degree" (B207). Or as it was stated in the first 'A' edition: "The **principle**, which anticipates all perceptions, as such, runs thus: In all appearances the sensation, and the **real**, which corresponds to it in the object (*realitas phaenomenon*), has an **intensive magnitude,** i.e., a degree" (A165). Earlier in the Schematism chapter, the categories under *quality* (i.e. reality, negation, limitation) had been given the following *a priori*-yet-sensible interpretation in terms of the empirical 'filling of time':

> [There is] a transition from reality to negation, that makes every reality representable as a quantum, and the schema of a reality, as the quantity of something insofar as it fills time, is just this continuous and uniform generation of that quantity in time, as one descends in time from the sensation that has a certain degree to its disappearance or gradually ascends from negation to its magnitude. (A143/B183)

Every moment of time is necessarily 'filled' (*erfüllt*) with some content (*Zeitinhalt*, 'time-content'), since as we have seen time itself just is a pure relational form in which all possible empirical contents are related. Intensive magnitude is the degree of reality given, not in a succession of times (as was the case with the Axioms), but rather at any given instant (A167/B209). But there is no manifold or 'many' to synthesize into 'one' quantity at a mere instant of time-filling sensation. As a result, a close reading of Kant's text reveals that the conceptual synthesis that represents the magnitude of intensive degree at any given moment concerns a manifold that results from considering what necessarily *can* or *could* be the case with any given sensation. The principle of the Anticipations thus starts from the modal or counterfactual assumption that any given sensation "*can* more or less fill the same time" at any given time (A143/B182, italics added). That is, despite the fact that "sensation, fills only an instant" (so that intensive magnitude as such is not extended in time), nevertheless it is an *a priori* formal feature of time that any possible empirical consciousness or time-content is such that it could be or could have been more, or less, intense (compare adjusting the brightness control on a computer screen):

> Now since sensation in itself is not an objective representation, and in it neither the intuition of space nor that of time is to be encountered in it, it has, to be sure, no extensive magnitude, but yet it still has a magnitude (and indeed through its apprehension, in which the empirical consciousness *can* grow in a certain time from nothing = 0 to its given measure), thus it has an **intensive magnitude,** corresponding to which all objects of perception,

> insofar as they contain sensation, must be ascribed an **intensive magnitude**, i.e., a degree of influence on sense.
> (B208, italics added)

> Every sensation is *capable of* a diminution, so that it can decrease and thus gradually disappear. Hence between reality in appearance and negation there is a continuous nexus of many possible intermediate sensations. (A168/B210, italics added)

The putative purely formal feature of time that Kant exploits here in the Anticipations is that any conceivable empirical content of sensory consciousness in inner sense must, as such, have *some* positive magnitude, however small or faint, in contrast to the total *absence* of empirical content in a *pure* intuition. This is Kant's *a priori* ground for the counterfactual assumption that the content of any sensation is such that it could be apprehended as continuously diminishing or increasing over time, and hence for the assumption that any *given* sensation must come in a degree that contrasts with arbitrarily greater or lesser degrees in which it could have come.

It is an important critical question to raise whether this initial assumption, which is supposed to concern a transcendental feature of time as the *a priori* form in which all possible empirical contents must be given, nonetheless illegitimately smuggles in *empirical* assumptions that depend in an essential way on our *a posteriori* knowledge of how our sensations actually can and do vary in degree over time or across cases. How can we know that our sensations can vary continuously in degree if we entirely abstract from our *a posteriori* experience of what happens in various cases? Kant is aware that "there must always be something striking about this anticipation of perception", and in particular "about the possibility of the inner variation of the sensation itself if one abstracts from its empirical quality" (A175/B217). It is not clear (to me), however, how the above *a priori* knowable general contrast between 'filled' empirical intuition and 'empty' pure intuition is by itself sufficient to support the assumption that such sensory fillings (i.e. sensations) must come in a continuously variable degree of intensity, without any appeal to the *a posteriori* fact that sensations *do* come in various degrees of intensity. Kant's intentions, at any rate, are clear: "All sensations are thus, as such, given only *a posteriori*, but their property of having a degree can be cognized *a priori*" (A176/B218).

From this *a priori* premise concerning the intensive degree of all possible 'sensory fillings' of pure time, Kant now argues for a conclusion concerning all possible *empirical realities* corresponding to such sensations. On grounds already established in the Aesthetic and the Deduction, we know that sensation in general is the "merely subjective representation, by which one can only be conscious that the subject is affected, and which one relates to an object in general" (B207). Sensation is thus the subjective correlate of the objective empirical *reality* that affects the subject (B208). (The latter phenomenal reality is of course not to be confused with the empirically empty idea of a 'thing in itself'.) The particular application-deduction that takes place in the Anticipations then requires that the above *a priori* formal feature of sensory consciousness in time must be represented as a rule governing the presented empirical realities or objects of possible experience themselves. The real in appearances, as the *object* of sensation (B207), must therefore itself be represented as an intensive magnitude. That is, since time itself is merely the form in which empirical contents stand related, the empirical realities indicated by the sensory 'fillings' of time must themselves be quantifiable as to their degree of intensive magnitude (greater than 0). The principle of the Anticipations thus requires only that the real in time, *whatever* its empirical nature, must exhibit an intensive magnitude of some degree: "the real, which corresponds to sensations in general, in opposition to the negation = 0, only represents something whose concept in itself contains a being, and does not signify anything except the synthesis in an empirical consciousness in general" (A175/B217).

This argument raises questions about the nature of the relationship between sensation and "the **real**, which corresponds to it in the object (*realitas phaenomenon*)" (B207), and thus about the soundness of Kant's argument from premises concerning what is (allegedly) necessarily true of our sensations to what is therefore supposed also to be necessarily true of the realities that 'correspond to' our sensations in the object. For example, even if we accept Kant's initial contention that sensation as such necessarily "has an **intensive magnitude**" (B208), why does it follow that any corresponding empirical object that *causes* our sensations (i.e. by affecting our senses) must itself necessarily have an intensive magnitude? Surely Kant would not want to rule out on *a priori* transcendental or metaphysical grounds (in Kant's own sense of an 'immanent metaphysics of experience') the *empirical* hypothesis in physics that an increase in the intensive magnitude of a sensation of heat might be due, *not* to any increase in intensive magnitude in any reality in the corresponding object, but rather (say) to an increase in the rapidity of motion of the object's otherwise unchanging constituent particles or atoms?

There are difficult issues here, but we should note Kant's statement in the Anticipations that in relation to its synthetic *a priori* principle he is not "dealing with causality", and in particular not with "reality as cause (whether of the sensation or of another reality in appearance, e.g., an alteration)" (A168–9/B210). Kant pauses to raise this sort of causal consideration only in order to give an empirically grounded example of such a corresponding "degree of reality" in physical objects: in this case, in the Newtonian physicist's conception of an object's instantaneous "moment of gravity" (A168–9/B210) "or weight" (A173/B215). Kant also cites colour and warmth as examples of sensations with intensive degree without pausing to explore the empirical question of what might be the physical realities corresponding to such sensations that thus necessarily also admit of variance in intensive degree (A169/B211). It is important to recognize that in the strictly *a priori* investigations of the First *Critique* – as opposed, for example, to the 'mixed' empirical and transcendental metaphysical inquiries of Kant's subsequent *Metaphysical Foundations of Natural Science*, about which more later – the transcendentally justified notion of *the real* that "corresponds to" sensation is left entirely indeterminate as to its empirical content. Perhaps the force of the objection raised in the previous paragraph could be diminished if one began by recognizing that Kant's transcendental conclusion in the Anticipations directly concerns the corresponding empirical realities not in so far as they are *causes* of our sensations, but rather in so far as their contents are necessarily *cognized* in terms of the sensations in us that are 'worked up' into the concept of an empirically real object of experience.

I shall not pause to pursue this particular issue further here, but our brief foray into some of the details of Kant's conception of empirical reality will be continued during the course of the rest of this chapter, as we now move from the 'mathematical' to the 'dynamical' principles of pure understanding. Two further points should at least be mentioned before leaving the Axioms and Anticipations, however.

First, Kant holds that the mathematizable "continuity" of space and time as "*quanta continua*" follows from the above mathematical principles of pure understanding. For example, it follows that 'points' of space and 'instants' of time are not ultimate indivisible entities (cf. Kant's Antinomies), but rather every stretch of space or time is necessarily perceptually cognized as divisible into endlessly smaller spaces and times, with points and instances in every case being "only boundaries [or limits], i.e., mere places of their limitation" (A169/B211). So all "appearances whatsoever are accordingly continuous magnitudes, either in their intuition, as extensive magnitudes, or in their mere perception (sensation and thus reality), as intensive ones" (A170/B212).

Second, Kant argues that from the "infinite gradation of ever lesser degrees" in the sensory 'filling' of time it follows that no perceptual experience could ever "*prove* an entire absence of everything real in appearance, i.e., a proof of empty space or of empty time can never be drawn from experience" (A172/B214, italics added). Note, however, that Kant is not here attempting to prove on *a priori* philosophical grounds that no 'vacuum' or materially empty space can ever be coherently hypothesized to exist in nature by physicists, for example. Rather, he is arguing that it follows from the Anticipations that no such physical hypothesis of empty space or time could ever be shown to be necessary on *a priori metaphysical* (i.e. transcendental philosophical) grounds having to do with the nature and possibility of experience (see A172–5/B214–16). As Kant later remarks during his argument in the Third Analogy on simultaneous material 'coexistence', "I do not in the least hereby mean to refute empty space; that may well exist where perceptions do not reach, and thus where no empirical cognition of simultaneity takes place; but it is then hardly an object for our possible experience at all" (A214/B261; but cf. A229/B281–2; see also Falkenstein [1995: 203–16]).

In the application-deductions contained in the Axioms of Intuition and the Anticipations of Perception Kant has attempted to demonstrate that the application of synthetic *a priori* principles of extensive and intensive quantitative magnitude to all possible objects of experience is rationally warranted. The justification ultimately traces back, as we saw earlier, to the idea that only if such an application of *a priori* concepts to the objects of experience is warranted in general is our potentially self-conscious sensible experience possible at all. The proofs of the two *constitutive* (as opposed to *regulative*) 'mathematical' (as opposed to 'dynamical') principles of quantitative and qualitative magnitude have thus attempted to show how it could be possible – indeed, why it is necessary – that the sensible world with all its multifarious and heterogeneous content is nonetheless throughout directly "constituted" in a way that warrants the application to it of principles of pure and exact mathematics. This is a striking conclusion. To put it in sweeping historical terms, the eternal mathematical forms and archetypes that had been exalted in Plato's intelligible realm of non-sensible noumena have turned out to have a very different home. Brought down to earth, so to speak, they have been 'deduced' to be determinations and applications of the *a priori* necessary forms of sensibility and understanding that constitute any humanly experienceable world of sensible phenomena in space and time.

5.2 SUBSTANCE AND CAUSALITY, SELF AND NATURE: A METAPHYSICS OF EXPERIENCE

Throughout the previous chapters we have seen that two of the most important principles, not only of common sense and theoretical science, but also of traditional speculative metaphysics, have always been: (i) the principle that persisting *substance* necessarily underlies all the changes we observe in the world; and (ii) the principle that each happening or event in the world necessarily has some determining *cause*. In the three Analogies of Experience, Kant now famously attempts to prove that the principles of substance and causality, as well as a third principle concerning mutual causal interaction, are in fact synthetic *a priori* principles that necessarily apply to, and are restricted to, the world of possible sense experience in space and time. In particular he will argue that these principles are necessary for the possibility of our experiencing three objective temporal features of any experienceable world, namely, the "three modi of time" of "persistence [or duration], succession, and simultaneity" (A177/B219). Kant's overall arguments in these cases will again take the form of what I have called 'application-deductions', and as such they are ultimately based in part on premises supplied from earlier conclusions in the Aesthetic, the Deduction, and the Schematism.

In an important introductory section Kant states the general principle of the Analogies of Experience as follows: "**Experience is possible only through the representation of a necessary connection of perceptions**" (B218); or in A: "As regards existence, all appearances stand *a priori* under rules of the determination of their relation to each other in **one** time" (A176). Kant's "Proof" of this general principle articulates several of the key premises that are common to each of the three Analogies, several of which I have briefly discussed above in connection with the general idea of the Principles as 'application-deductions'. Accordingly, after emphasizing (i) the necessary role of the transcendental unity of apperception in experience and in particular its requirement of a synthetic *a priori* unity, under objectively valid concepts, of all the manifold of possible empirical consciousness in time; as well as (ii) the fact that nonetheless "time itself cannot be perceived" or intuited directly in the given empirical contents of experience (A176/B219); Kant concludes that the:

> **synthetic unity** in the temporal relation of all perceptions, **which is determined** *a priori*, is thus the law that all empirical time-determinations must stand under rules of general time determination, and the analogies of experience, with which we will now deal, must be rules of this sort. (A177–8/B220)

In this introductory section Kant also further clarifies the distinction between the *constitutive principles* of the ('mathematical') Axioms and Anticipations, and the *regulative principles* of the ('dynamical') Analogies and Postulates. Kant later in the *Critique* introduces a *second* 'constitutive–regulative' distinction according to which all four of the pure principles of understanding just named are constitutive of the *a priori* form of our experience in general, when contrasted with the *merely regulative maxims of reason* (see A664/B692; we encountered these regulative maxims toward the end of Chapter 2). The general idea that will be common to both distinctions, I suggest, is that regulative principles or regulative maxims entitle us to make certain *existence claims* about objects or appearances that go beyond what can be shown to constitute the *a priori* form of all possible empirical intuitions (in relation to the first constitutive–regulative distinction), or beyond the *a priori* form of every possible experience of objects in general (in relation to the second constitutive–regulative distinction). As Kant puts the general point, *the existence of appearances cannot be constructed a priori* (cf. A179/B221–2), but nonetheless certain 'regulative' principles of understanding and maxims of reason concerning the existence of appearances can be rationally warranted in general, as necessary for the possibility of experience.

For example, the regulative principle of causality in the Second Analogy will entitle us to judge that, necessarily, *something* must have existed in the preceding appearances that was sufficient to cause, for instance, the shattering of this window here and now; but we cannot determine merely on *a priori* grounds, independently of experience, *what* that particular cause must have been or must be like. By contrast we *can* 'anticipate' *a priori* that every possible object of empirical intuition, simply as something that is to be directly presented to us, will be *constituted* by a form and a content that are necessarily subject to quantification as to their extensive and intensive magnitudes (i.e. the Axioms and Anticipations). In the concluding chapter below a structurally similar but different contrast will be seen to obtain in the case of the *second* constitutive–regulative distinction concerning the 'regulative maxims of reason' to be met later on (for example, in the "Appendix to the Dialectic"). According to this latter contrast between the principles of understanding and the maxims of reason, *all four* of the Principles of Pure Understanding can be shown, *a priori*, to *constitute* the *lawful form* that every possible object of our experience must take. In this case, the 'merely regulative' maxims of reason will by contrast entitle us to conclude only that nature itself must exhibit (i.e. there must *exist*, if our experience is to be possible) at least *some* degree of uniformity in its discoverable empirical details (for example), but *how much* or *what kind* of empirical uniformity actually exists in the appearances in nature is something that is beyond our power to determine merely *a priori*. (For further details, see O'Shea [1997] and the concluding chapter below.)

In the case of both contrasts, in sum, the *regulative* principles are the ones that justify certain *indeterminate existence claims* about empirical realities (e.g. about *something* having caused a given event to happen, or about *some* degree or other of empirical uniformity or systematicity existing in nature), the nature of which cannot be 'constructed' merely *a priori* but rather requires empirical hypotheses and discoveries to determine. My hope is that the nature of both of Kant's 'constitutive–regulative' distinctions will have become more clear by the time we are done.

But let us turn now to the Analogies of Experience themselves. Roughly put, Kant explains that these regulative principles are called philosophical 'analogies' in a way that is comparable to the *mathematical* "qualitative analogy" that '*a* is to *b* as *c* is to *x*'. In transcendental philosophy as opposed to mathematics, the general idea is that on the basis of some things that are known or directly 'given' in experience we can also thereby determine *a priori* at least the *relation* to something else (*x*) that must exist in nature, although we are not in a position to determine merely *a priori* what kind of object *x* is: "although I [thus] have a rule for seeking it in experience and a mark for discovering it there" (A179–80/B222–3). We shall see what all this means in due course. (For an excellent discussion of Kant on 'analogy' in this context, see Callanan [2008].)

The First Analogy: the persistence of substance through all change

The "**principle of the persistence** [or 'permanence', *Beharrlichkeit*] **of substance**" is stated in the first edition as follows: "All appearances contain that which persists (**substance**) as the object itself, and that which can change as its mere determination, i.e., a way in which the object exists" (A182). In the second edition the principle is restated this way: "In all change of appearances substance persists, and its quantum is neither increased nor diminished in nature" (B224). In the Schematism Kant had expressed the '*a priori* sensible interpretation' of the category of substance, that is, in terms of experienceable reality in time in general, as follows: "The schema of substance is the persistence of the real in time, i.e., the representation of the real as a substratum of empirical time-determination in general, which therefore endures while everything else changes" (A143/B183). Since Kant holds that the idea of 'immaterial substances' or souls is demonstrably problematic (as we saw in relation to the Paralogisms at the end of Chapter 4), it is not surprising that in the course of the First Analogy he will identify 'the real' that is persisting substance with *matter* in space. As he puts it a bit later on in the Principles, we do not "have anything persistent on which we could base the concept of a substance, as intuition, except mere **matter**" (B278, in the Refutation of Idealism). Let us take a moment to peek still further ahead, for clarity's sake, to Kant's eventual conclusions about material 'substance' or 'substances' in writings after the First *Critique*, since this might prove to shed some light on his highly condensed and much disputed argument in the First Analogy.

When Kant later moves beyond the non-empirical domain of the First *Critique* and seeks to apply its synthetic *a priori* principles to empirical reality in the *Metaphysical Foundations of Natural Science*, it turns out that with the single additional empirical assumption that matter involves *motion* in space (motion, Kant argues, being the only means by which our senses are affected by matter in general; *MFNS* 191=4:476), substance as 'persistence of the real' for Kant ultimately turns out to be *matter as the movable in space*. For example, a physical body with its constituent parts 'acting in mass' is an instance of a persisting material substance, for Kant, and in this sense Kant frequently uses 'count nouns' to refer to substances as individuated, countable objects. More comprehensively, however, Kant also uses 'mass terms' to characterize this same persisting substance-as-matter as a 'substratum' of physical stuff. In *Metaphysical Foundations of Natural Science*, Kant argues that this matter composes an experienceable 'material space' that is always perceived against the background of potentially wider material spaces, and so on without end. (Interestingly, Kant in fact constructs the *regulative idea* of an 'absolute space' out of this sequence; cf. *MFNS* 264–9=4:558–63.)

Furthermore, in *Metaphysical Foundations of Natural Science* Kant argues that this material substance necessarily 'fills' any sensible space to an intensive degree, and this turns out to be the first and most general *empirical instantiation* of 'the real' that was first discussed in relation to the Anticipations of Perception. The 'filling' of space with substance-as-movable-matter, Kant argues, is necessarily due to *repulsive forces* and counteracting *attractive forces* that he contends must be operative across any experienceable physical universe in space (this is a conception of the 'relative' rather than 'absolute' *impenetrability* of any material body). This is all part of Kant's eventual *a priori metaphysics of nature* as foundational for natural science, as argued in *Metaphysical Foundations of Natural Science*, a topic that is beyond our scope to further examine here. It is important, however, to be aware of what kind of empirical reality Kant sees as the most general and necessary instantiation of the synthetic *a priori* principles that he defends in the First *Critique* (for more on this topic see Butts [1986]; Friedman [1992]; O'Shea [1996b]; and Watkins [2001]).

So that is the concept of material substance that Kant eventually develops on the basis of the Principle of the Persistence of Substance to be proved in the First Analogy. In previous chapters we have seen why the very idea that *all changes are necessarily alterations of persisting substance* is a synthetic *a priori* (or '*every ... must ...*') principle that, as Hume argued, cannot be warranted either by merely analytic logical considerations or by the data given *a posteriori* in sense experience. So the '*quid juris*' question of the source of our rational entitlement to *apply* such a principle to experience has arisen, and in the Aesthetic, Deduction, and Schematism Kant has defended some of the premises needed finally to carry through this justification or 'application-deduction', as I have called it. Before turning to Kant's argument for the *a priori* necessity of the persistence of substance throughout all experience, let us first continue with some further clarifications of what he means in the First Analogy by his particular version of the traditional concept of 'substance' and related terms.

Kant's basic category of *substance*, as we know from the Metaphysical Deduction, corresponds to the logical subject-predicate form of judgment, S is P. This logical form of judgment, when employed in the thought of an object of our cognition, is the thought of "something that could exist as a subject but never as a mere predicate" (B149; cf. A147/B187, A80/B106). As Kant explains, "if I bring the concept of a body under" the category of substance, then "it is determined that its empirical intuition in experience must always be considered as subject, never as mere predicate; and likewise with all the other categories" (B129). A substance for Kant is thus what I shall call an *ultimate subject* of properties: a substance is, so to speak, the 'unhadhaver' of the various changing empirical qualities and relations (e.g. changing colours, shapes, motions, forces, etc.) that positively characterize or 'determine' the substance over time.

In the First Analogy Kant stresses that these changing 'empirical determinations' are the ways "in which a substance is positively determined" (A187/B230). Substance, for Kant, is not a propertyless 'bare substratum' as it was for Locke (on traditional readings). Substance for Kant does not stand in a *real* relation of 'underlying' to the changing properties that 'inhere' in it (i.e. inherence is not a real relation either). The substance and its accidental determinations are not separate or separable real existences. Rather, as we might put it, there is just the *substance-as-positively-determined* in different ways over time. Or as Kant puts it, it is only "thanks to the conditions of the logical use of our understanding" that it is "unavoidable for us to abstract out, as it were, that which can change in the existence of a substance while the substance remains" (A187/B230). The substance is conceived as *one identical object* ("the object itself", as Kant put it above) that persists throughout all the changes in its positive characteristics, and the substance–accident 'relation' is merely a logical relation as opposed to a real relation between two separable ontological existences. If we were to suppose that a dog is a material substance, for instance, then the dog would be that which persists throughout all the changes in the qualities and constituents that fully make up the dog throughout its life. So the category of substance "stands under the title of relations, but more as their condition than as itself containing a relation" (A187/B230).

By the 'persistence' of substance Kant makes it clear in the First Analogy that he means to refer to substance as what necessarily persists throughout *all possible changes*, and hence to what persists throughout *all time*. This means that any object that is not 'sempiternal' and does not exist throughout the entire history of the universe will not qualify as a substance, on Kant's view. This will rule out dogs and many other finitely persisting entities that have traditionally been regarded as 'substances' in the philosophical sense of being *ultimate subjects* that bear properties without themselves being predicated as mere properties of anything 'deeper', so to speak. We shall discuss this issue further below.

One more distinction is needed before we attempt to sketch the argument of the First Analogy. Kant distinguishes between an "**alteration**" (*Veränderung*) and a "change" (*Wechsel*) as follows: "Arising and perishing are not alterations of that which arises or perishes. Alteration is a way of existing that succeeds another way of existing of the very same object. Hence everything that is altered is **lasting**, and only its **state changes**" (A187/B230). For example, when a substance persists through an alteration in its colour from red to green, its colour 'changes' in the sense that its state of being red ceases to exist and is replaced by its state of being green. Call the latter a *replacement-change*. Since any substance for Kant absolutely persists throughout all time, and hence never came into existence and never ceases to exist, substances alter but they do not themselves undergo replacement-changes.

As we saw in the previous chapter on the Deduction, all of our experiences, as sensory apprehensions, are in one sense *subjectively successive* in time, as I shall put it. In the representation of substantial permanence Kant claims to have discovered a basic conceptual precondition for representing either an *objectively successive* existence (to be further discussed in the Second Analogy) or an *objectively simultaneous* existence or 'coexistence' (to be discussed in the Third Analogy). To use Kant's example in the Second Analogy (A192/B237), to perceive a ship moving downstream is to perceive an objective succession in time (an event, a happening), whereas the perception of first the front and then the back of an unchanging house is the successive perception of *non*-successive, objectively coexisting parts of a house. Kant's principle of substantial persistence is supposed to be necessary for the possibility of representing *either* of those types of objective states of affairs (i.e. either an objective succession or an objective coexistence):

> Our **apprehension** of the manifold of appearance is always successive, and is therefore always changing. We can therefore never determine from this alone whether this manifold, as object of experience, is simultaneous or successive, if something does not ground it **which always exists**, i.e., something **lasting** and **persisting**, of which all change and simultaneity are nothing but so many ways (*modi* of time) in which that which persists exists. Only in that which persists, therefore, are temporal relations possible (for simultaneity and succession are the only relations in time), i.e., that which persists is the **substratum** of the empirical representation of time itself, by which alone all time-determination is possible.
> (A182–3/B225–6)

So both the successive perception of an objective coexistence (e.g. the parts of a house) and the successive perception of an objective succession (such as a ship movement) require and thus presuppose the possibility of successively apprehending a *duration of existence* in general. The 'application-deduction' of the First Analogy is thus intended to establish that the persistence of substance through change is necessary for the possibility of any cognition of any objective empirical duration through time at all. In very general terms Kant argues that the persistence of substance (or matter) follows from the Deduction (and the Schematism) in conjunction with certain *a priori* formal features of *time*, established in the Aesthetic, as *a singular and unitary representation of all possible existence*. I will call this Kant's 'Single Time' argument.

Its general idea is that persisting matter is required in order to represent empirically the permanency of the single, itself unperceivable time that is the form of inner sense. We have already discussed the sense in which 'time itself' and 'space itself' are not perceivable. Again, the Deduction has shown that the possibility of any potentially self-aware sense-perceptual cognition requires a synthesis of all possible sensible diversity under the concept of a unified *object* of experience. Recall especially our earlier discussion (in §4.2) of the lawful 'modal constraints' of necessity and possibility that must be conceived to govern any object that is capable of being cognized as existing *objectively* in contrast to our particular subjective experiences of it. Temporal ordering, that is, existence at a time and over time, is the *a priori* relational structure of all possible appearances (the Aesthetic). Since, however, time itself is a form rather than an empirically given content, the empirical representation of the formal 'modes of time' can be achieved only by means of conceptually represented modal constraints on the necessary and possible relations of the given empirical contents themselves.

In the First Analogy Kant now contends that temporal "**duration**", as a "**magnitude**" of "**existence**" through time (A183/B226), can be empirically represented only by means of the concept of persisting substance (or matter). The key question thus becomes *why* it is that the concept of persisting substance is supposed to be required in order to empirically represent any duration of time in existence. In the Aesthetic, Kant had argued for the necessary *unity* or *singularity* of time:

> [Time] has only *one* dimension: different times are not simultaneous, but successive ... Different times are only parts of *one and the same time* ... The infinitude of time signifies nothing more than that every determinate magnitude of time is only possible through limitations of *a single time* grounding it.   (A31–2/B47–8)

Throughout the Analogies of Experience, Kant's emphasis on the one single time, on time as a unitary representation, makes essential reference to the necessary *unity of apperceptive consciousness* (the single 'I think'), and thus (given the argument of the Deduction) to justified objectivity principles in general. For example, any determination as to when something happened that could in principle be determinable as part of *my experience* must in principle bear a determinate relationship to the *now* of my experience. The *a priori* formal feature of time to which Kant here appeals in the First Analogy is that the representation of appearances as ordered in time (an order of 'before-during-after') requires a single time topology. (Kant further argues that it would be incoherent to suppose that this single time-ordering could itself 'change', i.e. undergo a 'replacement-change' in the sense explained above: "For change does not affect time itself, but only the appearances in time ... If one were to ascribe such a succession to time itself, one would have to think yet another time in which this succession would be possible" [A183/B226]. But the claim that time does not 'change' in *this* sense basically reasserts, on different grounds, the idea just defended that time, as the form of our unitary experience, is necessarily a *single* system of ordered relations of simultaneity and succession.)

Given that "time cannot be perceived by itself" (B225), the 'Single Time' argument now takes the familiar form of an application-deduction. In this case, the singularity of the 'unchanging' time-order can only find its representation as an *a priori* rule or law (a modal constraint) governing the *empirical* contents themselves. Kant thus concludes that in order to empirically represent either simultaneity or succession, and so *a fortiori* any possible duration, all possible changes of content in experience must be conceived to be the merely changing determinations or alterations of a single persisting substance (or aggregate of substances – in short, a *matter-in-space*) that never itself 'changes', that is, never itself ceases to exist only to be replaced by something else. The *a priori* conceptual constraint of *substantial persistence through change* is thus claimed to be the only way to fulfil the demands set ultimately in the Deduction. Kant's Single Time argument in the opening paragraphs of the First Analogy can thus be summed up, in rough terms, as the following application-deduction:

(1) The perceptible items of experience must in general be conceived to stand in objective relations independent of the subjective features of my apprehension of them. (This follows from the Deduction.)
(2) *A priori* formal principles of *time* (as form of inner sense) must therefore find representation in the contents of experience. (This follows from (1) and the Schematism.)
(3) That time is a *single* 'unchanging' ordering of all possible experienceable contents, determinable as before/during/after, is an *a priori formal*

feature of time as the form of inner sense. (This was discussed above in relation to the Aesthetic and the Deduction, as well as in relation to the idea that 'time itself cannot change'.)

(4) Time itself, and so *a fortiori* its necessary singularity and 'unchangeability', cannot be perceived. (As discussed earlier, time is a form, not a content.)

(5) Therefore, we must judge *a priori* that all possible changes in the perceptible contents of experience are changing modifications or alterations of some single ('unchanging') substance or matter that persists throughout those changes.

On this simplified reconstruction of what I have called Kant's Single Time argument in the First Analogy, the representation of an identical persisting substance through change is necessary for the possibility of representing the necessary single temporal ordering of all possible coexistent and successive existence. Put loosely, we need substance to stand as the empirical correlate of the single unchanging time, since time (as a pure form) cannot be perceived in itself.

However, even if the above is taken to represent Kant's main intended argument in the opening paragraphs of the First Analogy, commentators have rightly sought further resources in the text of the First Analogy in the attempt to fill out why exactly the *persistence of substance* is really supposed to be necessary for the possibility of cognizing any *duration of time* in experience. Why, for example, couldn't a *single succession* of discrete events or 'replacement-changes', that is, without any identical substance persisting through those changes, be sufficient to give us the cognition or experience of an objective duration of time?

That is a fair challenge to Kant, and in fact Hume's view was that a *succession of perceptions* is all that is needed in order to give us the idea of a real duration of time (cf. Hume, *Treatise*, 1.2.3). Commentators have in effect tried to answer this challenge in a variety of different ways based on additional materials in the text of Kant's First Analogy. However, Hume's position just mentioned should remind us of what Kant's answer to this particular challenge would be. Based on Chapter 4 and the Deduction we know that a mere *succession of perceptions*, for example, is insufficient for the *perception of a succession* in the relevant sense, and that the latter requires the concept of an *object* of our ever successive perceptions. Now consider in this light the following passage from the opening paragraph of the First Analogy in A:

> Only through that which persists does **existence** in different parts of the temporal series acquire a **magnitude**, which one calls **duration**. For in mere sequence alone existence is always disappearing

and beginning, and never has the least magnitude. Without that which persists there is therefore no temporal relation.

(A183/B226)

My view is that Kant is here assuming an application of the general requirement of the Deduction for object-identity, just mentioned above, to the particular case appropriate to the First Analogy: here, the alleged cognition of a *succession of vanishing and recommencing existences in time without any identical object* conceived to persist *through* that change. Call such a succession a 'flux'. A mere flux considered alone – that is, without sneaking in any background assumptions about *something* that persists, including one's own body, or even one's own identical Self – is no more a possible object of our cognition, for Kant, than were the mere sequences of representations without the representation *of an object* that were treated in the Deduction, and for essentially the same reasons.

I call Kant's key assumption here the 'No Identity, No Duration' thesis. That is, without the warranted application of the concept of an identical object of our successive representations over time in general (i.e. 'No Identity'), no mere succession or 'flux' of sensible contents alone would be sufficient for us to cognize any sequence whatsoever *as either an enduring unchanging object or as an objective succession* over time (i.e. 'No Duration'). Kant's warranted conclusion, therefore, is that the concept of substantial object-identity and persistence through any 'flux' of sensible contents (whether a 'house case' or a 'ship case', as it were) is necessary for the possibility of cognizing any objective empirical duration in time. This view of Kant's concerning an *a priori* conceptual connection in experience between temporal duration and object-identity contrasts favourably, I believe, with a (seldom noticed) parallel connection posited by Hume between two separate *fictions* of the imagination. On Hume's account, the imagination's fiction of an object-identity through time (*Treatise*, 1.4.2.26–30) rests on another fiction of *temporal duration without change* (*Treatise*, 1.2.5.29), but this turns out to be an uncomfortably tight circle of fictions once one examines it closely. (This issue was the central topic of my 1992 doctoral thesis, "Problems of Substance: Perception and Object in Hume and Kant".)

Most commentators on Kant, however, take an interesting different route and suggest that Kant's key argument occurs towards the end of the First Analogy at A187–8/B230–31. It is suggested, contrary to my reading above, that what Kant is arguing is that the persistence of substance is ultimately required if it is to be possible for us to cognize any *objective change* as such – that is, as an objective succession involving a replacement-change from one state to another – as *distinguished from* the successive perception of unchanging (i.e. objectively coexisting) items such as the parts of a house.

Very roughly, the idea is that only with the assumption that all changes are alterations from one state to another state *of the same persisting substance* can it be possible in principle for us to determine that a change has occurred as opposed to the mere perception of an objective coexistence. I do not myself agree that the First Analogy is concerned primarily with the possibility of the distinction *between* objective change and objective coexistence, but these interpretations are well worth the reader's following up (cf. e.g. Allison 2004: 236–46).

Furthermore, many commentators on Kant's First Analogy have quite reasonably distinguished between what they call the *absolute persistence* (or permanence) as opposed to the merely *relative persistence* of substances, where the former but not the latter are required to exist throughout *all* time (see e.g. Bennett 1966; Van Cleve 1999). The need for such a distinction is felt not only on common sense and traditional philosophical grounds, but also in part because of the seeming implausibility of any direct argument for the absolute persistence of substance throughout all time. The result is that Kant is presented (incorrectly, I believe) as implicitly relying on a two-stage argument of the following kind.

The first stage allegedly involves the attempt to prove the merely relative persistence of some substance or substances throughout any given change, without requiring that a substance, as such, must exist at all times. In a second stage Kant is then portrayed as attempting to infer from that more moderate thesis to the more extreme thesis of the absolute persistence of all substances throughout all possible changes, and hence as existing at all times. Some commentators (such as Bennett) have argued that such an inference would be fallacious. Roughly, from the thesis that 'any given change must be the alteration of some relatively persisting substance or other' it does not follow that 'there must be some absolutely permanent substance of which all possible changes are the alterations'. (Compare the 'quantifier-shift fallacy': from 'every child owns some toy' it does not follow that 'there is some one (mega-) toy that every child owns'.) Others, however, have attempted to defend the validity of Kant's alleged two-stage inference (see esp. Van Cleve 1999: ch. 8).

I have argued elsewhere that no such two-stage argument, whether valid or invalid, is either explicit or implicit in Kant's First Analogy. The 'Single Time' argument and the 'No Identity, No Duration' thesis, as explained above, represent Kant's main intended argument in the First Analogy. But seeing why there is no 'two-stage' view in Kant does require carefully distinguishing, once again, the 'second-order' *a priori* transcendental level from the 'first-order' empirical level of Kant's analysis, which in this case works out briefly as follows (cf. O'Shea 1996b).

The transcendental principle of the persistence of substance that is defended in the First Analogy, as I shall state it, is that *identical substance must persist throughout any possible succession of apprehended sensible contents that may be given to us in experience.* Using an example of such an empirical judgment in the *Metaphysical Foundations of Natural Science*, Kant explains that "if I represent it to myself as *determined in the object* that the stone must be thought only as subject, but hardness only as predicate," then the subject-predicate logical function becomes the pure concept of "*substance* and *accident*" (*MFNS*: 4:475 n.). But of course, we know that wider experience teaches us that hard stones are perishable and undergo destruction and dispersal into smaller constituent materials. So we should, on reflection, consider what would be preserved throughout the latter kinds of changes. Having done so, now take this process of reflection further: suppose one now considers in imagination (or more importantly for Kant, in scientific theorizing, or most importantly, as is done in the First *Critique*, in *a priori* transcendental reflection) what would be preserved throughout all possible kinds of experienceable changes in nature in general.

If we go on in this way to consider ever wider kinds of experiences then, in accordance with the Principle of Kant's First Analogy articulated above, it follows that *for each case* considered separately we must judge that there exists some fundamental kind of matter that would be preserved throughout such an envisaged sequence of changes, *however extensive* such a succession is imagined to be. In the sorts of all inclusive 'nature-of-the-world' hypotheses that are typically considered in ongoing scientific and philosophical inquiry, there will be a variety of conceptions as to what kind of stuff (or what substances or elements) must be lawfully preserved throughout all possible transformations and changes in experience. For example, perhaps it is the atoms or other fundamental elements of things, or energy, or matter-energy, or water (Thales); or Earth–Water–Air–and–Fire (Empedocles); or those plus the eternal species of living things and heavenly bodies (Aristotle); and so on. In short, we are confronted with an ongoing variety of 'best explanatory hypotheses' as to what are the fundamental substances or matters that must be preserved throughout all possible changes.

But as just noted, to get to the transcendental perspective of Kant's First Analogy we must go yet one step 'higher', so speak. What the second-order, non-empirical, *transcendental* context of the *Critique of Pure Reason* asserts is the principle that was just stated a moment ago: namely, that *identical substance must persist throughout any possible succession of apprehended sensible contents that may be given to us in experience.* My view is that none of this, contrary to the various 'two-stage' interpretations of Kant, requires any (same-level) *inference from* an alleged thesis about the 'relative persistence' of 'substances' to Kant's principle concerning the 'absolute persistence' of matter-as-substratum. What is required is a proper grasp of the complex relationships between the *a priori* transcendental principle of the First

Analogy, on the one hand, and our ongoing fallible inquiries into the proper empirical instantiation or realization of that transcendental principle of persisting substance at the empirical level. (I shall also briefly suggest in the concluding chapter that an analysis of Kant's conception of the role of the *regulative maxims of reason* within ongoing empirical inquiry would further support this account of his view.)

Finally, for insight into the question of why Kant restated the principle of the First Analogy in the B-edition in terms of the "quantum" of substance being "neither increased or diminished" (B224), one should begin by consulting a pertinent passage in the *Metaphysical Foundations of Natural Science* in which Kant attempts to prove a "*First Law of Mechanics*: In all changes of corporeal nature the total quantity of matter remains the same, neither increased nor diminished" (*MFNS* 249=4:541). We should recall that this work was published in 1786, just before the B-edition of the First *Critique* in 1787; hence it is particularly relevant to Kant's changed statement of the principle for the B-edition. Kant's application-deduction in this particular case is based on the idea that, as he puts it, "the *quantity of matter*, with respect to its substance, is nothing else but the *aggregate of substances* of which it consists" (*MFNS* 249–50=4:541–2, italics added). Note, by the way, that this last sentence nicely confirms our earlier discussion of the ultimate irrelevance of the '*substances* (count noun)–*substance of* (mass term)' distinction as far as Kant's univocal conception of substance-as-matter is concerned, both in the First Analogy and beyond, and contrary to what some commentators have understandably attempted to argue. In general, the *Metaphysical Foundations of Natural Science* is fertile territory for anyone who is interested in further exploring how Kant's views on substance and causality in the First *Critique* were intended to find their primary empirical realization or instantiation in various 'impure' synthetic *a priori* principles concerning movable material bodies that are subject to universal attractive and repulsive forces pervading all of nature. Which brings us conveniently to the notorious topic of Kant's views on causality.

The Second Analogy: the universal principle of causality in nature

We have discussed the fundamental role of the principle of causality in common sense, science and metaphysics at several points in the preceding chapters, and we need not repeat those discussions here. In particular I shall assume that we now have a firm grip on the details of Hume's sceptical challenge to this alleged synthetic *a priori* principle of pure reason, as explained in §2.1. Kant will now attempt to prove that the objective validity of the principle of causality is necessary for the possible experience of any objective succession in time, that is, for the cognition of any 'happening' or event in nature as such.

In the Second Analogy, Kant states the principle as follows in the first edition: "Principle of Generation: Everything that happens (begins to be) presupposes something which it follows in accordance with a rule" (A188); and then in the second edition: "**Principle of temporal sequence according to the law of causality**: All alterations occur in accordance with the law of the connection of cause and effect." Earlier in the Schematism chapter the "schema of cause" had been stated to be "the real upon which, whenever it is posited, something else always follows. It therefore consists in the succession of the manifold insofar as it is subject to a rule" (A144/B183). How does Kant set about demonstrating the objective validity of this principle?

The 'application-deduction' of the Second Analogy will have something like the following overall form, although the real insights will again be seen to lie in the details of the argument. That all appearances must occur as *either successive or simultaneous* in time, as the *a priori* form of our inner sense, was a result of the Aesthetic. That we are rationally entitled to the *a priori* categorial distinction between *objective* and *subjective time-order* in general was a result of the Deduction and the Schematism. The question that will now gradually come into focus is this: how is it possible for our ever-changing perceptions (the subjective succession of apprehension) to represent the perception of a ship movement, for example (an objective succession), as *opposed to* the successive perception of the parts of an unchanging house (an objective coexistence)? For the mere succession of sensible contents itself considered merely as such, as we shall see, does not determine the relevant difference. Kant's answer will be a clear illustration of *the 'modal' conception of objectivity* that was discussed in relation to the Deduction in §4.2, where the 'concept of an object' was explicated in terms of the idea of *rules* that determine objective necessities and possibilities in the objects as appearance. Let us see how all of this unfolds in the Second Analogy.

As was the case in the First Analogy, Kant once again begins by emphasizing that the "apprehension of the manifold of appearance is always successive. The representations of the parts succeed one another" (A189/B234). I shall again call this the *subjective succession* of our apprehension, for Kant immediately follows it with the question: "Whether they also succeed in the object is a second point for reflection, which is not contained in the first" (*ibid.*). To use the 'house/ship' example that I introduced above in connection with the First Analogy (but which is in fact used by Kant here in the Second Analogy), suppose that Smith's subjectively successive apprehensions are in fact, objectively speaking, the successive representation of the front and then the back of a house, that is, as coexisting parts of an unchanging house. In this case the subjective succession of sensible contents in Smith's apprehension ('front → back') represents what I shall call an *objective coexistence*.

Whereas if Smith is successively apprehending a ship moving downstream, the subjective succession ('upstream → downstream') represents an *objective succession* or change – that is, an *event* – in nature. (To avoid confusion, note that it is true that *Smith's moving around the house* is an objective succession or event, yes. But that is not the perceptible content that is at issue, which is rather: *front of the house, and then back of the house*. The latter 'succession' of sensible contents represents items that are objectively *unchanging* or coexistent: the parts of a house.)

In short, the subjective succession in our ever-successive sensory apprehensions in some cases constitutes, when considered objectively, the representation of an objective coexistence (the parts of a house), while in other cases it represents an objective succession or event (a ship movement).

We can also put this in terms of a familiar example in which the apprehended sensible contents of the subjective succession – call them *A* and *B* – are the same in both cases. You are sitting in a train stopped next to another stationary train, and then it appears to you that the adjacent train is slowly departing: there goes *train-car-1 followed by train-car-2* outside your window. Then you are unsure: is it perhaps *your own* train that is departing? Suddenly, when the last car 'goes whizzing by' and you now see the distant fields and hills passing by, you realize that it was all along *your* train that was departing, and that the succession of perceived sensible contents, *car-1 followed by car-2*, was in reality merely the perception of two parts of a stationary train (an objective coexistence) rather than the perception of the event of the other train departing (an objective succession). Kant's question is then this: *what is it that constitutes or makes possible our representation of the objective difference in the two cases?* What makes the latter but not the former the perception or cognitive representation that an *event* has occurred?

The crucial point is that there is a sense in which the mere succession of perceptible contents itself (i.e. *car-1-followed-by-car-2*), considered merely as such, cannot be what determines your representation of the difference between the two cases. For that can be *the same* in the two cases, as indeed it was for a time, from your perspective, in the case just considered. In a deeper transcendental sense we can thus initially philosophically 'suspend' or 'phenomenologically bracket' our judgments and commitments concerning the corresponding difference in the object itself (a method later developed in impressive detail by the great phenomenologist, Edmund Husserl [1859–1938]), and in this sense we can see that the 'connected' sensible contents themselves do not *by themselves* determine the relevant difference. Or as Kant puts it here, with reference to the *imagination* as the faculty that coherently connects our sensory intuitive representations in time in general (but again, we begin by carefully methodologically bracketing or initially prescinding from the objective difference in the two cases):

> I am therefore conscious that my imagination places one state before and the other after, not that the one states precedes the other in the object; or, in other words, through the mere perception the **objective relation** of the appearances that are succeeding one another remains undetermined. (B233–4)

This is yet another manifestation of the point that *time itself cannot be perceived*. Time is a relational form of sensible contents rather being itself a special kind of further content. Objective temporal relations and distinctions are not *given* in the sensible 'data' of perception considered as such. The passage then continues by supplying the relevant difference in *conceptual*, rule-governed content (rather than sensory content or associational processes) that turns out to make all the difference:

> Now in order for this to be cognized as determined, the relation between the two states must be thought [i.e. be conceptualized in a rule] in such a way that it is thereby necessarily determined which of them must be placed before and which after rather than vice versa. The concept, however, that carries a necessity of synthetic unity with it can only be a pure concept of understanding, which does not lie in the perception, and that is here the concept of **the relation of cause and effect**, the former of which determines the latter in time, as its consequence, and not as something that could merely precede in the imagination (or not even be perceived at all). (B234)

This opening passage, which appropriately occurs in Kant's opening reformulation of the "**Proof**" of "**the law of causality**" in the B-edition, contains in compact form most of the crucial ideas in the Second Analogy. So let us continue to dig into it for a while.

Why, as the passage asserts, must "the relation between the two states" (say, *A and then B*) be conceived "in such a way that it is thereby necessarily determined which of them *must* be placed before and which after rather than vice versa" (italics added)? What is the source of this "*must*"? Kant's analysis during the course of the Second Analogy reveals a key difference in our conception of an event (such as the ship case) as opposed to our conception of an objective coexistence (such as the parts of the house). The house case exhibits what Strawson (1966: 133) once helpfully called an "order-indifference": Smith *could* – note the *modal* notion – just as well have looked at the back of the house before the front (*B and then A*). By contrast, there is a different modal notion of *irreversibility* built into Smith's conception of any happening or event, such as a ship's moving from upstream (*A*)

189

to downstream (*B*). In conceiving the latter succession of sensible contents to be the representation of something that *happened* from time t_1 to t_2 (i.e. *ship-upstream-at-t_1-(A)-and-then-downstream-at-t_2-(B)*), Smith is committed to denying the sort of order-indifference that he conceives in the house case. It is *not* true that in this very case of a particular ship-movement, conceived as a succession that *occurred*, Smith conceives that he might just as well have seen the ship downstream (*B*) at the earlier time t_1 and then upstream at t_2. (Of course, ships can also move upstream in general, but that is not the event that is under consideration in this case.)

In fact, in conceiving the contents he perceives, '*upstream-and-then-downstream*', to be something that happened out there, rather than being (as in the house case) merely a product of his own changing perspective on an unchanging scene, Smith implicitly conceptually commits himself to the idea (a modal or counterfactual 'if had … then would have …' idea) that *wherever* he had been situated at time t_1, what he would then have perceived would be determined by, or must at least be consistent with, the fact that the ship was upstream at that time. The point is really a simple one. If a fireworks display really went a certain way, for example, then what everyone in the audience in fact saw, as well as what they *would have seen if* they had been located in a different seat, must be a function of or determined by or "bound to" (A192/B237) the order that really occurred in the fireworks display. So the order of the actual contents apprehended is in this sense conceived to be *irreversible* in the case of the representation of any objective event as such, "making the combination of representations necessary in a certain way" (A197/B242–3), as Kant puts it; whereas, by contrast, there is a modal 'order-indifference' in the case of the contents successively apprehended in the representation of any unchanging scene as such.

But this distinction, though a simple one, is pregnant in its consequences if the next step in Kant's argument is sound (something that is a matter of much controversy among Kant scholars). For suppose that such a modal irreversibility is indeed built into our conceptual cognition of any sequence *as* an objective happening or event: for example, in the conception or perception of a ship as *moving* from upstream to downstream. The crucial question now is: *how is that modal irreversibility represented in the event perceived*? (And similarly in the house case, how is the modality of 'order-indifference', i.e. the 'could have gone either way' aspect, represented in the successively apprehended contents of an unchanging scene?) Do we, for example, *see* the irreversibility in the movement of the ship from upstream to downstream?

Here the ghost of Hume arises with a resounding no. On Hume's view – and in this respect Kant agrees – when one moving billiard ball is about to collide with a stationary one, our belief that the second ball *must* move on contact is not based on any 'sense impression' of an 'objective necessitation' or 'force' between them. Hume's conclusion, as we know, was that our modal beliefs in causal necessitation are simply based on the fact that the past repetition of similar such sequences in past experience led us to form, by our animal nature, habits of expectation that similar cases will also follow suit outside our experience, now and in the future. For Hume, the necessity thus turned out to be a felt compulsion to infer in accordance with past regularity: we subjectively *feel* the necessitation that we 'project' onto the objects.

Kant's answer is that the irreversibility that is part and parcel of our representation of any successively apprehended appearance *as an event* is neither 'seen' in the objects nor (*contra* Hume) 'felt' in oneself, but rather must be *thought as a rule* of necessitation that governs the objects themselves: the later state of affairs (say, *ship downstream*) *had to follow* due to something in the preceding state of affairs itself (in this case, *ship upstream* plus wind, gravity or whatever other empirical factors our hypotheses might bring to bear on the given case). And that rule of objective necessitation just *is* the law of causality! The principle of causality demands that for any given event there must have been something in the preceding event or wider state of affairs that determined that the given event *must* follow (and so *would* follow again, other things being equal, whenever the same or a relevantly similar preceding type of state of affairs obtains). Hence the objective validity of the principle of causality is necessary for the possibility of representing and experiencing any sequence of appearances as an objective event in the first place. Before examining whether what just happened was a sound argument or a sleight of hand, let us see one among the many ways in which Kant expresses this idea during the course of the Second Analogy (the following passage particularly clearly illustrates the structure of what I have been calling 'application-deductions' in the Principles):

> Understanding belongs to all experience and its possibility, and the first thing that it does for this is ... to make the representation of an object possible at all. Now this happens through its conferring temporal order on the appearances and their existence by assigning to each of these, as a consequence, a place in time determined *a priori* in regard to the preceding appearances, without which it would not agree with time itself, which determines the position of all its parts *a priori*. Now this determination of position cannot be borrowed from the relation of the appearances to absolute time (for that is not an object of perception), but, conversely, *the appearances must determine their positions in time for each other*, and make this determination in the temporal order neces-

sary, i.e., that which follows or happens must succeed that which was contained in the previous state in accordance with a general rule. (A199–200/B244–5, italics added)

Now, it is crucial to remember with respect to the argument above that although the Deduction has already warranted our concept of objective relations among the appearances as distinct from our subjective apprehensions of them *in general*, it is the 'application-deductions' exhibited here in the Principles chapter that are supposed to show what is necessary for the possibility of actually *achieving* the representation of the various objective temporal distinctions thus demanded by the Deduction (in conjunction with the Aesthetic and the Schematism). The Second Analogy has thus just *shown* what it takes for our successive apprehensions to represent any objective succession or 'happening' in the first place, as opposed to their successively representing a mere objective coexistence (an unchanging scene). Kant's argument, as we have seen, begins by 'bracketing' or prescinding from the relevant 'objective–subjective' temporal distinction that is to be achieved: namely, that our ever-successive subjective apprehensions should constitute the representation of an event (e.g. a ship movement) as opposed to an unchanging coexistence (e.g. the parts of a house). The very possibility of representing any objective event as such is then argued to require that the principle of causal determination applies *to the apprehended contents themselves*, the objectivity of which is thereby *achieved* by means of that very representation.

In my view some of the most famous criticisms of Kant's argument in the Second Analogy are a result of overlooking that crucial point. Here is how to overlook the point and launch a popular but (I believe) mistaken objection to Kant. Suppose we take it as just given – as Hume would take it as given with respect to the successiveness of his own 'perceptions', for example, and legions of philosophical 'transcendental realists' would take it as given with respect to the successiveness of outer things – that an event occurs in which one state, A (say, a ship upstream), is followed by another state, B (the same ship downstream). Now suppose that we also take ourselves to be entitled to assume, from the start, the validity of the common-sense distinction between those objectively successive events or states of empirical objects on the one hand (i.e. A *and then* B) and our corresponding subjective perceptions of them: call the latter, our *perception-of-A* and *perception-of-B*. (The objectors also usually make the additional common-sense assumption that our perceptions are *caused by* the corresponding states in the object, e.g., the perception-of-A is caused by A, but our response to the following objection will apply whether or not this additional assumption is made.)

With those common-sense assumptions in place, the critic is now ready to accuse Kant's central argument in the Second Analogy of committing what

Strawson (one such critic) once memorably called "a *non sequitur* of numbing grossness" (1966: 137). For it is true, given those assumptions, that if state A is assumed to in fact be followed by state B in the object (in this case, the ship movement as an objective happening), *then* the corresponding empirical ordering of my subjective perceptions of those states, that is, *perception-of-A* and *perception-of-B*, can occur only in a corresponding order that is a determinate function of the objective states of which they are the perceptions. That is, assuming it as given that B *did* follow A 'out there', then this will *determine how any corresponding perceptions of* those events can be empirically ordered in the mind. Strawson now 'grants' all of this to Kant: that is, yes, it is *necessary* that the order and character of my subjective perceptions will be determined in general by the order and character of corresponding objective events out there. But this does *not* require, Strawson objects, that the objective sequence, 'A and then B', must *itself* be a *causally necessary sequence*! According to Strawson, Kant has confused the necessity that our perceptions are determined in intelligible ways by the objective events that we perceive (a 'conceptual' point with which Strawson agrees), with a supposed proof that the events themselves must always be governed by necessary causal laws determining their successiveness in time.

We can perhaps see this more clearly, the objection continues, if we were to suppose that it is in fact just a contingent accident that state A is followed by state B in the object. Still, it would follow from Kant's premises (the objector holds) that my *perception-of-A* and my *perception-of-B* must be determined or 'bound to' that objectively sequential (although accidental) order in intelligible ways, given the above common-sense premises. So once again, Kant's inference that B must be *causally necessitated* by some prior state of affairs is revealed to be just a flatly unsound inference, according to Strawson (and before him according to Arthur Lovejoy [1906] 1967): "a *non-sequitur* of numbing grossness".

But in this case, I believe, it is the objectors rather than Kant who have missed the point. For the objection simply *assumes* the justified distinction between our subjective perceptions and corresponding objective temporal relations among events that Kant is arguing is itself a distinction that cannot be represented in the first place *unless the principle of causality is conceived to govern the objects themselves*. Kant's argument was that our cognition of any apprehended sensible contents 'A-and-then-B' *as a sequence or happening at all* (rather than a coexistence) is itself possible only if the irreversible ordering that is thereby implied is conceptually represented as a necessity that governs the relations *among A and B themselves*, there being no other candidate contents available to us (for reasons discussed above). The objectors fail to see that the application-deduction in the Second Analogy attempts to show that (i) representing any 'event' as an objective sequence in time in the first place, and (ii) representing any such event as governed by the principle of causality, are *the same representational achievement*. If Kant is right, then we achieve (i), the cognition of any appearance as an event in the first place, only by (ii) subsuming that event under the law of causality. So the critics cannot simply help themselves from the start to the idea of an objective event that is *empirically distinguishable from our subjective perceptions of it* – as the objector has above – and then accuse of Kant of committing a fallacy by *inferring* the principle of causality *from* just the common-sense idea of an event assumed as already given. That *would* be a *non-sequitur* of numbing grossness!

I think that any successful objection to the Second Analogy on causality is going to have to attack Kant's philosophy 'further upstream', so to speak, most likely by attempting to cast doubt on the Transcendental Deduction itself. For Kant's argument in the Second Analogy, in my view, when properly interpreted, has never been successfully undermined by its many critics. I shall consider just a few more examples of such objections before moving on to close with a brief consideration of Kant's "Refutation of [Empirical] Idealism".

Another well-known type of objection takes Kant's Second Analogy to entail the absurdity that whenever state A is followed by state B as an objective event, state A itself must be the cause of state B (or at least A must be a relevant causal factor in whatever produced B). Thus, absurdly, *night* would have to be regarded as the cause of *daylight*, and so on. But not so. What Kant in fact holds is that the present state B, "(insofar as it has come to be) points to some preceding state as a correlate, to be sure still undetermined, of this event [i.e. B] that is given, which is, however, determinately related to the latter, as its consequence" (A199/B244). That is, what Kant's principle of causality requires is this: for any given event, B, there must have been *some* kind of event in the preceding state of affairs, call it X, such that states or events of X's empirical kind are such as to causally necessitate states or events of B's empirical kind in general.

So consider again the example of daylight (B) as an event that objectively follows night-time (A). That I cognize B as an event does indeed require me to judge (usually, of course, this principle will be implicit rather than explicit) that the coming to be of daylight was caused by *some* empirical kind of event or complex of events or other, call it X, in the preceding state of affairs. Of course, what is in fact, in this case, the empirical kind of event, X, that is the cause of empirical kinds of events such as B, is not something that can be established merely *a priori*. That is, what the prior cause actually is in any given case is a matter of empirical inquiry that remains, as Kant says above, "undetermined" as far as anything we can prove merely *a priori* by transcendental reflection. Such matters, on Kant's view, are the business of *empirical hypotheses* guided by various 'regulative maxims of reason' (see the end of Chapter 2 as well as the discussion of substance above, and also the Conclusion, below). A good empirical causal hypothesis in this case would be, for example, that it is *the rotation of the earth relative to the sun* that causes (i.e. necessitates, in the right circumstances) the change from night to day in general. There is no absurd requirement, in Kant's view, that the actual perceptual antecedent of *B*, in this case *A* (night-time), must be either the cause or a relevant causal factor in whatever is in fact responsible for causally producing *B*. (Of course, if our explanatory concerns are abstract enough, as for example in the case of predictions based solely on the *laws of motion* in physics, then there will always be available *some* inclusive description of the prior state of affairs of what caused *B* that will take into account the particular perceived antecedent state, *A*. But so construed, this is now a plausible idea rather than an objectionable consequence of Kant's view.)

If one keeps in mind the above account of what Kant's principle of causality in the Second Analogy does and does not entail, then I believe that one has the resources to answer these and more objections that have been raised against Kant's account. For example, the account just given can explain how Kant's position can consistently allow for 'merely contingent sequences' in experience while also defending universal causal determinism. To adapt an example ultimately due to a criticism of Kant by Arthur Schopenhauer (1788–1860), suppose that my walking out of the door of my house (*A*) is followed by a brick landing on my head (*B*). That's an accident: fortunately, *house exits* do not causally necessitate *head alterations* in general. What we should do now, on Kant's actual view of the matter, is to cast about for a plausible empirical hypothesis as to what prior kind of empirical event (call it *X*) was such as to causally necessitate the alteration of my head (*B*). In this case, as it happens, the empirical kind of event that was my exiting my house (*A*) was not itself the cause. Rather, a quick look around suggests the empirical hypothesis that the cause (*X*) in this case was in fact the event of a *rapidly descending builder's brick* landing on my head. And that is the general kind of empirical event that *would* lawfully determine and causally necessitate the alteration of any comparatively soft head that were to come directly in its path. Accordingly this is the best *empirical causal hypothesis* as to what is the 'empirical realization' of the *a priori* transcendental principle of causality in the present case. Of course, that empirical hypothesis could turn out to be wrong, and then the 'regulative' inquiry for the true cause would continue. Here Kant's views match up well, I think, with the epistemic practices and implicit assumptions of both common-sense and theoretical science.

I shall let the above stand for a brief introduction to the sorts of issues that are raised by Kant's ingenious defence of the principle of causality in the Second Analogy. One final thing to bear in mind, however, is this. The general causal principle of the Second Analogy *does* entail that (if experience of objective events is to be possible in the first place, etc.), for any given event, there must exist in nature *some particular empirical causal law* or other that subsumes or 'covers' that particular kind of event (e.g. as *brick impacts* can be the right empirical kind of event to causally explain *head alterations* in the relevant circumstances). But just *which* empirical law really is the correct causal explanation in any given case is not, according to Kant, something that can be determined 'constitutively' merely *a priori*, by sitting in one's armchair, so to speak. Which kinds of things cause which other kinds of things are questions for empirical hypothesis formation, in a way that Kant argues is governed by what we have now several times seen him call the *regulative maxims of reason*. We shall see a bit more on the role of such regulative maxims in the concluding chapter.

All in all, *if* the argument and approach of the Transcendental Deduction in general is regarded as defensible – an issue of considerable controversy that was discussed at the end of the previous chapter – then I think that Kant's Second Analogy constitutes a convincing defence of the principle of causality as governing all possible events of which we could have any objective perceptual cognition. (For an exceptionally clear discussion and defence of other aspects of Kant's Second Analogy, including the problem of 'simultaneous causation' and other issues not discussed here, see Rosenberg [2005: ch. 10].)

Kant's Refutation of Idealism: against the modern 'way of ideas'

Let us conclude this chapter with at least a brief look at one of the most important passages in the First *Critique*: Kant's "Refutation of Idealism" in the B-edition (B275–9). This rightly much-discussed argument was written for the second edition and inserted by Kant into the section on those principles of pure understanding he calls the "Postulates of Empirical Thought". It might be recalled that the three Postulates – which are not to be confused with *practical* reason's moral need-based *a priori* 'postulates' concerning God and immortality in the Second *Critique* – fall under the category of *Modality* and occur directly after the Analogies of Experience (under the category of *Relation*). Here is how Kant states the three Postulates:

The postulates of empirical thinking in general

1. Whatever agrees with the formal conditions of experience (in accordance with intuition and concepts) is **possible**.
2. That which is connected with the material conditions of experience (of sensation) is **actual** [*wirklich*].

3. That whose connection with the actual is determined in accordance with general conditions of experience is (exists) **necessarily**. (A218/B265–6)

The modalities involved here are not the purely *logical* modalities of possibility and necessity, for example as understood in terms of logical consistency and entailment. Rather, they concern what Kant characterizes as the *real* possibility (or necessity, actuality) of an object of our cognition. As he puts it later in the third chapter of the Transcendental Analytic, entitled "On the Ground of the Distinction of all Objects in General into Phenomena and Noumena" (A235/B294), as part of his discussion of the vain attempt to apply the categories to 'things in themselves' or noumena lying beyond the knowable phenomena of possible experience:

> [T]he deception of substituting the logical possibility of the **concept** (since it does not contradict itself) for the transcendental possibility of **things** (where an object corresponds to the concept) can deceive and satisfy only the inexperienced. [Footnote added in B:] In a word, all of these concepts could not be **vouched for** and their **real** possibility thereby established, if all sensible intuition (the only one we have) were taken away, and there then remained only **logical** possibility, i.e., that the concept (thought) is possible is not the issue; the issue is rather whether it relates to an object and therefore signifies anything. (A244/B302–3)

First, a thought or concept represents a real possibility, for Kant, if that concept can be shown to agree with the synthetic *a priori* forms and principles of sensibility and understanding that have been discussed throughout this book. Thus, for example, the concept of a mind that could "*intuit* the future" or could communicate with the minds of long gone or distant people:

> are concepts the possibility of which is entirely groundless, because it cannot be grounded in experience and its known laws, and without this it is an arbitrary combination of thoughts that, although it contains no contradiction, still can make no claim to objective reality, thus to the possibility of the sort of object that one would here think. (A222–3/B270)

In an important "Appendix" occurring at the end of the Analytic after the 'Phenomena and Noumena' chapter and known as the 'Amphiboly' (entitled "Appendix: On the Amphiboly of the Concepts of Reflection Through the Confusion of the Empirical Use of the Understanding with the

Transcendental" [A260/B316]), Kant offers trenchant criticisms of Leibniz's rationalist metaphysics. (For a recent book that emphasizes a certain reading of the Amphiboly and which provides a very different understanding of Kant from the one I offer in this book, see Langton [1998]. I offer a brief synopsis and criticism of Langton's reading of Kant in O'Shea [1999].) These criticisms are based partly on the charge that Leibniz and his followers confused purely intelligible or 'noumenal' *logical* relations, possibilities and necessities with *real* relations, possibilities and necessities. The former pertain merely to the 'pure understanding' considered in abstraction from its necessary relationship with sensibility in space and time; and hence, like all 'transcendental realists', "Leibniz took the appearances for things in themselves, thus for *intelligibilia*, i.e., objects of the pure understanding" (A264/B320). Once we recognize that real possibility depends on the categories and space and time as the *a priori* forms of any possible cognition of objects for us, Kant argues, then Leibniz's rationalist metaphysics collapses. (Compare our discussion of Kant's resolution to the Antinomies in §2.3.)

Second, that a thought or concept represents something as *actual* (i.e. as existing) and not just as a real possibility requires more than simply consistency with the *a priori* formal conditions of experience:

> The postulate for cognizing the **actuality** of things requires **perception**, thus sensation of which one is conscious – not immediate perception of the object itself the existence of which is to be cognized, but still its connection with some actual perception in accordance with the analogies of experience, which exhibit all real connection in an experience in general. (A225/B272)

In this connection Kant discusses how we can have 'mediate' or inferential cognition of "the existence of a magnetic matter from the [immediate, non-inferential] perception of attracted iron filings" (A226/B273, interpolation added), a passage that we discussed earlier in §1.2.

Third, and finally, Kant rounds out the Postulates with a very interesting discussion of his principle of "material necessity in existence" conceived in terms of the *laws of causality*:

> Now there is no existence that could be cognized as necessary under the condition of other given appearances except the existence of effects from given causes in accordance with laws of causality. Thus it is not the existence of things (substances) but of their state of which alone we can cognize the necessity, and moreover only from other states, which are given in perception, in accordance with empirical laws of causality. ... Necessity therefore con-

cerns only the relations of appearances in accordance with the dynamical law of causality. (A226–7/B279–80)

"Everything that happens is hypothetically necessary", as Kant puts it (A228/B280): roughly, *if* something happens, *then* something else necessarily follows. Kant's ensuing discussion of this principle includes an interesting argument involving his rejection of the seemingly intuitive idea that "Much is possible that is not actual" (A231/B283–4). However, I shall not pause to examine that complex issue here, since we must close this chapter with a more pressing topic.

It is in the context of having just raised the distinction between inferential (or mediate) as opposed to non-inferential (or immediate) knowledge of the *actual* existence of something, in connection with the second Postulate, that Kant chose to insert his new Refutation of Idealism into the B-edition version of the Postulates. This was presumably because the traditional view, certainly in the early modern period following Descartes and up to Kant's time, was that we have *immediate, non-inferential knowledge of our own conscious inner mental lives* (ordered in time), whereas we have knowledge of outer material objects in space – if we have such knowledge at all – only by means of an *inference* from the safe confines of inner consciousness to the existence of outer objects in space. As we shall see in a moment, in the Refutation of Idealism Kant's aim is to invert and thereby subvert that traditional picture of our alleged epistemological predicament.

Kant takes the argument of his Refutation of Idealism to depend directly on the principle of the persistence of substance that was proved in the First Analogy. The 'idealism' that Kant is here rejecting is *empirical idealism* in the sense that was explained earlier in §1.2, and which Kant here calls "**material** idealism" (B274). (For Kant's use of the term 'empirical idealism', see A369–80 of the Fourth Paralogism in A, which contained the material that Kant radically revised and moved to its new location here in B.)

In previous chapters we have encountered numerous times the early modern 'way of ideas' or 'idea-ism' that is traditionally attributed to Descartes, Locke, Berkeley and Hume (where 'idea' here means something radically different from Kant's 'ideas of reason'). According to this outlook, which is what Kant calls empirical (or material) idealism, the only things we are capable of knowing *directly* or immediately, that is, without having to venture any 'mediate' *inferences* beyond them, are our own inner perceptions or mental states: our 'ideas'. Inner mental states are thus known directly or immediately (non-inferentially), while outer material things in space are known only indirectly or mediately (by an inference). The familiar potted history of early modern philosophy then builds on this picture as follows (for our immediate purposes I am not concerned with the deep

199

historical inadequacies of the caricature): Descartes attempted to prove God's benevolent existence, solely on the basis of our idea of God, in order to warrant our inference from the 'inner' to the 'outer' (this is the 'problem of the external world'); Locke declared that somehow the inference from our ideas to their outer material causes was just obviously justified; but then Berkeley argued compellingly that it was not only unobvious but impossible, and he concluded that physical objects are *really* just collections of ideas (this was Berkeley's idealism); and this led inevitably to Hume's scepticism, which declared the entire dispute to be irresolvable by reason but settled in fact by our unavoidable reliance on our natural instinctive belief in external bodies.

Although of course that potted history would not bear the slightest close examination, it does bring out a general issue that remains as important and controversial today as it was for these early modern philosophers. For many contemporary philosophers and scientists continue to contend, or simply to assume, that we know our own inner conscious states more directly and certainly than we know 'outer things', and that we know the latter only indirectly and by inference from the former. (For example, many philosophers today argue that our common-sense belief in the existence of external objects is justified only by an implicit inference [or 'best explanation' or hypothesis] as to what *causes* us to have our inner perceptions or 'ideas' as the psychological *effects* of those outer material causes. And then other philosophers challenge the soundness of such an alleged inference or explanation.)

Kant's contention, by contrast, is that our knowledge of outer material objects in space is not, in the most basic cases, by means of any such inference or explanatory hypothesis, causal or otherwise, from our inner mental states to the existence of those outer objects. Rather, Kant argues, we cognize the existence of outer objects in space *directly*; and in fact (this is the striking claim) our being able to do so is necessary for the possibility of our having any knowledge of our *inner* mental states in the first place; and this, rather than any inference, is the true *a priori* transcendental source of the justification for our judgments about outer material bodies in general. This thesis is clearly closely related to, and in fact depends on, a central claim already established in the Deduction: roughly, that the 'I think' can accompany any of my representations (i.e. I can be aware of them *as* my representations) *only if* my representations constitute the rule-governed cognition of *an object* that is represented as existing independently of them. With the First Analogy having further established in relation to such objects that in "all change of appearances substance persists" (B224), the 'application-deduction' of the Refutation draws out a further necessary condition of the possibility of experience.

Kant states the "Theorem" of the Refutation of Idealism this way: "**The mere, but empirically determined, consciousness of my own existence proves the existence of objects in space outside me**" (B275). The "empirically determined" aspect here distinguishes this sort of self-knowledge from the transcendental unity of apperception, and would be exemplified by my 'inner' knowledge that, for instance, roughly an hour ago I had a certain thought about Paris. It is important to note that this sort of knowledge of our inner conscious lives would typically be granted (in fact, emphasized) by empirical idealists or 'way of ideas' philosophers of whatever stripe. Thus Kant begins his "Proof" as follows (the second sentence in this quotation follows Kant's own recommended emendation of the passage in the B-Preface at Bxxxix, footnote):

> I am conscious of my existence as determined in time. All time-determination presupposes something **persistent** in perception [i.e. based on the First Analogy]. This persistent thing, however, cannot be an intuition in me. For all grounds of determination of my existence that can be encountered in me are representations, and as such require something persistent that is distinct even from them, in relation to which their change, thus my existence in the time in which they change, can be determined. Thus the perception of this persistent thing is possible only through a **thing** outside me and not through the mere **representation** of a thing outside me. Consequently, the determination of my existence in time is possible only by means of the existence of actual things that I perceive outside myself. ... [Thus,] the consciousness of my own existence is at the same time an immediate consciousness of the existence of other things outside me.   (B275–6)

Kant then nicely adds that "in the preceding proof the game that [empirical] idealism plays has with greater justice been turned against it": for here it is shown "that outer experience is really immediate, that only by means of it is possible not, to be sure, the consciousness of our own existence, but its determination in time, i.e., inner experience" (B276–7). A tremendous amount of rich and interesting philosophical commentary has rightly been devoted to this short argument (for a start one might look at Bennett's [1966: ch. 14] comparison of it with Wittgenstein's Private Language Argument). Here I must be brief.

Put metaphorically, the claim is that inner mental autobiography, so to speak, is possible only within the context of a real external geography. That is, determining temporal facts about one's own states of consciousness would be impossible if the only objects of consciousness immediately available to one were one's own inner 'representations' or 'ideas' themselves. Why? Kant's own reasoning appears to be as follows. First, the possibility of any determination of time requires the objectively valid concept of *something persisting* or enduring through such changes (as was argued in the First Analogy). But second, our mental lives, as presented in inner sensory intuition in time, *present nothing persisting* of which such changing inner states could be cognized as the alteration. As Kant clarifies in "Note 2" to the Refutation, "this **I** does not have the least predicate of intuition that, as **persistent**, could serve as the correlate for time-determination in inner sense, as, say **impenetrability** in matter, as **empirical** intuition, does"; or again, we can "perceive all time-determination only through the change in outer relations (motion) relative to that which persists in space (e.g., the motion of the sun with regard to the objects on the earth)" (B278), or for example by means of the motion of the hands of a persisting clock (cf. Melnick 1973: ch. 2).

The First Analogy had proved, in effect, that temporal questions such as 'How long?' (an example of an 'empirical time-determination') depend on the general applicability of the concept 'How long *what*?' – that is, for how long did some substantial thing persist? But the 'I think' and its inner intuited states does not by itself provide us with any substantial persisting thing (as we saw in relation to the Paralogisms at the end of Chapter 4) against which our ever-changing mental episodes can be apprehended and ordered in time. Therefore, we must be *directly* conscious, not merely of our own inner mental states alone (as the philosophers of the 'way of ideas' and their contemporary descendents would have it), but of persisting substances as *outer* material bodies in space, objects that are distinct from our inner states. That is why, as the final sentence of Kant's proof concludes, "the consciousness of my own existence is at the same time an immediate consciousness of the existence of other things outside me".

The above is really only an introductory prelude to the many deep and controversial interpretive and philosophical issues that subsequent philosophers have raised in relation to Kant's Refutation of Idealism, an argument that many philosophers have found to be compelling but to stand in need of various proposed lines of argumentative support and revision. If Kant's argument is sound, however, then the modern turn toward subjectivity initiated by Descartes – which, crudely put, emphasized the primacy of consciousness and the certainty of inner knowledge over outer knowledge – has, according to Kant, led many philosophers into a radically mistaken way of thinking about our cognition, not only of the world, but of our own selves. For if Kant is right, then the possibility of our inner self-knowledge is in certain crucial and provable ways already dependent on our cognition of persisting material objects in space in general. As many later philosophers have argued, building upon Kant, perhaps our knowledge of our inner life is itself possible only in the context of our gradual initiation into a public 'form of life' (Wittgenstein) or a 'space of reasons' (Sellars) that is constituted by certain social-linguistic normative rules and intersubjective standards of cognitive correctness. Or as Hegel and other German idealists would already go on to argue in criticizing and transforming Kant's Critical Philosophy in the nineteenth century, perhaps the seeming certainty and even the very identity of any 'inner' life as such are in fact already 'mediated' by the socially and historically developing conceptual frameworks that make it possible for any conscious being to take in, conceive and navigate a rationally intelligible course through one intersubjectively shared world.

In this chapter we have not been able to explore in any detail some of the other important synthetic *a priori* principles that make up Kant's principles of pure understanding as a whole. In his very interesting Third Analogy, for example, Kant argues that cognition of the simultaneous existence of substances requires the *a priori* principle that any such substances stand in mutual causal interaction in general. We have also only briefly discussed the Phenomena and Noumena chapter and the Amphiboly appendix to the Analytic. But I hope we have gone far enough in our examination to have achieved a good grasp of what is surely, whether one agrees with all its details or not, a profound conception of the warrant for our *a priori* and empirical cognition of *one law-governed natural world* of material and psychological phenomena in space and time. Kant nicely sums up his own overall picture of this lawful nature at the end of the Analogies of Experience, in a passage that also helpfully displays the various connections to the arguments of the earlier Aesthetic, Deduction and Schematism:

> By nature (in the empirical sense) we understand the combination of appearances as regards their existence, in accordance with necessary rules, i.e., in accordance with laws. There are therefore certain laws, and indeed *a priori*, which first make a nature possible; the empirical laws can only obtain and be found by means of experience, and indeed in accord with its original laws, in accordance with which experience itself first becomes possible. Our analogies therefore really exhibit the unity of nature in the combination of all appearances under certain exponents, which express nothing other than the relation of time (insofar as it comprehends all existence in itself) to the unity of apperception, which can only obtain in synthesis in accordance with rules. Thus together they say: All appearances lie *in one nature*, and must lie therein, since without this *a priori* unity no unity of experience, thus also no determination of the objects in it, would be possible.
> (A216/B263, italics added)

For my money it would be difficult to find any other stretch of argument in the history of philosophy to match the profundity of the long chain of argument that is summarized in this paragraph. Not that I think that all of it is right. But I think enough of it is right, warts and all, that, as continually transposed into new keys, it continues to represent one of the most compelling outlooks in philosophy today.

CHAPTER 6

CONCLUSION: PURE REASON'S ROLE IN KANT'S METAPHYSICS OF NATURE

> Now that, the concept of which, contains within itself the 'Because' to every 'Why?' – that which is in no part or respect defective, that which is in all ways sufficient as a condition – seems to be the being suited to absolute necessity just because by itself possessing all the conditions for everything possible, it itself needs no condition, and is indeed not even susceptible of one. (A585/B613)

> I will establish that reason accomplishes just as little on the one path (the empirical) as on the other (the transcendental), and that it spreads its wings in vain when seeking to rise above the world of sense through the mere might of speculation. (A591/B619)

> One might have believed that this is merely a device of reason for achieving economy … Yet such a selfish aim can easily be distinguished from the idea, in accordance with which everyone presupposes that this [systematic] unity of reason conforms to nature itself; and here reason does not beg but commands, though without being able to determine the bounds of this unity.
> (A653/B681)

6.1 CLIPPING THE WINGS OF PURE SPECULATIVE REASON

Kant's overriding emphasis in the First *Critique* is on the need for a *critique* of pure reason: that is, for a strict intellectual *disciplining* (see "The Discipline of Pure Reason", 738/B766ff.) of the overreaching pretensions of the lofty and inevitable ideas and ideals of our totalizing rational faculty. This was announced right from the start of the *Critique of Pure Reason*, in the quotation from the preface to Francis Bacon's *The Great Instauration* (or *The Great*

Renewal; 1620) that Kant chose as the motto for his book in its second edition. As Bacon writes: "each may hope from our instauration that it claims nothing infinite, and nothing beyond what is mortal; for in truth it prescribes only the end of infinite errors, and this is a legitimate end" (Bii).

In Chapter 2 on the Antinomies we examined in detail Kant's diagnosis of the internal conflicts and the systematic *transcendental illusions* that arise whenever reason "spreads its wings in vain" (A591/B619) and launches on its inevitable attempts to draw inferences from our potentially unending experiences of the natural world in space and time to various alleged 'unconditioned' conditions of the ever-conditioned phenomena of our cosmos. Notable among the putative 'objects' of such ideas of reason were the ideas Kant takes to be supportive of religion: those of a 'necessary being', of free will as an 'uncaused causality', and of the soul as immaterial and immortal. But also among such ideas of pure reason were the opposed pretensions of the empiricists and scientific naturalists, and in particular the idea that the infinitely expansive material world and its physical causality could be known to be *exhaustive* of all of reality. The latter metaphysical claim, Kant argued, embodies the equally illusory conclusion that the existence of God, freedom and immortality can be conclusively *ruled out* by theoretical reason. In Chapters 3–5 we then saw that on Kant's view a *true a priori metaphysics of nature* must, by transcendentally demonstrable necessity, concern only the *a priori* grounds of the strict lawfulness and objectivity of the phenomenal universe in space and time: the single unified nature that is the object of all possible human experience. All theoretical speculation by pure reason concerning any alleged purely intelligible 'noumenal' objects or ultimately unconditioned causes has been shown to be delusive by its very nature, however inevitable such apparent 'conclusions' may be for our reason.

On Kant's view, as we saw especially in §1.1, and at the end of Chapter 3, all such theoretical speculations ought to be abandoned. The apparent 'space' that was to be occupied by the putative objects of such theoretical speculations, so to speak, was in fact – unbeknown to the philosophers – always intended by our rational nature to be filled by the very differently grounded *a priori* principles and ideas of *pure practical reason* and morality rather than by any speculative theoretical reasoning. On Kant's moral philosophy the obligations and ideals of our practical rationality show themselves, not in our speculations, but in the moral constraints and ends that Kant argues inform the very basis of our *free intentional actions* in the sensible world. Such principles of practical reason are ultimately based on the undeniable 'fact of reason' (as we earlier saw Kant put it in the *Critique of Practical Reason*) concerning our rational moral obligations and the moral freedom that those obligations presuppose. As Kant in fact already claimed towards the end of the *Critique of Pure Reason* itself, in a section of the Doctrine of Method entitled "The Canon of Pure Reason" (A795/B823ff.): "if there is to be any legitimate use of pure reason at all" in relation to pure reason's ideas of God, freedom and immortality – the objects of which do indeed constitute the "final aim to which in the end the speculation of reason in its transcendental use is directed" – then such a legitimate doctrine or "**canon**" of pure reason must, as we have seen, "concern not the speculative but rather the **practical use of reason**" (A797–8/B825–6).

In light of all of this it might seem that as far as the ideas of pure theoretical reason are concerned – as opposed to the principles of pure understanding in relation to sense experience and as opposed to the principles of pure practical reason in relation to our intentions and actions – Kant's *Critique of Pure Reason* is all about the need for *critical discipline*. It certainly is about that. But as has been noted several times throughout this book, on Kant's view the ideas and principles of pure theoretical reason do have various epistemically legitimate 'immanent' roles when interpreted as *regulative maxims* that necessarily govern our inquiries *within* the realm of sense experience, rather than in their illusory guise as 'transcendent' principles allegedly constitutive of various 'unconditioned' conditions or totalities beyond experience. By way of conclusion let us examine both the negative and the positive roles of theoretical reason's ideas, respectively, in the final chapter of the Transcendental Dialectic, "The Ideal of Pure Reason" (A567–642/B595–670) and in the "Appendix to the Transcendental Dialectic" that immediately follows it (A642–704/B670–732).

6.2 KANT'S CRITIQUE OF SPECULATIVE THEOLOGY IN "THE IDEAL OF PURE REASON"

In "The Ideal of Pure Reason" (the Ideal), Kant famously criticizes what he characterizes as the "only three kinds of proof for the existence of God possible from speculative reason": (i) the "**physico-theological**" proof, usually called the 'Design Argument' (discussed in section six of the Ideal); (ii) the "**cosmological**" proof (section five); and (ii) the "**ontological** proof" (section four). "There are no more of them", Kant contends, "and there also cannot be any more" (A590–91/B618–19). Kant's critical analyses of these traditional arguments were systematic and revolutionary, although we should immediately include within that same revolution Hume's earlier and penetrating (not to mention delightfully readable) *Dialogues Concerning Natural Religion* ([1779] 1993). Together these important criticisms have become standard fare in any introduction to philosophy and in the philosophy of religion, and I shall not attempt to introduce all of those classic issues here. But the Ideal does contain some crucial material for understanding Kant's overall position in the *Critique of Pure Reason*. (For a comprehensive treatment of Kant's views on theology, see Wood [1978]; for very helpful brief overviews of the Ideal, I recommend Buroker [2006: ch. 10] and Grier [2010]; and for Kant's own further writings on religion, see the Cambridge Edition of Kant's writings on *Religion and Rational Theology*.)

The chapter on the Ideal begins with three difficult but important sections on the nature and origins of our rational idea of God as the necessarily existent and supremely real being. Broadly similar to his earlier conclusions in the Antinomies, Kant will contend that, on the one hand, our *idea* of God as the supreme being is a "**faultless ideal**" (A641/B769), one that has its origin in *reason's own legitimate search for completely sufficient explanations*. But on the other hand, all classic attempts to conclude on such theoretical grounds that therefore *God exists* are based on a deep-seated transcendental illusion and are doomed to failure. A particularly important point that underlies Kant's critique of theology throughout the chapter on the Ideal was examined earlier in relation to the Antinomies, in §§2.2–3. There we explored Kant's diagnosis of the inevitable confusion between broadly explanatory *logical conditions* as opposed to *causal-empirical conditions* that he argues generates the transcendental illusion that is involved in all of the fallacious arguments for any ultimately 'unconditioned' condition or absolute totality of conditions. The idea of a 'necessary being' as the ground of all empirical contingency in the Fourth Antinomy was a prime example of such an allegedly unconditioned being.

Each of the opposed theses and antitheses of the Antinomies, as we may recall, began with a series of empirically conditioned, law-governed phenomena in experience and then attempted to infer the existence of some unconditioned condition or totality as allegedly required in order to fully explain the conditioned empirical phenomena. The inferences to the unconditioned on both sides were governed by the logical postulate and corresponding real transcendental principle of pure reason: "**If the conditioned is given, then the whole sum of conditions, and hence the absolutely unconditioned, is also given,** through which alone the conditioned was possible" (A410/B436; cf. §2.2, above). In the case of pure reason's inevitable demand for an unconditioned freedom and for an unconditionally necessary being in the Third and Fourth Antinomies, Kant's conclusion was that such supersensible conditions in principle *cannot be ruled out* as impossible. In this sense, Kant argued, the theses and antitheses in these two cases "can **both be true**" (A562/B590). In fact the thought of such unconditioned supersensible conditions was argued to be the *only* solution that is consistent with reason's own inherent explanatory demands, if our reason is not to "remain in conflict with itself" (A564/B592).

CONCLUSION: PURE REASON'S ROLE IN KANT'S METAPHYSICS OF NATURE

On Kant's view we are thus *rationally entitled to the thought* or idea that there exists a necessary being 'outside of' and as the necessary causal 'ground' of the realm of contingent appearances in spatiotemporal nature – but not to any knowledge claim concerning the existence of such a being. As we have seen in earlier chapters, the latter 'postulate' can ultimately only be justified on moral grounds supplied by pure *practical* reason. The 'Solution' to the Fourth Antinomy was thus based on the problematic but coherently thinkable and inevitable idea of an "unconditionally necessary being" as the "non-empirical condition of the entire series" of all contingent existences in general, "thought of as entirely outside the series of the world of sense ... and merely intelligible" (A560–61/B588–9). But any attempt by theoretical reason to conclude the real existence of any such being was shown by the Antinomies to be demonstrably unwarranted. In the Ideal of Pure Reason Kant now proceeds to offer a complex diagnosis of the ways in which speculative philosophers and theologians have nonetheless perennially managed to convince themselves that pure reasoning *can* demonstrate the existence of such a necessary being, and more particularly of *God* as the supremely perfect being (the *"ens realissumum"*).

He begins the Ideal by reminding us that the "**ideas**" of reason concerning the unconditioned, as just recounted, "contain a certain completeness that no possible empirical cognition ever achieves"; and that "with them reason has a *systematic unity* only in the sense that the *empirically* possible unity seeks to *approach* it without ever completely reaching it" (A567–8/B595–6, italics added). But now he adds that "even further removed from objective reality than the idea is what I call the **ideal**": that is, "an *individual thing* which is determinable, or even determined, through the idea alone" (A568/B596, italics added). Many philosophers, Kant explains, have conceived of various ideally complete or 'perfect' individual beings as the ideal archetypes that correspond to and 'ground' the imperfectly realized beings that we encounter in sense experience: such were Plato's eternal 'ideal Forms' (of the Good, the Beautiful, the Just, Triangularity, and so on), and also the ideally wise 'sage' envisaged by the Stoics. On Kant's view such ideals of pure reason, "even though one may never concede them objective reality (existence), are nevertheless not to be regarded as mere figments of the brain; rather, they provide an indispensable standard for reason...in order to assess and measure the degree and the defects of what is incomplete" (A569/B597). Kant thus contends that the ideal of reason in the sense he will articulate "always rests on determinate concepts" (A570/B598), despite the fact that such a *transcendent* concept or ideal of reason in principle cannot be realized in any possible experience, and hence cannot be *understood* by us as an objectively real object in that crucial sense.

In section two of the Ideal, Kant contrasts a formal *logical principle* of the "determinability" of any concept, resting merely on "the principle of contradiction" – namely, "that of **every two** contradictorily opposed predicates only one can apply to" a given concept – with a corresponding *a priori transcendental principle* (A574/B602) "of **thoroughgoing determination**, according to which, among **all possible** predicates of **things**, insofar as they are compared with their opposites, one must apply to it" (A571–2/B599–600). The latter principle specifies what the 'rationalist' philosophers Leibniz and Wolff conceived as the *complete individual concept* of a thing: a concept, fully graspable only by God, of all the possible predicates belonging to any existing thing, as the real ontological ground of that individual thing. This "idea of the **sum total of all possibility**" as the allegedly real *a priori* (hence 'transcendental', but in this case also *transcendent*) ground of the existence of each thing then becomes the "concept of an individual object that is thoroughly determined *a priori* … merely through the idea": that is, "an **ideal** of pure reason" (A573–4/B601–2). As we shall see, however, such an *a priori* transcendental principle of thoroughgoing determination will have validity for us in relation to real objects only when it is interpreted merely *regulatively* as opposed to *constitutively*: that is, as "prescrib[ing] to the understanding the rule of its complete use" (A573/B601), rather than as allegedly *determining a corresponding ideally complete real object.*

Traditional rational theology, however, attempts to make a constitutive yet experience-transcendent use of this Ideal as proving the existence of a corresponding ideally perfect being: God. During the course of sections two and three of the Ideal, Kant explains that there is a perfectly legitimate (indeed, indispensable) sense in which the "transcendental **ideal**" is "the one single genuine ideal of which human reason is capable" (A576/B604). Here reason's genuine aim is "solely that of representing the necessary thoroughgoing determination of things", doing so in such a way, however, that "reason does not presuppose the existence of a being conforming to the ideal, but only the idea of such a being" (A577/B605). Kant also explains, somewhat turgidly, how it comes about by means of an inevitable transcendental illusion that this ideal of pure reason is "**hypostatized**" and "**personified**" into the theological concept "of **God**" as the necessarily existent, "simple, all-sufficient, eternal" being, "the object of a transcendental **theology**" (A580/B608ff.). The crucial underlying "natural illusion", as was indeed the case earlier in the Antinomies, involves reason's mistakenly thinking of some principle that *does* have a valid (if indeterminate) interpretation within the realm of possible experience – in this case, the idea "that nothing is an object **for us** unless it presupposes the sum total of all *empirical* reality as condition of its possibility" – as if it were "a principle that must hold of all things in general" and unconditionally (A582/B611, italics added). In section three (A584/B612ff.), Kant explains how reason adds a further mistake, specific to the Ideal, to the original natural error of reason that was involved in the Fourth Antinomy in attempting to prove the existence of a *necessary being* as the allegedly required ground of all contingency in the world:

> This, therefore, is how the natural course of human reason is constituted. First, it convinces itself of the existence of **some** necessary being. In this it recognizes an unconditioned existence. Now it seeks for the concept of something independent of all conditions, and finds it in that which is the sufficient condition for everything else, i.e., in that which contains all reality. The All without limits, however, is absolute unity, and carries with it the concept of one single being, namely the highest being; and thus reason infers that the highest being, as the original ground of all things, exists in an absolutely necessary way. (A586–7/B614–15)

Very roughly, Kant is arguing that reason first naturally (but problematically) makes an inference from the experienced world to the alleged need for a 'necessary being' as the ground of the contingency within the world. The traditional *cosmological* and *physico-theological* (or 'design') arguments for God's existence, as Kant goes on to explain in sections five and six of the Ideal, each accordingly sets out from an *a posteriori* experiential starting-point. And objectively speaking, each 'proof', on Kant's view, really gets no further than had the problematic argument for a necessary being in the Antinomies. But as explained above, reason naturally 'bulks out' and strengthens the latter idea, as it were, by further idealizing it into the conception of a being containing the sum total of all reality; and then into 'the ideal' of an all-sufficient, individual being as the highest being; and finally into that original ground of all things that exists with *absolute* necessity. Let us turn now to a brief look at how Kant's criticisms of the three traditional arguments for God's existence unfold on this basis.

The ontological argument for God's existence had been offered by St Anselm, the Archbishop of Canterbury (1033–1109) and was also defended by Descartes in the Fifth of his *Meditations on First Philosophy* in 1641. It is an argument that continues to be much debated today (on Kant's version, cf. Buroker [2006: 267–74]; Grier [2010: 275–80]; Van Cleve [1999: ch. 12]). Very briefly, from the premise that we can *conceive* of a supremely real being possessing all positive realities or 'perfections' (an *ens realissimum*) – that is, as *that than which nothing greater can be conceived* – it is supposed to follow just from that concept that such a being must really *exist*. Descartes states the key move pithily: "it is just as much of a contradiction to think of God (that is, as a *supremely perfect* being) lacking existence (that is, lacking *a perfection*), as it is to think of a mountain without a valley" ([1641] 1985: 2:46, italics added). But both Kant and Hume (*Treatise*, 1.2.6) in effect raise the objection that *existence* cannot be considered one among the properties or determinations that an object is conceived to have, but rather plays a fundamentally different logical role. In the predication '*x exists*', Kant argues, 'exists' functions as a 'logical' rather than a 'real' predicate. For example, if you conceive of a red apple on a table and list its properties, and then you conceive of an *existing* red apple and list its properties, the list of properties or 'perfections' you conceive is the same in both cases. To judge that a red apple of the conceived kind *exists* is not to attribute a further real property to the red apple, but rather to assert or 'posit' (to use Kant's term) that the conceived properties are in fact *instantiated* by some object. Although these matters remain subject to much debate, many philosophers would see Kant's criticism of the ontological argument as having been supported by later developments in modern symbolic logic, according to which the logical role of the 'existential quantifier' ($\exists x$) is not to ascribe a property to an object, but rather to assert that at least one object satisfies or instantiates a given property or set of properties.

Kant has other objections to the ontological argument in this section – he objects, for example, that the concept of a supremely perfect being does not succeed in being a determinate concept of any object in the first place – but we shall pass over these here. Kant's view (as was indeed the view of Aquinas) is that rather than thus attempting in vain to prove the existence of God directly from the mere *a priori idea* or concept of such a being, the only natural and plausible path for reason, as we have already partly seen in the Antinomies, is to begin with our *a posteriori* experience of the phenomena in the natural world, and then attempt to argue that God must exist as the ultimately necessary ground of the latter. The cosmological proof (e.g. Leibniz's proof from the contingency of the world [A604/B632]) and the physico-theological proof (the argument from design) are both arguments of this kind: they attempt to infer that God or the supreme being must exist as, respectively, the necessary ground of all of the contingently existing beings that we find in nature in general, and as the intelligent source of all of the wonderfully adaptive 'design' or *purposive* ordering of things that we find, in particular, in the case of *living* things.

As Kant curtly formulates it, the cosmological argument at bottom contends that "If something exists" – for example, himself or any other object in nature – "then an absolutely necessary being also has to exist" (A604/B632). However, in "this cosmological argument", he writes, "so many sophistical principles come together that speculative reason seems to have summoned up all its dialectical art so as to produce the greatest possible transcendental illusion" (A606/B634). At B637–8 Kant rapidly cites four objections to the cosmological argument (several of which resonate with criticisms Hume had given). For example, the inference "from the contingent to a cause" existing outside

CONCLUSION: PURE REASON'S ROLE IN KANT'S METAPHYSICS OF NATURE

the world of sense involves the attempt to apply the concepts of contingency and causality beyond the only domain in which such concepts have sense for us. Or again: the "inference from the impossibility of an infinite series of causes one upon another to a first cause" mistakenly assumes to be impossible what neither reason nor experience can really show to be such. And so on.

Kant also introduces an important and novel criticism at this point in the Ideal. First, Kant holds that the cosmological argument, even if it were successful, would at best deliver as its conclusion only the indeterminate idea of a 'necessary being', and not the conclusion of the God of theism as the supreme being in particular. (This is a point that Hume had also urged in his *Dialogues*.) But now Kant argues that, as a result, the *a posteriori* cosmological argument, against its own intentions, in the end covertly relies on the same dubious inference that was required by the *a priori* 'ontological argument': that is, an inference from the mere *a priori* idea of a 'necessary being' to the more specific conclusion of God as the 'supreme being'. In a nice dialectical twist, Kant thus argues that (i) the *a priori* ontological argument from the mere concept of God to the real existence of God would never have had any initial plausibility for us were reason not already covertly convinced by the more natural *a posteriori* arguments from experience to the (alleged) need for a necessary being (A603/B631). And yet (ii) the latter *a posteriori* argument itself does not succeed in getting one from the merely indeterminate 'necessary being' to the existence of *God* as the supreme being unless reason (in what is often just a quick final step, such as the announcement that 'This all men call God') covertly relies on the same type of inference that it *rejects* in relation to the ontological argument. When all is said and done, on Kant's view, in the domain of theoretical (as opposed to practical) reason it turns out that the theological idea of an "unconditioned necessity, which we need so indispensably as the ultimate sustainer of all things, is for human reason the true abyss": "Here everything gives way beneath us, and the greatest perfection as well as the smallest, hovers without support before speculative reason" (A613/B641).

Finally, and very briefly, the 'physico-theological proof' or traditional argument from design for God's existence basically argues that the purposive or goal-directed, adaptive ordering of particular (especially living) things that we encounter in the world cannot be explained in terms of the *purposeless* physical mechanisms of mere matter in motion. Rather, such organic "purposiveness" (*Zweckmässigkeit*) in nature appears to be an entirely *contingent* product of matter in comparison with the broadly Newtonian causal mechanisms in terms of which, Kant has argued, our understanding has genuine insight into the nature of the material world. For instance, it is hopeless to attempt to explain how the parts of the human eye cooperatively function so as to produce the adaptive end of *vision* by appealing merely to the complex 'pushes and pulls' of the Newtonian physics of matter, no matter how complex such 'blind' processes might be. (Of course, the triumph of Darwinian evolutionary biology a century later was to throw a permanent wrench into the basis of this argument, but unfortunately we cannot pause here to speculate on the relationship between Kant's views and that later revolution in biology.) Our explanations in biology do generally seem to require appeal, in *some* sense, to the purposive ordering or ends that such complex natural mechanisms are supposed to (i.e. are by nature 'designed to') achieve. Thus, Kant argues, we inevitably require a problematic appeal to the model of *teleological purposiveness* in order to explain the workings of such organized products of nature:

> This purposive order is quite foreign to the things of the world, and pertains to them only contingently, i.e., the nature of different things could not by themselves agree in so many united means to determinate final aims, were they not quite properly chosen for and predisposed to it through a principle of rational order grounded on ideas. (A625/B653)

The eventual conclusion of the physico-theological argument from design – again only by means of a deep-seated transcendental illusion and exhibiting various other errors similar to those already discussed – is that there must exist "a sublime and wise cause" (A625/B654) of the idea-conforming purposiveness exhibited by nature and its products. Reason thus inevitably forms the problematic idea that nature as a whole is the product of an all-perfect divine intelligence, and through a natural illusion takes itself to have proved that such a being really exists corresponding to that ideal.

In the next section, however, we shall turn finally from the perennial errors of pure speculative reason in its vain hope for a genuinely *transcendent* use of such ideas and ideals – a noble but misguided aspiration that Kant thinks has long stood in need of a crushing and systematic critique – to Kant's own conception of the *real a priori transcendental* but strictly *immanent* use that theoretical reason makes of its high-flying ideas and principles *within* the realm of possible experience. Let us close, then, with a few words on the crucial role of the *regulative* principles or 'maxims' of pure reason within experience.

6.3 THE VALIDITY OF PURE REASON'S IMMANENT REGULATIVE PRINCIPLES

At the end of his critique of the cosmological proof of God's existence in section five of the Ideal, Kant offers an "explanation of the dialectical illusion in all transcendental proofs of the existence of a necessary being" (A614/B642). As was the case in the Paralogisms and the Antinomies, Kant here argues that pure reason's mistake has been to treat a "**regulative principle** of reason" as if it were a principle that is *a priori constitutive* of the nature and existence of some object (in this case, of the highest being or God):

> The ideal of the highest being is ... nothing other than a **regulative principle** of reason, to regard all combination in the world **as if it** arose from an all-sufficient necessary cause, so as to ground on that cause *the rule of a unity that is systematic and necessary according to universal laws*; but it is not an assertion of an existence that is necessary in itself. But at the same it is unavoidable, by means of a transcendental subreption, to represent this formal principle to oneself as constitutive, and to think of this unity hypostatically. (A619/B647, italics added)

Pure reason's ideal of a highest, most perfect being is valid, on Kant's view, only if it is treated *regulatively* as a way of representing the ideal of a *completely systematic and unified explanation of the natural world*. We have, in fact, already met the underlying sources of this regulative ideal in the nature of reason in §2.2 (see "What is 'Reason'?" and "Reason's Quest to Explain the Cosmos as a Whole"). There we examined the *a priori principle of pure reason* and the ideally complete *unity of reason* that is, as it were, 'built in' to our rational explanatory aims. Pure reason has as its legitimate regulative *quest* an unconditionally complete and systematic explanation of all the lawful empirical phenomena of nature that are continuously presented to reason by our understanding in its ongoing engagement with the world. Transcendental illusions arise when this rationally warranted *goal* of an ideally complete understanding of nature's intelligible lawfulness is inevitably mistaken for a *proof* that a corresponding ideal completeness therefore *exists* as an objective reality. The most adequate representation of such an ideally complete explanatory grounding of nature's conditioned phenomena has now been found in reason's 'pure ideal' of God as the unconditionally necessary and sufficient purposive ground of all actual and possible realities.

Kant tells us in the Ideal that pure reason's *a priori* ideal of completeness, when properly treated as a regulative ideal rather than as an object-constituting principle, generates two warranted maxims or "subjective principles of reason":

> namely, on the one side, for everything given as existing to *seek* something that is necessary, i.e., *never to stop anywhere except with an a priori complete explanation*, but on the other side *also*

> *never to hope for this completion, i.e., never to assume anything empirical as unconditioned*, thereby exempting oneself from its further derivation. In such a significance both principles can very well coexist with one another, as merely heuristic and **regulative**, taking care of nothing but the formal interest of reason. For the one says that you should philosophize about nature **as if** there were a necessarily first ground for everything belonging to existence, solely in order to bring systematic unity into your cognition by inquiring after such an idea, namely an imagined first ground; but the other warns you not to assume any single determination dealing with the existence of things as such a first ground, i.e., as absolutely necessary, but always to hold the way open to further derivation and hence always to treat it as still conditioned.
>
> (A616–17/B644–5, italics added)

These two regulative principles of our reason in effect demand that all our inquiries into nature must be governed by two rules: (i) always to presuppose that in principle there is some ideally complete explanatory ground *to be sought* for any given phenomena that we encounter in nature; but (ii) never to assume that one *has found* any such unconditionally or ideally complete ground or explanation of the phenomena, since every proposed real explanatory ground will always itself be a contingent phenomenon within nature.

The ideal set by our pure reason is thus basically the idea that nature in all of its potentially infinitely discoverable empirical detail, in all its beauty and organic purposiveness, and in all its unending expansiveness, is through and through entirely the designed product of an *all-wise and all-powerful supreme being* that exists "**outside the world**" (A617/B645) as its ultimate ground. When this ideal is properly treated in a merely regulative "**as if**" manner, it is equivalent to the rational prescription always to continue searching for a completely sufficient and systematically unified explanation of nature's phenomena.

In the fascinating but elusive "Appendix to the Transcendent Dialectic", Kant finally turns directly to the investigation of the nature and validity of the totalizing and idealizing ideas of pure reason in their "**immanent** use" (A643/B671), that is, within the realm of our cognition of nature. One of the things that has made Kant's Appendix so difficult for his readers is that he seems both to deny and yet also to assert that the regulative principles or 'maxims' of reason are *objectively valid* transcendental principles. So it will perhaps be fitting to end our examination of the *Critique of Pure Reason* by sketching a possible resolution of this vexed question concerning Kant's own view of the credentials of the intellectual products of pure reason in their immanent theoretical use. (See Grier [2001: 268–79] and O'Shea [1997] for two attempts to resolve this particular interpretive problem.)

During the course of the first half of the Appendix "On the Regulative Use of the Ideas of Pure Reason", Kant puts forward three regulative principles of reason as encapsulating the "good and consequently **immanent** use" that we make of reason's maximal ideal of a *complete and purposive systematic unity* as the explanatory ground of nature's phenomena ("**as if**" nature were the purposive creation of an all-perfect, supreme intelligence):

> Reason thus prepares the field for understanding: 1. by a principle of **sameness of kind** in the manifold under higher genera, 2. by a principle of the **variety** of what is same in kind under lower species [or kinds]; and in order to complete the systematic unity it adds 3. still another law of the **affinity** of all concepts, which offers a continuous transition from every species to every other through a graduated increase of varieties. We can call these the principles of the **homogeneity, specification** and **continuity** of forms.
> (A658/B686)

These general assumptions concern (1) nature's generic simplicity (for instance, in our assumption that nature in all its details will always exhibit some underlying uniformity or sameness in its empirical kinds); and yet also (2) the potentially infinite variety of specifiable empirical differences and further species to be discovered within those generic kinds; and combining both of those, (3) the thoroughgoing 'affinity' or continuous gradation of sameness-in-diversity waiting to be discovered nature. Each of them expresses an aspect of the *maximal ideal* of the *complete systematic unity* of nature: the idea that nature is characterized by a *purposive organization* throughout all of its discoverable empirical phenomena. We assume, in short, that nature is 'as if' it were purposefully 'designed' to exhibit a maximal organization of intelligible unity-within-diversity.

Kant nicely illustrates by means of multiple examples from the history of scientific and metaphysical inquiry how each of these general principles functions as a "transcendental presupposition" (A651/B679) that structures our investigation of nature. For example, when nature in its observed details presents us with a bewildering variety of empirical kinds and data, the scientist or philosopher will assume that the diversity observed is not simply 'brute' or ultimate but is rather ultimately to be explained in terms of some more basic, generic kinds or simpler principles to be discovered upon inquiry (the principle of **homogeneity**). Kant's discussion throughout the Appendix makes clear that this assumption of an underlying sameness or *simplicity of principles* (A652/B680) is not merely a subjectively useful or desirable attribute of a theory, making it easier to use or apply, for instance. Rather, the assumption embodied in the regulative principle is that the observed diversity in nature is ultimately to be explained by the fact that *nature itself, objectively, is governed by some parsimony of principles and uniformity of kinds or other*, to be discovered by ongoing empirical inquiry. "It is thereby said that the nature of things themselves offers material for the unity of reason, and the apparently infinite variety should not restrain us from conjecturing behind it a unity of fundamental properties" (A652/B680). All three of the regulative maxims or 'laws' of reason are in this way assumptions about the ideal systematic organization of empirical nature itself:

> [O]ne can see clearly that the laws judge the parsimony of fundamental causes, the manifoldness of effects, and the consequent affinity of the members of nature in themselves reasonably and in conformity with nature, and these principles therefore carry their recommendation directly in themselves, and not merely as methodological devices. (A661/B689)

> [T]he parsimony of principles is not only an economical requirement of reason, but is one of nature's own laws.
> (A650/B678; in this case I have preferred Kemp Smith's translation of Kant's "nicht bloß ein ökonomischer Grundsatz der Vernunft, sondern inneres Gesetz der Natur wird")

But granting that the three regulative maxims of reason are such that we apparently *assume* that they apply to nature itself, this immediately raises the critical question of how any such supposition could really be *objectively valid* at all. For Kant is clear that however indispensable for us it may be, reason's conception of such an ideal maximum of purposive organization in nature – no less than the idea of a Divine Designer of nature that ultimately sums it up – ultimately outstrips anything that could be exhibited in *any possible human experience*, however extensive. It is thus quite clear that on Kant's view "the transcendental ideas are never of constitutive use" and hence are not objectively valid in the way that was the case for the pure principles of understanding (see A670/B698; A306/B362–3). As he puts it in the Appendix, such ideas:

> have an excellent and indispensably necessary regulative use, namely that of directing the understanding to a certain goal respecting which the lines of direction of all its rules converge at one point, which, although it is only an idea (*focus imaginarius*) – i.e., a point from which the concepts of the understanding do not

really proceed, since it lies entirely outside the bounds of possible experience – nonetheless still serves to obtain for these concepts the greatest unity alongside the greatest extension. (A644/B673)

Thus the complete "systematic unity (as a mere idea)" that is the goal of the regulative principles of reason "is only a **projected** unity, which one must regard not as given in itself, but only as a problem" (A647/B675). The regulative idea of a maximal systematic unity in nature is "indispensably necessary" as *setting the goal to be pursued* as far as possible by the strictly *constitutive understanding* within experience. As such "systematic unity or the unity of reason … is a **logical** principle" that guides our understanding towards greater systematicity in its knowledge of nature's particular causal laws and empirical kinds. "But whether the constitution of objects" in nature "are themselves determined to systematic unity" *is an idea of reason that cannot be constitutively determined a priori by our understanding*: "that would be a **transcendental** principle of reason, which would make systematic unity not merely something subjectively and logically necessary, as method, but objectively necessary" (A648/B676).

So in one fundamental sense, Kant clearly holds that reason's regulative idea of nature's maximal systematic unity is a *merely subjectively valid* "logical" or methodological principle. In relation to this "pursuit of the principle of affinity resting on the interests of reason", for example, our constitutive understanding's experiential "observation and insight into the arrangements of nature could never provide it as something to be asserted objectively" (A668/B696). Reason's regulative "maxim" of a complete systematicity in nature has *only subjective validity* as an indispensable projected goal and methodological aid to the understanding: "I call all subjective principles that are taken not from the constitution of the object but from the interest of reason in regard to a cetain possible perfection of the cognition of this object, **maxims** of reason", which "may seem as if they were objective principles" (A666/B694). Such regulative maxims accordingly have *no objective validity* in so far as they are considered as providing us with any supposed *a priori* constitutive insight that a *maximum* of systematic organization really exists in nature.

Despite all of this, however, Kant does argue that such principles, when properly interpreted, "nevertheless have objective but indeterminate validity, and serve as a rule of possible experience" (A663/B691). (The "indeterminate" here will turn out to be important.) On his view, as we shall now see, the regulative maxims of reasons are not only "logical" or methodological principles; they are also *transcendental* principles that are necessary for the possible experience of any objective reality at all. They *do* tell us something objective about what the real objects in nature must be like in general, if we are to be able to have any possible experience of them. Let us take as our sample regulative maxim Kant's further remarks on the principle of "genera" or "homogeneity" discussed above. This principle, Kant tells us, ascribes a uniformity or simplicity to nature itself: "everyone presupposes that this unity of reason conforms to nature itself; and here reason does not beg but commands, though without being to determine the bounds of this unity" (cf. the "indeterminate" objective validity above). Here is Kant's argument that the 'logical' maxim of generic sameness or homogeneity presupposes a real 'transcendental' one:

> If among the appearances offering themselves to us there were such a great variety ... that even the most acute human understanding, through comparison of one with another, could not detect the least similarity (a case which can at least be thought), then the logical law of genera would not obtain at all, no concept of a genus, nor any other universal concept, indeed no understanding at all would obtain, since it is the understanding that has to do with such concepts. The logical principle of genera therefore presupposes a transcendental one if it is to be applied to nature ... According to that principle, sameness of kind is necessarily presupposed in the manifold of a possible experience (even though we cannot determine its degree *a priori*), because without it no empirical concepts and hence no experience would be possible.
> (A654/B682)

What is Kant arguing for in this passage? This will constitute the final piece of synthetic *a priori* cognition that we shall attempt to mine from the *Critique of Pure Reason* on this occasion. In my own opinion, however, this is a piece of the puzzle that is crucial for the proper understanding of Kant's subsequent development of the Critical Philosophy throughout the next decade and beyond, but in particular in the Third *Critique*, the *Critique of the Power of Judgment* (1790).

The passage asks us to form the bare "thought" of an experience in which the spatiotemporal "appearances offering themselves to us" would be so thoroughly chaotic as to exhibit not "the slightest similarity" or sameness in empirical content or kind over time. The argument is that such a completely chaotic experience is merely *logically* possible or thinkable but is not *really* possible for us in Kant's transcendental sense: that is, such a thoroughgoing lack of empirical uniformity could not for us constitute the possible cognition *of any object* at all. It follows, as a synthetic *a priori* transcendental principle, that *if* any experience of objects is to be possible for us at all, then *at least some minimum degree* of 'generic homogeneity' or empirical sameness in kind must be found in the appearances that present themselves to us. Reason's 'merely regulative' maxim of homogeneity is thus a real *a priori* transcendental principle that is necessary for our possible experience of any object whatsoever, which as we saw in Chapter 4 is just what it takes for a principle to be *objectively valid* for Kant.

But how can a regulative maxim of reason be objectively valid given all that has been said above concerning the merely subjective validity of the experience-transcending ideas of reason? What is usually overlooked here in the Appendix (and, I think, in the Third *Critique* as well; cf. O'Shea [1997]) is just how carefully Kant qualifies the claims that the various regulative maxims of reason make about objective empirical reality. We have seen that reason gives us the transcendent idea of a *maximum* of systematic unity and purposive organization in nature (i.e. of empirical homogeneity, specification and continuity). But what the argument just given explicitly concludes is only that *some minimum degree or other* of such empirical systematicity must be found in the appearances, if experience is to be possible for us. This is what Kant means by the "indeterminate" objective validity of the regulative maxims of reason: we cannot determine merely *a priori*, merely in our philosophical armchairs without ongoing empirical research, what is the *nature and extent* (i.e. what kind and how much) of the empirical uniformity, diversity and continuity that exists waiting to be discovered in brute empirical nature. As he puts it later in the Appendix, "the principle of such a systematic unity is ... objective but in an indeterminate way (*principium vagum*): not as a constitutive principle for determining something in regard to its direct object, but rather as a merely regulative principle" (A680/B708). That is, reason's *a priori* ideas and ideals do not *constitutively determine* any corresponding *maximal object* or completely systematic organization as existing in nature. But the regulative maxims *do* lay down that it *must* be true of any possible appearances or objects that we could ever encounter in nature that they must be characterized by at least *some* degree or other of empirical orderliness or uniformity. And Kant gives similar arguments for the *a priori* necessity of at least *some degree* of empirical differentiation and continuity in nature, too, although again just how much or of what kind cannot be determined merely *a priori*. This is the sense of the "indeterminate" objective validity possessed by such regulative maxims of reason.

What is particularly significant here is that Kant's various 'application-deductions' (to recall the term I introduced in Chapters 4 and 5) or arguments for the objective validity of the maxims of reason do not appeal *directly* to the systematic and maximizing *interests of reason*. This is not surprising, since the latter ideals by their very nature transcend the limits of possible experience. Rather, Kant's fascinating strategy is to argue that such maximizing ideals of systematic purposiveness can and must be put to a regulative and yet *a priori* objectively valid immanent use in which their content is strictly limited to an anticipation of nature's empirical details that is 'indeterminate' in the sense that it cannot be legislated *a priori*.

This is precisely the difference between the regulative maxims of reason on the one hand and all four principles of pure understanding on the other. The principles of pure understanding (the Axioms, Anticipations, Analogies and Postulates) are *a priori* constitutive of the lawful form of any possible experience whatsoever. Hence we can know in advance, for example, that for any happening that might present itself to us as an appearance in nature, this event must have *some* determining cause or other (and thus must fall under *some* empirical causal law or other). By contrast, we cannot know *a priori* or in advance either what kind or what degree of empirical uniformity, continuity and so on actually exists in brute nature waiting to be discovered through our empirical inquiries. But nonetheless we can and do know *a priori*, Kant argues in the passage quoted above, that if there were *no* degree of empirical systematicity at all in nature's appearances, then in that imagined case *we could have no concepts of any objects whatsoever* (however generic or specific they might be), hence *we could have no possible application for the pure categories of understanding* either.

Recall the discussion Kant's Second Analogy and the universal principle of causality in Chapter 5. It is a universal law of understanding that every particular event encountered in nature must have some determining cause or other. But in order to successfully *apply* this universal principle of causality to some particular empirical kind of event, we must investigate and offer hypotheses concerning what kind of empirical causal law in particular subsumes the given case at hand. What *this* will be we cannot legislate *a priori*, constitutively. But what the regulative maxims assure us is that nature in its discoverable details *must* be governed by *some* appropriate empirical uniformities and kinds, if any experience of nature's objects is to be possible for us. On Kant's view nothing guarantees *a priori* that any *particular degree* of empirical systematic unity or purposiveness lies waiting for us to discover in nature. Nature can always turn out to be more chaotic and diverse than we expected, but the regulative maxims of reason ensure that a *complete* chaos is not even a *possible* nature for us. The very possibility of any coherent empirical inquiry into nature thus requires that reason's regulative maxims are not only subjectively valid, as setting useful methodological or heuristic goals for the understanding to seek to approximate. The maxims of reason are also objectively valid, although only indeterminately and not constitutively so, as representing that nature in its brute empirical details will necessarily be characterized by some degree of orderliness that is cognizable by us, the particular nature of which awaits our patient scientific discovery.

CONCLUSION: PURE REASON'S ROLE IN KANT'S METAPHYSICS OF NATURE

I have only touched on a few aspects of Kant's intriguing and, I believe, deeply insightful discussion of the regulative maxims of reason in the Appendix to the Transcendental Dialectic. In the second half of the Appendix, entitled "On the Final Aim of the Natural Dialectic of Human Reason" (A669/B697), Kant continues the investigation of the proper use of the experience-transcending ideas of theoretical reason in light of the above justification of both their subjective validity and their indeterminately objective validity within the realm of possible experience. Now, however, he returns to focus once again on the ideas of reason in their role as representing those ideal *maxima* and unconditioned conditions that have been with us since the start of Chapter 1: reason's inevitable sense-transcending ideas of God, freedom and immortality. And here Kant argues that if such ideas are properly treated 'merely regulatively' in ways that are similar to those briefly discussed above, then the *ideas* of such 'maximal objects' can be justified as demonstrably *never hindering and always promoting* the properly 'immanent' aims of both our understanding and our reason, in our never-ending investigation of nature's inexhaustible secrets. Kant sums up these results, and in fact the *Critique of Pure Reason* as a whole, this way:

> Thus pure reason, which initially seemed to promise us nothing less than an extension of our knowledge beyond all the boundaries of experience, if we understand it rightly contains nothing but regulative principles, which certainly command greater unity than the empirical use of the understanding can reach, but just because they put the goal we are approaching so far off, they bring this goal to the highest degree of agreement with itself through systematic unity; but if one misunderstands them and takes them to be constitutive principles of transcendent cognition, then they produce a dazzling but deceptive illusion, persuasion and imaginary knowledge, and thus also eternal contradictions and controversies.
>
> (A701–2/B730)

BIBLIOGRAPHY

WORKS BY KANT

References to Kant's works in this book that occur in the form 'volume:page number' (e.g. 6:232) are to the German Akademie-Ausgabe (Ak.) edition of Kant's works (listed below), and these pages are provided in the margins of the volumes of *The Cambridge Edition of the Works of Immanuel Kant* (also listed below). The only exception is the *Critique of Pure Reason*, references to which take the standard form 'A/B' referring to the Akademie pagination for the first 'A' edition (1781) and second 'B' edition (1787).

Kant, I. 1900ff. *Kants Gesammelte Schriften*, Königlich Preußische (spaeter Deutsche) Academie der Wissenschaften (ed.). Berlin: Georg Reimer, later Walter de Gruyter [Akademie-Ausgabe (Ak.)].

Kant, I. Various dates. *The Cambridge Edition of the Works of Immanuel Kant*, 13 volumes to date, P. Guyer & A. W. Wood (eds). Cambridge: Cambridge University Press. Volumes cited here:
- *Anthropology, History, and Education*, G. Zöller & R. B. Louden (eds & trans.), M. Gregor, P. Guyer, H. Wilson, A. W. Wood, A. Zweig (trans.).
- *Correspondence*, A. Zweig (ed. & trans.).
- *Critique of the Power of Judgment*, P. Guyer (ed.), P. Guyer & E. Matthews (trans.).
- *Critique of Pure Reason*, P. Guyer & A. W. Wood (eds & trans.).
- *Lectures on Metaphysics*, K. Ameriks & S. Naragon (eds & trans.).
- *Practical Philosophy*, M. J. Gregor (ed. & trans.), including: *Groundwork of the Metaphysics of Morals* [*Groundwork*] (1785); *Critique of Practical Reason* [*Practical Reason*] (1788).
- *Religion and Rational Theology*, A. W. Wood & G. Di Giovanni (eds & trans.).
- *Theoretical Philosophy, 1755–1770*, D. Walford (ed. & trans.) in collaboration with R. Meerbote (Kant's 'pre-Critical' writings in theoretical philosophy).
- *Theoretical Philosophy after 1781*, H. Allison & P. Heath (eds & trans.), including: *Prolegomena to any Future Metaphysics* [*Prolegomena*] (1783), G. Hatfield (trans.); *Metaphysical Foundations of Natural Science* [*MFNS*] (1786), M. Friedman (trans.); *On a Discovery Whereby Any New Critique of Pure Reason Is to Be Made Superfluous by an Older One* [*Kant–Eberhard Controversy*] (1790), H. Allison (trans.).

Kant, I. [1781/1787] 1929. *The Critique of Pure Reason*, N. Kemp Smith (trans.). London: Macmillan. Reprinted with additional apparatus in 1992. (The standard English translation before the *Cambridge Edition* version appeared in 1998.)

OTHER WORKS CITED

Al-Azm, S. J. 1972. *The Origins of Kant's Argument in the Antinomies*. Oxford: Oxford University Press.
Alexander, H. G. (ed.) 1956. *The Leibniz–Clarke Correspondence*. Manchester: Manchester University Press.
Allais, L. 2004. "Kant's One World: Interpreting 'Transcendental Idealism'". *British Journal for the History of Philosophy* **12**(4): 655–84.
Allais, L. 2009. "Kant, Non-Conceptual Content and the Representation of Space". *Journal of the History of Philosophy* **47**(3): 383–413.
Allison, H. 1990. *Kant's Theory of Freedom*. Cambridge: Cambridge University Press.
Allison, H. 1996. *Idealism and Freedom: Essays on Kant's Theoretical and Practical Philosophy*. Cambridge: Cambridge University Press.
Allison, H. 2004. *Kant's Transcendental Idealism: An Interpretation and Defense*, revised 2nd edn (1st edn 1983). New Haven, CT: Yale University Press.
Allison, H. 2007. "Debating Allison on Transcendental Idealism". *Kantian Review* **12**(2): 24–39.
Ameriks, K. 2003. *Interpreting Kant's Critiques*. Oxford: Clarendon Press.
Ameriks, K. 2006. "The Critique of Metaphysics: The Structure and Fate of Kant's Dialectic". In *The Cambridge Companion to Kant and Modern Philosophy*, P. Guyer (ed.), 269–302. Cambridge: Cambridge University Press.
Baiasu, S. & M. Grier (eds) 2011. "Revolutionary vs. Traditionalist Approaches to Kant: Some Aspects of the Debate". *Kantian Review* (Special Issue on *The Revolutionary Kant: Graham Bird Meets His Critics*) **16**(2): 161–73.
Beck, L. W. 1969. *Early German Philosophy: Kant and His Predecessors*. Cambridge, MA: Harvard University Press.
Bennett, J. 1966. *Kant's Analytic*. Cambridge: Cambridge University Press.
Bennett, J. 1971. "The Age and Size of the World". *Synthese* **23**: 127–46.
Bennett, J. 1974. *Kant's Dialectic*. Cambridge: Cambridge University Press.
Bieri, P., R.-P. Horstmann & L. Krüger (eds) 1979. *Transcendental Arguments and Science: Essays in Epistemology*. Dordrecht: Reidel.
Bird, G. 1962. *Kant's Theory of Knowledge*. London: Routledge.
Bird, G. 2006a. *The Revolutionary Kant: A Commentary on the Critique of Pure Reason*. Peru, IL: Open Court.
Bird, G. (ed.) 2006b. *A Companion to Kant*. Oxford: Blackwell.
Bird, G. 2006c. "The Neglected Alternative: Trendelenburg, Fischer, and Kant". In *A Companion to Kant*, G. Bird (ed.), 486–99. Oxford: Blackwell.
Boghossian, P. & C. Peacocke (eds) 2001. *New Essays on the A Priori*. Oxford: Oxford University Press.
Brandom, R. 2009. *Reason in Philosophy: Animating Ideas*. Cambridge, MA: Harvard University Press.
Buroker, J. V. 1981. *Space and Incongruence: The Origin of Kant's Idealism*. Dordrecht: Reidel.
Buroker, J. V. 2006. *Kant's* Critique of Pure Reason: *An Introduction*. Cambridge: Cambridge University Press.
Butts, R. (ed.) 1986. *Kant's Philosophy of Physical Science*. Dordrecht: Reidel.
Callanan, J. 2008. "Kant on Analogy". *British Journal for the History of Philosophy* **16**(4): 747–72.
Cassirer, E. [1918] 1981. *Kant's Life and Thought*, J. Haden (trans.). New Haven, CT: Yale University Press. Originally published in German as *Kants Leben and Lehre*, in E. Cassirer, *Gesammelte Werke*, vol. 8, Birgit Recki (ed.) (Hamburg: Felix Meiner, 2001).

Coffa, J. A. 1991. *The Semantic Tradition from Kant to Carnap*, L. Wessels (ed.). Cambridge: Cambridge University Press.
Collins, A. 1999. *Possible Experience: Understanding Kant's Critique of Pure Reason*. Berkeley, CA: University of California Press.
Descartes, R. [1641] 1985. *Meditations on First Philosophy*. In *The Philosophical Writings of Descartes*, vol. 2, J. Cottingham, R. Stoothoff & D. Murdoch (eds). Cambridge: Cambridge University Press.
Dicker G. 2004. *Kant's Theory of Knowledge: An Analytical Introduction*. Oxford: Oxford University Press.
Falkenstein, L. 1995. *Kant's Intuitionism: A Commentary on the Transcendental Aesthetic*. Toronto: University of Toronto Press.
Förster, E. (ed.) 1989. *Kant's Transcendental Deductions*. Stanford, CA: Stanford University Press.
Friedman, M. 1992. *Kant and the Exact Sciences*. Cambridge, MA: Harvard University Press.
Friedman, M. 2001. *The Dynamics of Reason*. Stanford, CA: CLSI Publications.
Gardner, S. 1999. *Kant and the Critique of Pure Reason*. London: Routledge.
Glock, H.-J. (ed.) 2003. *Strawson and Kant*. Oxford: Oxford University Press.
Grier, M. 2001. *Kant's Doctrine of Transcendental Illusion*. Cambridge: Cambridge University Press.
Grier, M. 2006. "The Logic of Illusion and the Antinomies". In *The Blackwell Companion to Kant*, G. Bird (ed.), 192–206. Oxford: Blackwell.
Grier, M. 2010. "The Ideal of Pure Reason". See Guyer (2010), 266–89.
Guyer, P. 1987. *Kant and the Claims of Knowledge*. Cambridge, MA: Harvard University Press.
Guyer, P. 2006a. *Kant*. London: Routledge.
Guyer, P. (ed.) 2006b. *The Cambridge Companion to Kant and Modern Philosophy*. Cambridge: Cambridge University Press.
Guyer, P. 2007. "Debating Allison on Transcendental Idealism". *Kantian Review* 12(2): 10–23.
Guyer, P. 2008. *Knowledge, Reason, and Taste: Kant's Response to Hume*. Princeton, NJ: Princeton University Press.
Guyer, P. (ed.) 2010. *The Cambridge Companion to Kant's* Critique of Pure Reason. Cambridge: Cambridge University Press.
Hanna, R. 2001. *Kant and the Foundations of Analytic Philosophy*. Oxford: Oxford University Press.
Hanna, R. 2006. *Kant, Science, and Human Nature*. Oxford: Oxford University Press.
Hanna, R. 2008. "Kantian Non-Conceptualism". *Philosophical Studies* 137(1):41–64.
Heidegger, M. [1929] 1997. *Kant and the Problem of Metaphysics*, 5th edn enlarged, R. Taft (trans.). Bloomington, IN: Indiana University Press.
Hume, D. [1739] 2000. *A Treatise of Human Nature*, D. F. Norton & M. J. Norton (eds). Oxford: Oxford University Press.
Hume, D. [1748] 2000. *An Enquiry Concerning Human Understanding*. Oxford: Clarendon Press.
Hume, D. [1779] 1993. *Dialogues Concerning Natural Religion*. In *David Hume: Dialogues and Natural History of Religion*, J. C. A. Gaskin (ed.). Oxford: Oxford University Press.
Jacobi, F. H. [1787] 1968. *David Hume über den Glauben, oder Idealismus und Realismus, in Ueber den transzendentalen Idealisus*. In *Werke*, vol. 2, F. Roth & F. Köppen (eds), 291–310. Darmstadt: Wissenschaftliche Buchgesellschaft.
James, W. [1907] 1978. *Pragmatism: A New Name for Some Old Ways of Thinking* & *The Meaning of Truth: A Sequel to "Pragmatism"*. Cambridge, MA: Harvard University Press.
Juhl, C. & E. Loomis 2009. *Analyticity*. London: Routledge.
Kitcher, P. 1990. *Kant's Transcendental Psychology*. Oxford: Oxford University Press.

Kitcher, P. 2006. "'A Priori'". In *The Cambridge Companion to Kant and Modern Philosophy*, P. Guyer (ed.), 28–60. Cambridge: Cambridge University Press.
Koch, A. F. 1990. *Subjektivität in Raum und Zeit*. Frankfurt: Klostermann.
Kripke, S. [1972] 1980. *Naming and Necessity*. Oxford: Blackwell.
Kuehn, M. 1983. "Kant's Conception of Hume's Problem". *Journal of the History of Philosophy* **21**: 75–106.
Kuehn, M. 2001. *Kant: A Biography*. Cambridge: Cambridge University Press.
Landy, D. 2010. "The Premise that even Hume must Accept". In *Self, Language, and World: Problems from Kant, Sellars, and Rosenberg*, J. O'Shea & E. R. Rubenstein (eds), 28–44. Atascadero, CA: Ridgeview.
Langton, R. 1998. *Kantian Humility: Our Ignorance of Things in Themselves*. Oxford: Clarendon Press.
Leibniz, G. W. 1989. *Philosophical Essays*, R. Ariew & D. Garber (eds & trans.). Indianapolis, IN: Hackett.
Longuenesse, B. 1998. *Kant and the Capacity to Judge*, C. Wolfe (trans.), Princeton, NJ: Princeton University Press.
Longuenesse, B. 2005. *Kant on the Human Standpoint*. Cambridge: Cambridge University Press.
Lovejoy, A. O. [1906] 1967. "On Kant's Reply to Hume". In *Kant: Disputed Questions*, M. S. Gram (ed.), 284–308. Chicago, IL: Quadrangle Books.
Matthews, H. E. [1969] 1982. "Strawson on Transcendental Idealism". In *Kant On Pure Reason*, R. Walker (ed.), 132–49. Oxford: Oxford University Press.
McDowell, J. 1996. *Mind and World* (with a new introduction). Cambridge, MA: Harvard University Press.
McDowell, J. 2009. *Having the World in View: Essays on Kant, Hegel, and Sellars*. Cambridge, MA: Harvard University Press.
Melnick, A. 1973. *Kant's Analogies of Experience*. Chicago, IL: University of Chicago Press.
Melnick, A. 1989. *Space, Time and Thought in Kant*. Dordrecht: Kluwer.
Neiman, S. 1994. *The Unity of Reason: Rereading Kant*. New York: Oxford University Press.
O'Shea, J. 1992. "Problems of Substance: Perception and Object in Hume and Kant". PhD dissertation, University of North Carolina at Chapel Hill.
O'Shea, J. 1996a. "Hume's Reflective Return to the Vulgar". *British Journal for the History of Philosophy* **4**(2): 285–315.
O'Shea, J. 1996b. "Kantian Matters: the Structure of Permanence". *Acta Analytica* **15**: 67–88.
O'Shea, J. 1997. "The Needs of Understanding: Kant on Empirical Laws and Regulative Ideals". *International Journal of Philosophical Studies* **5**(2): 216–54.
O'Shea, J. 1999. "Review of Rae Langton, *Kantian Humility: Our Ignorance of Things in Themselves*". *International Journal of Philosophical Studies* **7**: 253–7.
O'Shea, J. 2006. "Conceptual Connections: Kant and the Twentieth-Century Analytic Tradition". In *A Companion to Kant*, G. Bird (ed.), 513–27. Oxford: Blackwell.
O'Shea, J. 2007. *Wilfrid Sellars: Naturalism with a Normative Turn*. Cambridge: Polity.
O'Shea, J. 2011. "How to be a Kantian *and* a Naturalist about Human Knowledge: Sellars's Middle Way". *Journal of Philosophical Research* **36**: 327–59.
O'Shea, J. & E. Rubenstein (eds) 2010. *Self, Language, and World: Problems from Kant, Sellars, and Rosenberg*. Atascadero, CA: Ridgeview.
Posy, C. 1983. "Dancing to the Antinomy: A Proposal for Transcendental Idealism". *American Philosophical Quarterly* **20**(1): 81–94.
Prauss, G. 1974. *Kant und das Problem der Dinge an sich*. Bonn: Bouvier.
Putnam, H. 1981. *Reason, Truth, and History*. Cambridge: Cambridge University Press.
Quine, W. V. [1951] 1963. "Two Dogmas of Empiricism". In his *From a Logical Point of View*, 2nd edn, 20–46. New York: Harper & Row.

Reich, K. 1992. *The Completeness of Kant's Table of Judgments*, J. E. Kneller & M. Losonsky (trans.). Stanford, CA: Stanford University Press.
Rosenberg, J. F. 2005. *Accessing Kant: A Relaxed Introduction to the* Critique of Pure Reason. Oxford: Clarendon Press.
Russell, B. [1912] 1998. *The Problems of Philosophy*. Oxford: Oxford University Press.
Russell, B. [1914] 1956. *Our Knowledge of the External World*. New York: Mentor Books.
Savile, A. 2005. *Kant's* Critique of Pure Reason: *An Orientation to the Central Theme*. Oxford: Blackwell.
Sellars, W. [1956] 1991. "Empiricism and the Philosophy of Mind". In his *Science, Perception, and Reality*, 127–96. Atascadero, CA: Ridgeview.
Sellars, W. [1972] 2002. "... This I or He or It (the Thing) Which Thinks". In his *Kant's Transcendental Metaphysics: Sellars' Cassirer Lecture Notes and Other Essays*, J. Sicha (ed.), 341–62. Atascadero, CA: Ridgeview.
Stern, R. (ed.) 1999. *Transcendental Arguments: Problems and Prospects*. Oxford: Clarendon Press.
Strawson, P. F. 1959. *Individuals*. London: Methuen.
Strawson, P. F. 1966. *The Bounds of Sense: An Essay on Kant's* Critique of Pure Reason. London: Methuen.
Strawson, P. F. 1997. "Kant's New Foundations of Metaphysics". In his *Entity and Identity and Other Essays*, 232–43. Oxford: Oxford University Press.
Stroud, B. 1968. "Transcendental Arguments". *Journal of Philosophy* **65**: 241–56. Reprinted in Walker (ed.) 1982, 117–31.
Van Cleve, J. 1999. *Problems from Kant*. Oxford: Oxford University Press.
Van Cleve, J. & R. E. Frederick (eds) 1991. *The Philosophy of Right and Left*. Dordrecht: Kluwer.
Voltaire 2008. *Candide and Other Stories*, R. Pearson (ed.). Oxford: Oxford University Press.
Walker, R. (ed.) 1982. *Kant On Pure Reason*. Oxford: Oxford University Press.
Walker, R. 1999. *Kant*. London: Routledge.
Warren, D. 1998. "Kant and the A Priority of Space". *Philosophical Review* **107**(2): 179–224.
Watkins, E. (ed.) 2001. *Kant and the Sciences*. Oxford: Oxford University Press.
Watkins, E. (ed.) 2009. *Kant's Critique of Pure Reason: Background Source Materials*. Cambridge: Cambridge University Press.
Wenzel, C. H. 2005. "Spielen nach Kant die Kategorien schon bei der Wahrnehmung eine Rolle? Peter Rohs und John McDowell". *Kant-Studien* **96**: 407–26.
Westphal, K. R. 2004. *Kant's Transcendental Proof of Realism*. Cambridge: Cambridge University Press.
Westphal, K. R. 2010. "Kant's *Critique of Pure Reason* and Analytic Philosophy". See Guyer (2010), 401–30.
Wolff, M. 1995. *Die Vollständigkeit der Kantischen Urteilstafel: Mit einem Essay über Freges Begriffschrift*. Frankfurt: Klostermann.
Wood, A. W. 1978. *Kant's Rational Theology*. Ithaca, NY: Cornell University Press.
Wood, A. W. 2010. "The Antinomies of Pure Reason". See Guyer (2010), 245–65.
Wood, A., P. Guyer & H. Allison 2007. "Debating Allison on Transcendental Idealism". *Kantian Review* **12**(2): 1–39.

FURTHER READING

Brittan, G. 1978. *Kant's Theory of Science*. Princeton, NJ: Princeton University Press.
Caygill, H. 1995. *A Kant Dictionary*. Oxford: Blackwell.
Dryer, D. P. 1966. *Kant's Solution for Verification in Metaphysics*. London: Allen & Unwin.

Ewing, A. C. 1938. *A Short Commentary on* Kant's Critique of Pure Reason. London: Methuen, 1938.
Höffe, O. 1994. *Immanuel Kant*, M. Farrier (trans.). Albany, NY: SUNY Press.
Kemp Smith, N. 1923. *A Commentary to Kant's* Critique of Pure Reason, 2nd edn. London: Macmillan.
Kitcher, P. 1990. *Kant's Transcendental Psychology*. Oxford: Oxford University Press.
Kitcher, P. (ed.) 1998. *Kant's* Critique of Pure Reason: *Critical Essays*. Lanham, MD: Rowman & Littlefield.
Mohr, G. & M. Willaschek (eds) 1998. *Immanuel Kant: Kritik der reinen Vernunft*. Berlin: Akademie.
Paton, H. J. 1936. *Kant's Metaphysic of Experience*. London: Allen & Unwin.
Schaper, E. & W. Vossenkuhl (eds) 1984. *Reading Kant: New Perspectives on Transcendental Arguments and Critical Philosophy*. Oxford: Blackwell.
Ward, A. 2006. *Kant: The Three Critiques*. Cambridge: Polity.
Wood, A. 1978. *Kant's Rational Theology*. Ithaca, NY: Cornell University Press.
Wood, A. W. 2005. *Kant*. Oxford: Blackwell.

INDEX

actuality 196–9
Aesthetic, Transcendental 73, 78–105, 163, 165, 167, 170
  conclusions of 116–17
affection 31, 33, 109
  problem of 106–15
  empirical and noumenal 107, 112
affinity 137, 217
Al-Azm, S. J. 58
Allais, L. 38, 80, 106, 121
Allison, H. 37–8, 58, 66, 73–4, 83, 85, 88, 100–103, 106, 108, 110, 118, 184
Ameriks, K. 35, 97, 106
Amphiboly 103, 105, 197–8
Analogies 135, 159, 164, 173–96, 203–4; *see also* causality; substance
  Third Analogy (coexistence) 173, 179, 203
analytic/synthetic 22, 41–6, 49, 68, 94, 119, 164; *see also* synthetic *a priori*
Analytic, Transcendental 116–204
  sections of 132
animal cognition 122–3, 129, 143, 148
Anselm of Canterbury 211
Anticipations 159, 164, 168–73, 177
Antinomies x, 16, 50–77, 91, 206, 208–9, 212, 215
  sceptical representation of (too big/too small) 65
appearances 26–39, 69, 71–5, 96, 103–5, 139, 203; *see also* idealism, transcendental; phenomena/noumena; things in themselves
  non-sensible 'ground' of 107–8, 110–13
Appendix to the Dialectic 207, 216–23

apperception 141–3, 149–50, 203; *see also* 'I think'; self-consciousness
  analytical unity of 144–6
  empirical 146, 148, 150
  'I think' ability 144
  synthetic unity of 146–7
application-deductions 157, 159, 164, 168, 171, 173–4, 177, 180–81, 186–7, 191–4, 200, 221
apprehension (sensory) 134–6, 187
a priori/a posteriori 4–5, 14–15, 21–5, 42–6, 79–80, 85, 94, 130–31
Aquinas, Thomas 212
Aristotle 14, 129, 145, 168
assertion 129–30
Axioms 159, 164, 166–8

Bacon, F. 205–6
Baiasu, S. 106
Baumgarten, A. G. 3, 5
Beck, L. W. 40
Bennett, J. 58, 61, 99, 184, 201
Berkeley, G. 29–30, 160
Bieri, P. 154
Bird, G. 38, 43, 100, 102, 106–8, 153
blindness problem (intuitions without concepts) 80–81, 105, 122
Brandom, R. 129, 155
Buroker, J. V. 66, 73, 85, 94, 102, 104, 208, 211
Butts, R. E. 177

Callanan, J. 176
Cantor, G. 66
Cassirer, E. 1, 99

231

Canon 19, 207
categories 33–4, 57, 124, 126–32, 141, 148–9, 162–3
 as meta-conceptual 159, 184–5
causality 14, 16–18, 23–5, 43–6, 61, 74, 109, 117, 120, 125, 141, 159, 163, 171, 173, 186–99
 non-sensible 107–8
 Second Analogy on 120, 175, 186–96, 222
 Third Analogy on simultaneous 173
Clarke, S. (Leibniz–Clarke correspondence) 58, 87
Clue (guiding thread) *see* Deduction, Metaphysical
Coffa, A. 43
Collins, A. 107
concepts 33, 79–80, 90–91, 129, 138–9, 160–61; *see also* categories
 as predicates of possible judgments 129
 as rules (laws) 139, 142, 161, 189; *see also* objectivity, modal conception of
conditions of possibility *see* experience
constitutive principles *see* regulative principles
construction of concepts in intuition 93–4, 121, 136
 'existence cannot be constructed' 121
continuity 172
Copernicus, N. 4, 38
 Copernican turn 38–9, 107, 140–41, 155
cosmology 10, 57, 61, 65–7, 206
Critical/pre-Critical philosophy 6–10, 17, 104, 125, 220
critical solution 61, 65, 67
Crusius, C. A. 9

Darwinian evolutionary biology 214
Davidson, D. 155
Deduction 118, 126, 163–5, 170, 180, 182–3, 187, 197, 200; *see also* application-deductions; objectivity
 empirical 118
 Metaphysical 126–32, 141, 154, 178
 Transcendental 118, 125–6, 132–48, 152–7, 187
degree *see* Anticipations; magnitude, intensive
Descartes, R. 4–5, 22, 46, 145, 150, 199, 202, 211

Dialectic, Transcendental x, 18, 34, 50–51, 76, 152, 156
Dicker, G. 118, 128
Discipline 94, 205
Doctrine of Method 34
dogmatism 40–41, 49, 60, 63–4
double affection 107
dualism, empirical 152; *see also* Paralogisms
Dummett, M. 155
dynamical principles *see* mathematical

Einstein, A. 98
empiricism 4, 8, 12, 46–7, 77, 88, 92, 98–9, 111, 128–9, 133, 152–3, 156, 160–61; *see also* pure/empirical; realism, empirical
 principle of pure 63–4
epistemic conditions 100–102
Enlightenment 1–10, 19, 49
Euler, L. 8
experience 8, 42, 53, 122, 134; *see also* object
 conditions of possibility of 33–4, 53, 90, 92, 101–2, 133, 138, 149, 164
exposition *see* metaphysical expositions; transcendental, exposition

Falkenstein, L. 83–8, 90, 102, 173
forces, repulsive and attractive 171–2, 177, 186; *see also* matter
form 34, 79–80, 91, 107; *see also* matter; intuition, forms of
Förster, E. 154
Frederick, R. E. 104
freedom 9–10, 15–18, 37, 58, 62, 73–7, 109, 111, 113, 123, 156, 208; *see also* reason, fact of
Frege, G. 128
Friedman, M. 24, 99–100, 177

Galileo, G. 4
Gardner, S. 85, 125
Garve, C. x, 50
Geometry, argument from 92–100, 166; *see also* transcendental, exposition; non-Euclidean 98
Glock, H.-J. 153
God (idea of) 8, 10, 14–21, 37, 56–7, 62–4, 113, 123, 206–16; *see also* ideal of reason; religion

as necessary being 75, 208, 211
proofs of existence of 207–14
Grier, M. 56, 58, 69, 106, 110, 208, 211, 217
ground *see* appearances, non-sensible ground of
Guyer, P. xi, 38, 40, 74, 83, 85, 97, 102, 106, 118, 127, 155

Hanna, R. 43, 80, 99
Hegel, G. W. F. 36, 155, 203
Heidegger, M. 161
Herder, J. G. 3
Herz, M. x, 8, 40, 50, 125, 139, 143
highest good 19–20
homogeneity 160, 162
Hume, D. 3, 8–9, 40–51, 76–7, 92, 117, 119–20, 124–5, 128, 130, 133, 135, 142, 155, 160, 163, 177, 186, 190–92; *see also* scepticism
 on abstract ideas 128
 'bundle theory' of self 143–6
 on identity and duration 182–3
 on religion 207, 211–13
 on space and time 86–90, 182
Husserl, E. 188
Hutcheson, F. 9

ideas of reason 12, 37, 56, 58, 65–6, 113, 128, 152, 199, 206–23
 vs. innate 22
idealism 29–30; *see also* Refutation of
 empirical 29, 117, 199, 201
 transcendental x–xi, 28–39, 56, 74–5, 78, 81–2, 95–115, 155–7
 defence of 156–7
 indirect proof of (Antinomies) 72–3
 two-aspect vs. two-worlds 35–38, 74, 100–102, 155–6
Ideal of reason x, 206–16
illusion *see* Dialectic; transcendental, illusion
images 137, 161–2
imagination 93–4, 134, 136, 160–62, 166
 defined 137
 reproductive/productive 137, 160–62
immanent/transcendent 37, 39, 77, 171, 207, 214, 216
immortality *see* Paralogisms; soul
impenetrability (of matter) 177, 202
incongruent counterparts 104–5

inference 52–4
infinity 60, 65–6, 71
inner sense 82–3, 106, 146, 148, 150
intentionality (objective purport) 138, 141
intuition 15, 33, 79–80, 90–91, 121–2, 141, 160; *see also* sensibility
 space and time as pure forms of 78–106, 135
 intellectual 15, 110–11, 139
'I think' 142–5, 202; *see also* apperception
 as a 'form of representation' 146, 148–52
 as a merely logical (analytic) unity 145

Jacobi, F. H. 110
Jakob, L. H. 37, 105
James, W. 33, 64–5
judgment 41, 120, 129, 140, 154, 159; *see also* analytic/synthetic; Deduction, Metaphysical
Critique of (Third *Critique*) 7, 220

Kepler, J. 3–4
Kitcher, Patricia 118
Kitcher, Philip 22
knowledge, cognition 28, 30–31, 47
Knutzen, M. 5
Koch, A. F. 103
Kuehn, M. 1–2, 49, 51

Lambert, J. H. 8
Landy, D. 118
Langton, R. 97, 106, 110
laws (of nature, of experience, of understanding) 122, 130, 142, 148, 158, 163, 174, 180, 197–9, 203, 206, 221–2
Leibniz, G. W. (Leibnizian) 3, 5–8, 22, 41, 46, 58, 82–4, 86–8, 90, 103–5, 198, 210, 212
Locke, J. 8, 46, 56, 83, 86, 90, 145, 160, 178
logic 130
 general vs. transcendental 130
logical functions of judgment 126–131, 147 *see also* Deduction, Metaphysical
logical positivism/logical empiricism 98–9
Longuenesse, B. 36, 127
Lovejoy, A. 193

magnitude 61

233

INDEX

extensive 166–8
intensive 168–73
manifold (of intuitions, of thoughts) 84, 129, 135–6, 147, 167
materialism 152, 206
mathematical/dynamical principles 66, 73–4, 121, 172–5; *see also* regulative vs. constitutive
mathematics 94, 98–100, 164, 166–73; *see also* Discipline
matter 117, 119, 176, 202
  matter/form 34
  as the movable (motion) in space 176–7
Matthews, H. E. 100
McDowell, J. 80, 131, 155
Melnick, A. 73, 202
Mendelssohn, M. 49, 105
mereology (part/whole) 91
Metaphysical Deduction *see* Deduction, Metaphysical
metaphysical expositions of space and time 79, 81–92, 101–3
Metaphysical Foundations of Natural Science (*MFNS*) 23, 104, 172, 176–7, 185–6
metaphysics 5, 10, 13–19, 25, 39–41, 43, 49, 51, 57–60, 77, 125, 145; *see also* immanent; rationalism; reason
  of experience 173
  of morals 4, 9–10
  of nature 4, 8, 10, 23, 77, 206
  special/general 10, 14, 16, 56–7
monads 5, 7–8, 84, 151; *see also* Leibniz
morality 2, 4, 7, 9–10, 17, 19, 25, 63, 65, 75–6, 111, 113, 156, 206; *see also* metaphysics, of morals

naturalism 76–7, 111, 120, 152, 206
necessity 138, 197–9
neglected alternative 78, 102
Neiman, S. 53
Newton, I. (Newtonian) 3–4, 7–8, 23, 82–4, 87, 105, 171–2, 213

noumena 15, 25–6, 31, 57, 69, 102, 107, 110, 206; *see also* phenomena/noumena
  in the negative sense 109, 111
  in the positive sense 111

object 118–19, 121, 123, 125, 132, 139–40, 187, 191; *see also* Deduction; objectivity
  of possible experience 122, 133–41, 147
  of representation 125, 138
  transcendental 107–8, 112
objectivity (objective validity, objective reality) 18, 112, 117–22, 124–5, 131, 133, 139–42, 147–9, 153–8, 164, 188–9, 206, 218
  modal conception of 180, 187, 189–92
ontology 10
O'Shea, J. 43, 48, 56, 69, 154–5, 175, 177, 183, 198, 217, 221
outer sense 82–3

Paralogisms x, 10, 38, 57, 76, 145, 149–52, 202, 215; *see also* soul
perception 161, 198
phenomena/noumena 15, 26, 197; *see also* appearances/things in themselves; noumena
physics *see* science
Plato 15, 41, 46, 56, 84, 145, 167, 173, 209
Postulates 159, 164, 196–9
Posy, C. 66
pre-Critical period *see* Critical/pre-Critical philosophy
practical reason *see* morality; reason, theoretical/practical
Prauss, G. 38, 100, 106
Principles of pure understanding 119, 126–7, 133, 154, 158–9, 163–4, 191, 222
pure/empirical 15, 21–5, 80–81
purposiveness 213–14, 217
Putnam, H. 37, 155

quid juris 118–19, 124, 132, 139, 142, 149, 177
Quine, W. V. O. 42–3, 155

rationalism 4–8, 22, 46–7, 63, 145, 198, 210
realism 29
  empirical 30, 81–2, 96, 107, 112, 157, 170–71
  transcendental 30, 56, 69–70, 73, 79, 84, 139, 192, 198
real, the (corresponding to sensation) 168–73, 176; *see also* Anticipations
reason 13, 16–21, 49, 51–7, 65, 205–23;

234

see also ideas; morality; regulative principles
fact of   109, 113, 206
interests of   62–3
logical postulate or maxim of pure   53–6, 68–70, 73, 208
objective indeterminate validity of maxims of   219–23
principle of pure   55–6, 59–60, 62–3, 67–9, 111, 208, 215
real use/logical use of   69–70
regulative maxims of   *see* regulative principles
speculative   17, 25
systematic unity of   53–4, 68 209, 215
theoretical/practical   10, 17–21, 26, 28, 65, 75–6, 156, 206
receptivity   *see* affection; sensibility
recognition (conceptual)   134
Refutation of Idealism   144, 152, 196, 199–203
regulative principles   31, 37, 111, 152, 156, 207, 214–23
vs. constitutive   70, 73, 173–5, 210, 218
indeterminate objective validity of reason's   219–23
of reason (vs. of understanding)   174, 186, 194–6, 214–23
Reich, K.   127
religion   2–3, 18–21, 63, 111, 206–16
representation   12, 145
Rosenberg, J. F.   58, 66, 85, 88–9, 103, 118, 144, 196
Rousseau, J. J.   3, 9
rules   138–9, 142, 158, 161–2, 165, 187, 191, 203   *see also* concepts; laws
Russell, B.   66, 128, 154–5

Savile, A.   127
scepticism   43–9, 51, 77, 92, 117, 119–20, 142, 199–203; *see also* Hume
Schematism (schema, schemata)   137, 159, 160–65, 167, 169, 176, 187
unschematized concepts   113, 164
Schopenhauer, A.   195
Schultz, A.   2
Schultz, J.   168
science   62–4, 66, 98–100, 104, 171–2, 176–7, 185, 222
self, the   143–5, 149–53, 200
self-affection   36, 106

self-consciousness   142–3; *see also* apperception; 'I think'
Sellars, W.   80, 99, 141, 145, 155, 203
sensibility (sensation, sensible, sensory intuition)   15, 27, 30–31, 78–81, 85, 105, 116–17, 128, 196; *see also* intuition
sensory passivity   33, 110, 112
soul, immortal   4–5, 10, 13–17, 19–21, 37, 57, 113, 143, 145 , 149–52, 176, 206; *see also* Paralogisms
space   33–4, 60–61, 78–106, 135, 167; *see also* metaphysical expositions; transcendental, exposition; Newton; Leibniz
empty   172–3
regulative idea of absolute   177
Spinoza, B.   5, 22
Stern, R.   154
Strawson, P. F.   36, 38, 97, 99, 103, 110, 128, 153, 155–6, 189, 193
Stroud, B.   154–5
substance   14, 16, 18, 33, 117, 148, 150, 173, 176–86, 199–202; *see also* matter; monads; soul
First Analogy, principle of   150, 176–86
No Identity, No Duration thesis   183
Single Time argument   180–82
as ultimate subject of properties   178
supersensible   15, 63–4; *see also* appearances/things in themselves
synthesis   131–2
figurative   160
threefold   134–41, 165
synthetic *a priori*   24, 40–49, 51, 55, 77, 81, 92–9, 117, 125, 154, 159, 163–4, 177, 197, 220; *see also* analytic/synthetic
'relativized' to frameworks   100

teleology   213–14
Tetens, J. N.   8
theology   10, 57, 206–16; *see also* God; Ideal; religion
theoretical reason   *see* reason
things in themselves   26–39, 69, 71–5, 96, 103–15, 119, 139, 156, 171; *see also* affection; appearances; noumena
non-spatiotemporality of   102
unknowable but thinkable   106–9, 113, 123, 149

235

INDEX

time 33–4, 58–60, 79, 81–2, 85–91, 93, 103, 135, 159, 163; *see also* Analogies; inner sense; metaphysical expositions; Schematism; space
  cannot itself be perceived 84, 165, 174, 180, 182, 189
  Single Time argument 180–82
  three 'modi' of 174, 179
transcendental 10, 22; *see also* idealism; realism
  Deduction *see* Deduction, Transcendental
  exposition of space and time 81–2, 85, 92–7
  illusion 56, 60, 63, 65, 67–8, 71, 73, 206, 208, 210
  object *see* object, transcendental
  as 'second-order' (vs. empirical 'first-order') 184–6, 195
  vs. transcendent 22, 37, 39, 77, 207, 210, 214; *see also* immanent
Trendelenburg, A. 102
truth 129–30, 140

unconditioned, the 54–6, 60, 64–5, 67, 70, 74, 152, 156, 205–16
understanding 30–32, 52–3, 118, 120, 128–9, 206–7, 221–2; *see also* objectivity
  experiential principles of 52–3, 56–7, 67
  as faculty for judging 130
unity 129, 138
  analytical/synthetic 131

Van Cleve, J. 38, 104, 106, 118, 184, 211
Voltaire 5

Walker, R. 97
Warren, D. 83, 85, 88
Watkins, E. 8, 201
Wenzel, C. H. 80
Westphal, K. 121, 137, 154
Wittgenstein, L. 139, 155, 161, 203
Wolff, C. 2–3, 5, 210
Wolff, M. 127
Wood, A. xi, 56, 58, 73, 106, 208